Development and Challenge

Southeast Asia in the New Millennium

Edited by **Wong Tai-Chee & Mohan Singh**

TIMES ACADEMIC PRESS

© **1999 Times Media Private Limited**

First published 1999 by
Times Academic Press
An imprint of Times Media Private Limited
(A member of the Times Publishing Group)
Times Centre
1 New Industrial Road
Singapore 536196
Fax: (65) 2889254
E-mail: fps@corp.tpl.com.sg
Online Book Store: http://www.timesone.com.sg/fpl

ISBN 981 210 151 9

Printed by South East Printing Pte Ltd, Singapore

CONTENTS

ABBREVIATIONS

ABS	Australian Bureau of Statistics
ADB	Asian Development Bank
AEM	ASEAN Economic Ministers
AFTA	ASEAN Free Trade Area
AIA	ASEAN Investment Area
AIC	ASEAN Industrial Complementation Scheme
AICO	ASEAN Industrial Cooperation
AIDA	Australia–Indonesia Development Area
AIJV	ASEAN Industrial Joint Venture
AIP	ASEAN Industrial Project
AMM	Annual Ministerial Meeting
APEC	Asia-Pacific Economic Cooperation
ARF	ASEAN Regional Forum
ASEAN	Association of Southeast Asian Nations
ASEAN–CCI ASEAN	Chambers of Commerce and Industry
ASEANEUJCC	ASEAN–EU Joint Cooperative Committee

ASEM	Asia–Europe Meeting
ASEP	ASEAN Sub-Regional Environment Programme
BIMP	Brunei–Indonesia–Malaysia–Philippines
CAD	computer-aided design
CAM	computer-aided manufacturing
CEPT	Common Effective Preferential Tariff
CNC	computerised numerical control
COFAB	Committee on Finance and Banking
COFAF	Committee on Food, Agriculture and Forestry
COIME	Committee on Industry, Minerals and Energy
COTAC	Committee on Transportation and Communication
COTT	Committee on Trade and Tourism
EAAU	East Asia Analytical Unit
EAEC	East Asian Economic Caucus
EAEG	East Asian Economic Grouping
EAGA	East ASEAN Growth Area
EC	European Community
EDB	Economic Development Board
EMS	European Monetary System
EOI	export-oriented industrialisation
EOI	eradication of illiteracy
ESCAP	Economic and Social Commission for Asia and the Pacific
EU	European Union
FDI	foreign direct investment
FTAA	Free Trade Area of the Americas
GATT	General Agreement on Tariffs and Trade
GLC	government-linked companies
GNP	gross national product
GSP	Generalised System of Preferences

IEES	Improving the Efficiency of Educational Systems
ILO	International Labour Office
IMF	International Monetary Fund
IMS–GT	Indonesia–Malaysia–Singapore Growth Triangle
IUCN	International Union of Conservation of Nature and Natural Resources
LUAEE	Loosely United ASEAN Economic Entity
MFN	most favoured nation
MNC	multinational corporation
MOE	Ministry of Education
MOSTE	Ministry of Science, Technology and the Environment
MSC	Multimedia SuperCorridor
NAFTA	North American Free Trade Agreement
NCGUB	National Coalition Government of the Union of Burma
NCSRD	National Council for Scientific Research and Development
NGOs	non-governmental organisations
NIE	newly industrialising economies
NIE/NTU	National Institute of Education / Nanyang Technological University
NSTB	National Science and Technology Board
NT	Northern Territory
NTB	non-tariff barriers
NUS	National University of Singapore
OECD	Organisation for Economic Cooperation and Development
PCI	per capita income
PGDE	Post-Graduate Diploma of Education
PPP	purchasing power parity
PSC	Public Service Commission
PTA	ASEAN Preferential Trading Arrangement
R&D	research and development

RSE	Research Scientists and Engineers
S&T	science and technology
SEANWZ	Southeast Asian Nuclear Weapons Free Zone
SEM	Single European Market
SLORC	State Law and Order Restoration Council
SOE	state-owned enterprises
TAC	Treaty of Amity and Cooperation
TAFTA	Transatlantic Free Trade Agreement
UN	United Nations
UNCTAD	United Nations Conference on Trade and Development
UNEP	United Nations Environment Programme
UNESCO	United Nations Educational, Scientific and Cultural Organisation
UNIDO	United Nations Industrial Development Organisation
UPE	Universalisation of Primary Education
UPOU	University of Philippines Open University
WTO	World Trade Organisation

PREFACE

This book is the product of a geography seminar held at the National Institute of Education, Nanyang Technological University, on 8 November 1997, in commemoration of the 30th anniversary of the formation of the Association of Southeast Asian Nations (ASEAN). Thirty-two years have passed, and the Association has grown from its original five to the current ten members, hence covering the whole of Southeast Asia.

ASEAN has experienced turbulent changes since it was founded in 1967. From its primary concern about regional security arising out of ideological differences, ASEAN has moved towards a convergence between the two main systems of governments in the region. Whilst the Indochinese centrally-planned economies (Vietnam, Laos and Cambodia) undergo reforms, Myanmar, a long-standing self-isolating state, has implicitly acknowledged the advantages of market-oriented production system in improving the living standards of the population. It joined ASEAN in 1997. In parallel, domestic weaknesses of the more *laissez-faire* economies have been exposed following an unprecedented monetary crisis that broke out in July 1997. Reforms of financial systems have since been viewed as a prerequisite to support sustainable growth. In retrospect, the overall achievement is amazing as ASEAN develops its identity in its own right, shapes its own destiny, breaking barriers that once rendered them apart. Today, enjoying a total gross domestic product of S$800 billion and a population of 415 million, ASEAN is the third largest regional grouping in the world in terms of trade (after the European Union and North America Free Trade Area).

The post-Cold War era since 1990 has seen an increased mobility of technology, capital and labour in a globally integrated economic framework. The impact of globalisation on ASEAN will be substantial. There is growing pressure in the restructuring of its employment pattern to meet changing demands for a skilled workforce as information technology and high value-added products expand their world market share. Within ASEAN, despite regional integration efforts among its member states in terms of movements of capital and goods and services, free flow of labour has remained a dream because of disparities between countries in the region in terms of growth, wage levels and job availability. Large wage differentials induce employers to seek workers from low-wage and labour-surplus areas, and workers to seek jobs in more prosperous areas. We have now entered an era of skill and knowledge-based workforce flow in which education has a great role to play.

The current currency crisis has yet to go away and the way ahead is challenging. Development has also brought environmental degradation through domestic, traffic and industrial pollution. Collective efforts for the common good have yet to be strengthened, such as in the containment of transboundary pollution. Within ASEAN, cohesiveness is still weak, though aspiration and appeals for common prosperity are strong. This weak cohesiveness is best illustrated by the fact that 80 percent of ASEAN's trade is carried out with countries outside ASEAN. Unless intra-ASEAN trade is expanded significantly, interdependency will not be strong enough to bind its member states, which again will have to depend on rapidly rising regional living standards to bolster demand.

The book aims to provide some insights on the key issues currently of concern to academics, tertiary-level students and national governments. Concerns about the economic downturn, greater regional integration, environmental degradation, educational upgrading, labour flow and technological advancement can all be translated into challenging policies that call for appropriate actions. I am appreciative that Times Academic Press has agreed to put these concerns in print. We look forward to a bright future for everyone in ASEAN.

Professor Leo Tan Wee Hin
Director
National Institute of Education
Nanyang Technological University

May 1999

INTRODUCTION

The rise of Pacific Asia and the strengthening of trade blocs in the post-Cold War era arouses renewed interest in the geographic functioning of the Pacific Asian space. Pacific Asia where ASEAN is located finds that its developing nations need to interact more among themselves as well as with other world regions. While globalisation accelerates and ASEAN moves into the 21st century, it is also opportune to review some key development issues from within and deal with the challenges the region will face ahead. These issues such as regional economic cooperation, differences in socioeconomic variables between countries, sustainable urban development, cross-country environmental protection and population mobility as well as educational upgrading are interwoven and interdependent in one way or other. Convergence in socioeconomic variables between the ASEAN members, for example, will contribute towards greater regional integration and stability. This will, in turn, promote intraregional trade and help strengthen regional technological collaboration and collective efforts in countering transboundary pollution.

Chapter 1 examines three aspects in relation to Pacific Asia's geographic representation in this new era. First, it is the persistent continuity of the relationship of Pacific Asia with the former colonial powers as postcolonial independent states. This new posture is heavily dictated by the changing world power structure characterised by the globalisation of economic systems, in which national boundaries have remained fundamental but have become less distinctive as defensible lines of identity. Indeed, the impact of globalisation has brought new meaning questioning the entity of any region, such as Pacific Asia that is conceptual in origin. The purpose of ASEAN since 1967 has been to create political space and it has expanded ever since. The continued existence of such an invented space has changed focus, however, from a political to an economic one. Hitherto, in terms of economic significance, ASEAN's global linkages have much overshadowed its own trade relationship.

The second point of interest is how Australia is related to Pacific Asia, including ASEAN. Australia's position is ambiguous in this strange combination of emphasis on globalisation and regional "segregation" as trade blocs become an economic trend today. Australia's *rapprochement* with Asia was relatively recent, but their ties have strengthened in an accelerated pace as the sentimental and economic links of Australia with Europe begin to decline. On this basis, due to its geographic proximity to Asia, Australia has little option but to be more involved in Asian regional affairs, including the regional currency crisis and transboundary hazards such as the haze originating from Indonesia. The third concern is that the impact of the deregulatory globalisation, aided by the effectiveness of information technology could expose the weaknesses of regional economic frameworks to external influence, making them vulnerable to crises of tremendous scale such as the recent Asian currency crisis. This crisis is a test of national leadership, and ASEAN, as a relatively small regional grouping, could not manage its own crisis effectively but had to rely on international intervention and assistance.

Having laid the broad framework of ASEAN within Pacific Asia and the world as a whole, a number of selected issues in ASEAN are discussed. Chapter 2 investigates how ready a centrally planned economy, such as Myanmar, could contribute towards the ASEAN goals. It argues that in many aspects

Myanmar is in a good position to join the Association and be involved in its various activities. Compared to other centrally planned economies, the existing import tariffs of Myanmar are much lower than Cambodia and Laos, hence having little impact on Myanmar to join the ASEAN Free Trade Area (AFTA). Politically, the human rights issue raised by the West has not prevented Myanmar from joining ASEAN in 1997. Since joining ASEAN, Myanmar's bilateral relations with other Southeast Asian countries have improved. A constructive engagement with Myanmar is on the working agenda. Joining ASEAN also implies the military government's willingness to undertake further reforms, including perhaps democratisation and a more conciliatory attitude towards political opponents on the domestic front. Economically speaking, Myanmar is expected to gain from the ASEAN membership given its comparative advantages favourable to trade and investment: rich natural resources, a low-cost and literate workforce, and an English-speaking tradition in its urban populace.

Globalisation has positive effects on the economic survival of regional entities such as ASEAN. Chapter 3 examines ASEAN's potential economic cooperation and its ability to handle internal structural problems as the organisation enters the 21st century. This chapter first traces the development of ASEAN from a loose political association in the beginning to the more consolidated economic forum sharing many aspects of mutual interests at the later stage. Since 1990, the global ideological depoliticisation process has led ASEAN to break down barriers to accept the formerly less friendly neighbours into its organisation (e.g. Myanmar, the Indochinese states). It has gone even beyond the Southeast Asian boundary leading to APEC (Asia Pacific Economic Cooperation) and ASEM (Asia–Europe Meeting) negotiations to supplement the region's development interest. Indeed, when AFTA was proposed in 1993, it marked the move from a political-based to an economic-based strategy. The concept, however, was still in gestation and implementation was not immediate. The target date of formation in 2003 will allow adequate time for the member states to consolidate their foothold and new members from centrally planned economies to be prepared to commit to reforms. The nature of AFTA is different from the European Union. An economic union is foreseeable only after 2020, given the vast diversity in economic strength and base among the ASEAN member states. A monetary union is even more suspect in a globalising economy in which competition in pricing and quality is the rule of the game, though business networking may help to a certain extent.

In the next millennium, internal rivalry within ASEAN will remain a concern due to identical growth strategies adopted by member states, in particular in the pursuit of foreign capital and technology imports. Cooperation within ASEAN will, however, be a necessity if higher levels of economies of scale and economies of scope are to be achieved. The future global market place is projected to be persistently competitive and the nature of the workforce will undergo a dramatic change with the dominance of automation and knowledge-based industries.

Development has often led to uneven growth and change. Chapter 4 investigates the trend of divergence and convergence in ASEAN in the past two decades in the areas of educational attainment, health, demographics and economic change. Education, having received due consideration, has made much progress for both males and females throughout ASEAN. There is a convergence in male and female literacy rates but a widening gap has been observed between countries in the region in secondary school enrolment rates. This means that countries with better resources and stronger political will have leapfrogged at a much faster pace than some others. Variation in health facilities and services between ASEAN members is substantial but the gap is expected to narrow between lower-income countries, such as Vietnam, Laos and Indonesia, and higher-income countries, such as Singapore and Malaysia. Again, despite a general rise in income level throughout ASEAN, the gap between nations in terms of per capita income has widened over the past 20 years, largely as a result of the low starting base of lower income countries. A much higher growth rate is needed if gaps are to narrow down with more developed ASEAN nations in the short- and medium-term. Narrowing gaps between the ASEAN countries will further consolidate their cooperation efforts for a better common future.

Chapter 5 highlights the importance of technology in both developed and developing nations. Focus is centred on high value-added manufacturing and information and knowledge-intensive activities. For more than two decades, ASEAN has been able to attract the investments of multinational corporations (MNCs) from developed nations, in particular Japan and the United States, by providing conducive investment conditions. Nonetheless, ASEAN has not established its own internationally competitive industrial base. ASEAN is expected to continue to be highly technology-dependent on developed nations. Indeed, a new form of dependency has taken place within the global division of labour for ASEAN. For example, Southeast Asian engineers are managers of export-led MNCs that have invested heavily in the region. Despite the desire of the ASEAN countries to industrialise, their current working environment does not favour research by engineers and research scientists. In Singapore where comparatively more research funds are available, there are few research scientists and engineers. Research and development compete adversely for the small pool of science and engineering graduates who tend to be attracted to the brokerage and banking sectors which may offer higher incomes. Surveys also show that there is a general lack of interaction between research companies for fear of revealing information. The author feels that building an excellent technology infrastructure in support of R&D and innovation goes hand in hand with the sociocultural attitudes of the people. With the right attitude and institutional framework provided by national governments, a technological culture can be cultivated in the 21st century.

Chapter 6 deals with the problems of reconciling development of trade with the need for environmental protection in ASEAN. There are a series of agreements signed by the ASEAN member states designed to protect the environment as trade expands. Generally speaking, however, implementation has been inadequate as achieving environmental management objectives is almost tantamount to a trade-off to trade expansion and growth. Small and medium-sized enterprises are least willing to implement demanding and high standard measures since they are most affected by environmental protection requirements, for lack of skill, expertise, capital and technology to adapt them. Yet, the ASEAN governments cannot afford to ignore these requirements because environmental degradation would lead to a rise in cost or discrimination against their exports. Like it or not, environmental protection is a norm to be adopted, and will be an integral component of the development process. International and domestic pressures are bound to mount arising from the need to safeguard "collective survival" in the long term.

The environmental issue is then focused on the urban setting in Chapter 7 which discusses the sustainability of Southeast Asian primate cities. Urban sustainability has been a stimulating issue of development in the last two decades as cities experience the most acute environmental degradation due to their high concentration of production and consumption in relatively small areas. Added to this is the high incidence of urban poor in quarters of the Southeast Asian capitals or primate cities, deprived specifically of basic services and infrastructure. At the same time, these cities are centres of industrial capital investments and financial and administrative hubs accommodating a high-paying skilled workforce that supports a large consumer market. There is no direct relationship between the extent of environmental degradation and that of foreign direct investments in individual Southeast Asian countries. The degree of degradation is actually linked more to the enforcement capability of individual governments and types of domestic industries that are allowed to operate in the cities.

Sustainability indicators are needed in the form of guidelines for national governments to translate environmental policies into action. There should be different sets of indicators to suit the abilities of different countries to deal with the criteria for environmental sustainability. The use of sustainability indicators should be seen as an integral component of a developmental and incremental process.

Chapter 8 deals with transboundary migration of the ASEAN population. In general, the mobility of the population rises with urbanisation, advancement in transport technology and improvement in living standards that make travel more affordable. In Southeast Asia, there has been a dramatic increase in personal mobility resulting in both permanent and non-permanent redistribution of population. This redistribution is most significant in the form of rural-urban migration within countries. Globalisation as an agent of change has induced population flow in terms of job opportunities. Within Southeast Asia itself, cross-country labour flow, both legal and illegal, has originated from disparities in both economic and demographic aspects, facilitated by cheaper travel and improved social and information network.

Many countries in Southeast Asia are both importers and exporters of workforce. An overall net loss of permanent migrants is recorded in the region, most of whom have been absorbed by more developed nations, such as Australia, Canada and the United States. The status of migrants has evolved from the largely Indochinese refugees of the 1970s to more skilled and affluent individuals with investment potential in the recipient countries. Non-permanent migrants from Southeast Asia have been significant, in particular nationals from the Philippines, Indonesia and Thailand to West Asia, representing more than half of the foreign workforce in that region. The nature of work has also shifted from primarily infrastructure development to services, especially domestic services. Remittances, an important source of revenues for countries such as the Philippines, have surged dramatically over the past 20 years. More recently, Japan, South Korea, Taiwan and Hong Kong have become key destinations of these non-permanent migrants. Another feature is that because of a large influx of foreign direct investments into Southeast Asia, a sizeable number of well-qualified expatriate staff from developed nations now form part of this mobile foreign workforce.

The ASEAN workforce is expected to experience faster growth in labour-surplus countries but slower growth in countries enjoying higher economic growth. The overall trend will be characterised by rising numbers of younger cohorts of migrants. However, free movements of the labour force within ASEAN are in no way liberalised. In the light of a corresponding rise in undocumented migrants who are at times involved in criminal activities, more regulated flow is seen as necessary.

Chapter 9 looks at the relationship between the role of education and economic performance in ASEAN. Perhaps, with the exception of the Philippines, educational attainment in ASEAN somehow corresponds with the available resources of the national government in sponsoring universal education. For example, poverty in Vietnam means qualitative deficiencies in its educational system. Indonesia is another case in point. In spite of high achievement in universal primary school education, rural poverty in some remote regions has deprived many children of access to basic education. Lower-income groups are generally handicapped by restricted access to secondary education as well as the lower quality of their schools. School leavers from poorer schools are disadvantaged in the job market.

Without doubt, human capital formation through strongly committed formal schooling has contributed to growth by enhancing the skills and productivity of the workforce. This enhancement of productivity is inseparable from capitalising on modern technology that requires knowledge to operate. Education cannot and should not be completely tied up with the job market. Education has increasingly become a right rather than a means to equip learners with skills to meet job requirements. Mismatch of education and the labour market is inevitable when the economy fluctuates. In sum, schooling is merely a starting point. To link it with economic performance, one must not ignore the importance of training and retraining the workforce to meet the changing needs in the job place. On this issue, Chapter 10 examines lifelong learning using geography as a case study. Through the years of economic progress, an awareness has been firmly developed amidst national governments in ASEAN, in particular Singapore *vis-à-vis* the importance of education. The rapidly changing world environment and circumstances have called for sustained efforts to update the workforce. In Singapore, the in-service education programmes have been developed to keep teachers abreast of the changes in the discipline content. In-service learning helps place teachers at the forefront of professional training and as facilitators monitoring and maintaining the internal dynamism of a nation's education system. To be effective, in-service programmes need to be specifically tailored to the needs of the teacher upgraders. Long-term education policies should also be charted for an effective lifelong training of teachers. This will benefit both students and the workforce as a whole.

Summary

Southeast Asia has witnessed turbulent events in the past 30 years. Thus ASEAN was first formed with the primary objective of ensuring the regional security of the non-communist allies in the region. Ideological differences were then dividing the Southeast Asian nations into two conflicting blocs characterised by distrust, lack of dialogue and lack of regional cooperation. Since then ASEAN has moved towards a common destiny, surmounting barriers that once kept member states apart. Some of the issues treated in this book include the following:

- There is a trend towards convergence between the two main systems of government in Southeast Asia. On one hand, the current political economic reforms in the centrally planned economies, such as Vietnam, Laos, Myanmar and Cambodia, call for a greater role of market forces to minimise market failure. On the other hand, domestic weaknesses of the more *laissez-faire* economies have been exposed following an unprecedented monetary crisis. Reform of the financial systems seems inevitable.

- There is greater emphasis now on lifelong learning. Education will play a greater role in the region, contributing towards growth, environmental quality and, perhaps, a more democratic system tailored to the needs of ASEAN states.

- In an increasingly globalised economy, a greater mobility of workforce is anticipated across international boundaries.

- Urbanisation is an irreversible trend and cities have produced the most serious pollution problems. Greater international efforts will be required to safeguard the environment which is often transboundary in nature.

- Southeast Asia is still highly technology-dependent. Regional efforts in technological collaboration remain weak. The links between ASEAN countries and countries outside ASEAN, particularly in trade and technological cooperation, are much stronger than those within ASEAN itself.

ACKNOWLEDGEMENTS

The editors wish to thank the Continuing Education Committee, National Institute of Education, and all those who have helped in one way or another to make this book a reality.

Chapter 1

Imaginative Geography and the Postcolonial Spaces of Pacific Asia

Dean Forbes

Introduction

The approaching millennium has encouraged the critical review of representations of the structure and functioning of Pacific Asian space. Many of the key concepts which evolved under colonialism, and in the half century which followed the withdrawal of colonial powers, are being displaced due to the greater recognition being given to the postcolonial expressions of regionality emerging from Pacific Asia. New core functional regions are evolving through both government supported and spontaneous patterns of economic, political, social and cultural interaction. These imaginative geographies are harbingers of new ways of organising and representing space in the coming century.

This chapter addresses three related sets of issues. It begins by defining the use of the term postcolonial in relation to space/ geography and method. This conceptual distinction forms the basis for arguing that there are a number of contrasting manifestations of new spatial processes in the Pacific Asian region, and these have produced an array of new ways of representing the geographies of the region. The second part of the chapter examines a particular example of imaginative geographies expressed in the changing relationship between Australia and Pacific Asia. Finally the chapter discusses the implications of emerging representations of postcolonial space, focusing on the impact of the economic crisis, and new meanings of the state, identity and culture.

Constructing Postcolonial Space

Postcolonialism has two distinct, albeit intricately related, meanings in this essay. First, postcolonialism is a term used to describe the changing structures and relationships between the state, economy and society in nations able to find and develop a niche in the rapidly evolving global economy. The economic success of the newly industrialising economies (NIEs) of Asia is often cited as evidence of a decisive new period of Pacific Asian history with implications for the structures and functioning of these societies. A key institution, the postcolonial state, it is sometimes argued, has emerged largely free of the institutionalised influence of former colonial powers and other foreign states. The state thus has emerged as a relatively autonomous, even neutral institution, and potentially capable of achieving progressive ends.

New geographies have assembled and disassembled with each iteration of economy and politics, creating what I call postcolonial space. On a global scale the power relationships embedded in the economic domination of one nation over another have been superseded by the expanded role of global corporations. The emergence of a multipolar (some would say tripolar) global economy signals the end of the so-called Third World and the emergence of postcolonial space. Most significantly, state borders have been permeated and territories combined and reconstituted in new ways. The territorial units formed during decolonisation around mid-20th century, while still demarcating the formal space of the nation state, have been redefined.

A second meaning of postcolonialism is methodological. According to this usage, postcolonialism is an approach intended "to achieve an authentic globalization of cultural discourses ... abolish all distinctions between centre and periphery ... and to reveal societies globally in their complex heterogeneity and contingency" (Dirlik, 1994:329). A postcolonial approach to Asian space calls for serious, critical attention to the expression of other representations of change, alternatives to mainstream Western academic opinion. This is not a new argument, but is important nevertheless. Concerns about the need to heed the voices from the once colonised territories predates the emergence of the term postcolonial in the mid-1980s (for example, see Yeung, 1985; McGee, 1995).

The two dimensions of postcolonialism are related in that the emergence of postcolonial economies, societies and spaces creates the need for renewed articulations of identity and meaning. This, in turn, encourages the expression of alternative views of the way in which social and spatial processes are defined and analysed. Yet these are often mediated through concepts originating in Western social science, and predominantly expressed through English language texts. This imposes some rigidities on the expressions of postcoloniality, which require us to sometimes look beyond academic literature into other mediums of expression, such as cinema.

Edward Said (1978) made the distinction between "imaginative geography" and "positive" or "actual" geography. He went on to say that:

> ... imaginative geography and history help the mind to intensify its own sense of itself by dramatising the distance and difference between what is close to it and what is far away (Said, 1978:55).

The imaginative geographies to which Said referred were colonial in origin, and thus formed the basis of the caricature of "Eastern" societies as "orientalist". The imaginative geographies of the late 1990s, by contrast, are hybrid in origins.[1] They bring together ideas emanating from Western political economy, which are still the dominant stream of thought, with emerging postcolonial representations of place and space. Moreover, they do not seek to dramatise distance and difference, but recognise the homogenising impact of globalisation as well as the vast diversity of responses and momentums within local and regional communities. Thus the emerging imaginative geographies of the Pacific Asian region combine aspects of both meanings of "postcolonial" identified earlier.

The New Spaces of Pacific Asia

Since the heyday of political geography in the first half of the 20th century, geographers have gradually edged more and more to the periphery of contemporary discussions of global geopolitics or "metageography", as it is called by Lewis and Wigen (1997). Geographers' concerns about the way in which global regions are defined and redefined were replaced until recently by an intensified focus on fieldwork research and the detailed study of local change. However, the emergence of underdevelopment and world systems theories in the 1970s and 1980s, and the current concern with expressions of "globalisation", have encouraged renewed explorations of global geographies and especially the interaction between global processes and specific localities, especially cities.

Pacific Asia is proving to be fertile territory for thinking about the way in which space is reinvented and reconceptualised (Forbes, 1997b). The interplay between the inexorable impact of globalisation and the multifaceted responses of Pacific Asian economies and societies has encouraged governments to respond by facilitating the reinvention of major types of new spaces. Yet the production of global "metageography" itself is problematical. What precisely is meant by the term "Asia", and how is this particular regional entity justified?

Lewis and Wigen (1997:21–25) trace the origins of the term "Asia" to the view of ancient Greek mariners who distinguished between two continents: Europe (Greece) and Asia (Turkey). Africa was added later to the known world as a third continent. The idea of Asia grew and spread eastwards as knowledge of the world expanded, until it embraced the whole landmass east of a line running from the Ural Mountains to the Mediterranean. A continental fixation still dominates popular constructions of global geography. McGee (1995:196) has argued that the idea of Asia is essentially Western because there is no equivalent word in any Asian language. Asia has acquired a cartographic identity defined essentially by its non-Europeanness.[2]

In the same vein, the subcontinental, macroregional divisions within Asia have also been subject to different constructions. The conventional wisdom in scholarly writings has been to differentiate between East and Southeast Asia (Lewis & Wigen, 1997:186–87). Moreover, these terms are constantly being reinvented: as an example, the expansion of the Association of Southeast Asian Nations (ASEAN) over the years gives a tangible expression to what has been for many decades essentially a scholarly construction of "Southeast Asia", which defines the region as much by what it is not — it is not South Asia, nor is it East Asia or part of Australasia — as by what it is.

Because of the arbitrariness of such representations, other regional constructions compete for influence, depending on the purposes of the exercise: two constructions of regions in frequent use are the Asia–Pacific (Dirlik, 1993; Wilson & Dirlik, 1995) and Pacific Asia. Much of the contemporary usage of these terms is promoted by the postwar economic growth rates experienced by the eastern Asian seaboard countries. The Pacific Basin and the Pacific Rim have a different meaning, directly including both the small states of the Pacific Ocean as well as the Pacific coast states of North, Central and South America (Watters & McGee, 1997). Not all scholars support the evolution of new geographic labels: Cumings (1993) derides debates about the Pacific Rim as the growth of "Rimspeak". The lack of consensus over alternatives to the conventional definitions is indicative of the rethinking of the meaning of regional boundaries.

Within the Pacific Asian region, economic space in particular has been stretched and pulled as a result of both government and private sector initiatives. The result is that different organisations, and emerging patterns of interaction, have combined to suggest an emerging set of links and trends (Rimmer, 1997). Regional organisations oriented to macro-economic ends, as distinct from security arrangements, have emerged or changed shape, giving new structure and meaning to them as organisations. ASEAN,[3] which was established in 1967, has emerged as the most important regional organisation. It expanded to nine members in 1997, and recently included a new member, Cambodia, in early 1999. While ASEAN has had minor success as an economic unit, the announcement of the ASEAN Free Trade Area (AFTA) idea in the early 1990s signalled intentions to expand economic integration between member countries by gradually reducing the importance of tariff barriers to trade.

The recent expansion of ASEAN, and the difficulties of implementing the concept of AFTA, give expression to new ways of thinking about Southeast Asia. Significantly, ASEAN has been forced to bridge the ideological divide between "socialist" and non-socialist countries, an ironic move given that ASEAN's origins were an attempt to provide a bulwark against the expansion of socialist influence in the region. Moreover, the erosion of the tariffs, which were barriers to increased intra-ASEAN trade (or had forced trade through illegal channels), is recognition of the substantial economic benefits that could emerge from closer economic integration among these countries. Together these initiatives help to redefine ASEAN, highlighting the changing significance of the organisation and the countries it links, 30 years after its establishment.

The Asia Pacific Economic Cooperation (APEC) is of much more recent vintage and is less well entrenched in the institutional structures of its members than ASEAN. However, it has an ambitious economic agenda, which, like ASEAN, is centred around the desire to reduce tariffs and hence foster trade among its members. The commitment of APEC countries to the notion of "open regionalism", while sometimes considered naive, is an important institutional symbol of a pan-Pacific perspective set within a global context. A plethora of more specialised organisations devoted to issues ranging from economic interaction to urban development also seek to draw together people from both sides of the Pacific, though without seriously raising questions of regional identity.

A related group of emerging spatial formations is labelled regional economic zones. These are government created, economic regions, but represent a new organisation of space across national boundaries. Two examples of regional economic zones formed between ASEAN members illustrate this concept. The most prominent example is the Singapore growth triangle which links together Singapore with Indonesia's Riau Province and Malaysia's state of Johor. A rationale for the arrangement is the combination of Singapore's capital, technology and managerial talent with the land and labour resources of southern Malaysia and coastal Sumatra, thus sharing development among the three participants.

A newer regional economic zone is the awkwardly titled Brunei Indonesia Malaysia Philippines (BIMP) East ASEAN Growth Area (EAGA), which was officially formed in March 1994. The membership of BIMP–EAGA is drawn from four countries: Indonesia's provinces of west, central, south and east Kalimantan, north, central, southeast and south Sulawesi, Maluku and Irian Jaya. Malaysia's Sabah, Sarawak and the Federal Territory of Labuan, Mindanao and Palawan from the Philippines, and Brunei Darussalam, complete the membership. The objective of the group is "to increase cross border trade and investment/economic activity", with the ultimate aim of "the realisation of environmentally sustainable and socially acceptable economic development" (EAGA, 1997a).

Another variation on the interplay between state initiative and postcolonial space is illustrated by recent shifts in China's space economy (Linge, 1997). China's economic growth has been accompanied by significant internal restructuring of its space economy, most notably in a shift from its "third line" interior orientation in the 1960s to its coastal strategy of the 1980s which accompanied the opening up of the economy. Moreover, in the early years of the coastal focus, emphasis was given to the southern regions, particularly Guandong Province, followed by a shift in the early 1990s towards the central (e.g. Shanghai) and northern regions (Liaoning Province).

Independent states have taken the initiative in creating and sustaining the regional economic zones mentioned above. However, much of the momentum for the creation of new imaginative geographies stems from shifting patterns of economic engagement which, to a large extent, transcend (and sometimes deliberately ignore) the boundaries of the state. A continuation of China's economic opening up in the 1990s has prompted the view that China's domestic regional economies are increasingly engaging with neighbouring economies, exacerbating centrifugal forces. Research on the investment patterns of the Chinese diaspora (or the overseas Chinese) in southern China is an illustration of this process (Lever-Tracy et al., 1996). These investment activities often centre on the transfer of relatively small sums of private or family money, not the activity of corporations. The investments focus on small towns, not large cities, and the places chosen are generally the ancestral homes of the investors, and hence could not be described as footloose investments. Thus these accounts highlight the historically embedded and cultural meanings of space.

Finally the influence of the momentum of rural-urban migration in nations with still relatively low levels of urbanisation, combined with the polarisation effects of their accelerated integration into the global economy, has ushered into existence new urban forms throughout Pacific Asia (Forbes, 1997a). Scholars have invented a plethora of new labels to identify and distinguish between these places.

Megacities, or near magacities, such as Jakarta, Bangkok and Manila, extend the imagination as to how large cities might grow before residents and businesses alike start moving out of the city in larger numbers, thus precipitating some form of polarisation reversal. Moreover, the deep penetration of the largest cities into their once-rural hinterland and the creation of "extended metropolitan regions" (or desakota regions) challenge the binary urban-rural spatial divisions upon which much social science analysis is based. It is open to speculation that city-regions, many of which in population terms dwarf nearby nation-states, might inevitably become political rivals of the nations which host them, with serious implications for geopolitics.

Emergent "world cities" such as Singapore, and possibly Bangkok, represent another variation on the pattern of urban development (Forbes, 1996; Lo & Yeung, 1996). When the world cities are connected to major regional cities, such as

Jakarta, Kuala Lumpur, and to a lesser extent Manila, Ho Chi Minh City and Surabaya, by a spine of intensive transport and communications, so-called "megaurban corridors" are hypothesised (Rimmer, 1995).

Pacific Asia and Australia

For most of the past decade, Australia has occupied an ambiguous place within the restructuring of Pacific Asian space. The debate situating Australia *vis-à-vis* Pacific Asia has mainly concerned scholars in international economics and international relations. However, the recent expansion of the debate beyond its trade/investment and security core has opened the discourse to a divergence of views. Examining Australia's links to Pacific Asia in the broader context of the emergence of postcolonial space, demonstrates the important questions raised by the new imaginative geographies.

An intensifying discussion within Australia about its relationship to Pacific Asia intersects with another growing debate about identity and citizenship, not least in the context of whether Australia should shed its links with the British monarchy and become a republic. These debates are a manifestation of postcolonial preoccupations among some Australian scholars, specifically connected to a growing national angst about the plight of the country's indigenous population.

It is the conventional wisdom that Asia became a priority for Australian governments only after the election of the Labor government in 1983, this orientation reaching its pinnacle in the years when Paul Keating was Prime Minister (1991–96).[4] This is, however, disputed by the Liberal National Party Coalition government of John Howard, which argues that Australia has been concerned about its Asian future since the Menzies government in the 1950s, if not before (trade and shipping links go back to the 18th century). Certainly the United Kingdom's decision to enter the forerunner to the European Union was a catalyst for Australia's refocusing on Asia.

In recent years, both Labor and Liberal coalition governments have expressed Australia's Asian links as an economic imperative. Highlights of this connection are the high levels of trade between Australia and northeast Asia (Japan, South Korea and Taiwan) in particular, stemming from basic economic complementarities. Added to that are the growing economic links with Southeast Asian countries. For example, many overseas students studying in Australia are from Malaysia, Indonesia and Singapore. Putting the issue into long-term perspective, Asia's sheer population size, combined with uncertainty about the exclusiveness of potential European and North American trade blocs, makes closer economic links with Asia essential.

Nevertheless, questions have been asked about how well Australia as a whole has been able to realise this desire. According to FitzGerald (1997), the defining moment of recent years for Australia's Asian relations was its failure to be admitted to the Asia–Europe (ASEM) talks in 1996 (in addition to its exclusion from the East Asia Economic Caucus). FitzGerald overstates the case, but not by all that much.

The complexity of Australia's international links has many sources in history and geography. Perhaps the most important has been the endurance of sentimental links with Europe. Economic, military and cultural links with the United States have been grafted on to these for several decades. Added to all this is the overwhelming importance of Australia's trade links with northeast Asian countries, especially Japan and South Korea. Overall, therefore, there is a great degree of complexity, and inevitably confusion, in Australia's attempt to prioritise and position the nation, especially regarding Asia (Elegant, 1997).

This raises another issue — that of ambiguity. Australia is generally aligned with North American and European nations when voting in the United Nations, but at other times, it is seen as part of Asia. Sometimes it is seen as neither part of Europe, nor of Asia, such as in the preparations for the Asia–Europe summit. In the middle of a downward spiral of stock markets in October 1997, there were press reports that many currency traders in the United States sold Australian dollars because the country was seen to be enmeshed in Asia, whereas other traders in the US and especially in the United Kingdom resisted following suit because they saw Australia as external to the region and, therefore, less affected by the economic events (Radio National "PM", 24 October 1997).

The imaginative geographies of the last few decades have maintained a distinct separation between East and Southeast Asia on the one hand, and Australia and New Zealand on the other (e.g. Lewis & Wigen, 1997:187). Continental and archipelago societies are differentiated from island societies. Australia and New Zealand sometimes stand alone (as Australasia), or are sometimes lumped together with the states of Melanesia, Micronesia and Polynesia into a region known only in books as Oceania.

FitzGerald (1997:81) touchingly argues that greater attention to Asian history and geography in Australian schools is urgently needed to correct the perception that Australia is geographically outside Asia. As a geographer, of course, I strongly agree, as our students' knowledge of Asia's geography is limited (see Andressen, 1997), but FitzGerald (1997:118) fails to mention geography in his list of tertiary subjects deserving support. Yet there seems a need to go much further. Geography's "dramatisation of the differences" between Australia and Pacific Asia has created a distortion; the first priority must be, instead, that the postcolonial geography of Pacific Asia needs to be reassessed.

Growing Australian entanglement in Asia has been manifest in involvement in at least two new forms of economic space that need to be mentioned before I return to reflect on the new postcolonial geographies of Pacific Asia. The first is through participating in APEC, the most broad-based macro-economic organisation within the region. Then Australian Prime Minister Bob Hawke played a key role in the establishment of APEC in 1989 and his successors, Paul Keating and John Howard, have both maintained a significant level of support for the organisation. While seen as having primarily an economic role, APEC's most tangible achievements thus far have been symbolic. In particular, since 1993, the annual meetings of heads of government have provided both an attractive photographic opportunity and an important symbol of the ability of governments from both sides of the Pacific to meet to discuss matters of importance (Gallant & Stubbs, 1997).

However, unlike ASEAN, APEC represents a Western defined grouping rather than an indigenous construction. It is for this reason that FitzGerald (1997:13–14) considers APEC an irrelevance, as far as Australia is concerned. It represents a safe club for Australia, allowing it to avoid the hard decision to fully commit itself to Asia.[5] FitzGerald (1997:152, 156) would prefer to see APEC replaced by a more tightly defined East Asia community of which Australia was an integral part.

Since its conception, APEC supporters have urged that it remains almost exclusively an economic forum. This has helped to keep it focused, but it has created an artificially narrow range of goals. Other kinds of activities also intimately bind together the region, and change significantly with liberalisation of trade. For example, population movements lag behind, but inevitably follow, economic integration (Lloyd & Williams, 1996); and throughout 1997, the environmental consequences of the forest fires in Sumatra and Kalimantan seriously affected Malaysia and Singapore, and involved countries, such as Australia, in the effort to extinguish the fires.

The Asian currency crisis and stock exchange losses of 1997–98 have provided the most important economic crisis which affected all the economies of the region for many years. APEC seems to have played no significant role in the management of the crisis, which has been largely dealt with by the International Monetary Fund (IMF) and various bilateral arrangements between countries. As long as the problems were confined to Thailand, Malaysia and Indonesia, then the impact on Australia was likely to be relatively restricted. This is because Australia's more important economic links are with northeast Asia. But of course, the impact was very noticeable in specific sectors, particularly because trade with Southeast Asia has been growing rapidly. The Australian government's response, expressed by John Howard during a stopover in Jakarta, was to recognise this as a time of "regional mateship". More tangibly, the Australian government has provided short-term loans, under IMF-specified conditions, to Thailand and Indonesia.

The crisis may, on reflection, come to represent a more important defining moment for Australia's relationship to the region than its absence from the ASEM summit. It is much too early to fully understand the full dimensions of change, let alone the consequences. However, it is possible that this period of adversity will sharply reveal the real depths of Australian economic integration with Pacific Asia and provide a basis for greater levels of inclusion of Australia in the new imaginative geographies of Pacific Asia.

Regional economic zones are another way in which space in Pacific Asia has been restructured. Within Southeast Asia, it is the Indonesian government which has been the most active in creating these types of arrangements. Two have special importance for Australia. The BIMP–EAGA group, which incorporates parts of eastern Indonesia, is adjacent to Australia's northern coast. Its emphasis is on fostering cross-border economic activities, hence the majority of its 13 working groups, focus on either communications (air, sea transport, telecommunications) or on activities which transcend boundaries (joint tourist development, fisheries cooperation, environmental protection and management, population mobility). To give an illustration, the "people mobility" working group has focused on accreditation for health workers moving from Indonesia and the Philippines to Malaysia; travel tax exemption for those departing the Philippines through Mindanao; and predeparture trainer training in Sarawak. Together with initiatives just commencing, the thrust is on greater mobility for workers and business people within the BIMP–EAGA area (EAGA, 1997a; 1997b).

The government of Australia's Northern Territory (NT), based in Darwin, is actively building the linkages between the NT and Southeast Asia, especially in the context of the BIMP–EAGA region. This adds to a number of initiatives over the last few years. Indicative of the NT government's approach is a memorandum of understanding between the Republic of Indonesia and the NT government on Economic Development Cooperation, signed in Jakarta in 1992, and the existence of a Department of Asian Relations, Trade and Industry in Darwin to oversee this and other links with Asia.

A more recent initiative to develop another separate regional economic zone was the agreement between the

Australian and Indonesian governments to create an Australia–Indonesia Development Area (AIDA). The formal agreement was signed in Ambon in April 1997. Indonesian Foreign Minister Ali Alatas (1997) announced:

> The concept of this sub-regional cooperation is quite simple: we link adjacent areas with different but complementary factor endowments and different but complementary comparative advantages. The new and larger area thus formed consequently acquires a greater potential for economic growth. Indonesia is of the view that sub-regional cooperation will help ensure balanced development in the whole region.

Formally declared regional economic zones provide another mechanism for bringing together regions around an economic core. They supplement existing arrangements, such as the sister province/state agreement between the government of West Java and South Australia, which was signed in mid-1997. Clearly it would be premature to reflect on the long-term significance of these new forms of regional arrangements. Perhaps their fundamental, underlying flaw, though, is that while they are government-to-government in form, their intention is to lay the groundwork for greater private sector economic activity. Yet decisions by firms are based on profitability, not on the desires of government.

Economy, State and Identity

The representations of postcolonial space are founded on three key interrelated processes: the explicit power of economic integration to affect social processes; a reconstruction and slight erosion in the formal power of the nation-state; and the emergence of more complex, fragmented identities among Pacific Asian peoples. Each of these claims, however, involves a tangle of complex issues, and interpretations are contested.

The representation of emerging Pacific Asian postcolonial geographies was in the past set in the context of consistent, albeit unevenly distributed, economic growth throughout the region. The economic crisis that gained momentum in the first half of 1997, began with a rapid devaluation of the Thai baht, but subsequently spread to many other countries throughout the region. It has created the most serious economic crisis within Pacific Asia since the 1930s. At its core, the economic crisis stemmed from weaknesses in the financial sectors of a handful of countries, a product of bad bank loans which remain on the books but could not be repaid, partisan political involvement in banking, and a lack of overall transparency in financial management.

The growing economic integration within the region, and, even more importantly, the integration of Pacific Asia into the global economy, has facilitated the speed and spread of the impact of the crisis. Nevertheless, individual countries have been influenced unevenly. The economies most severely affected include Indonesia, Thailand, Malaysia and South Korea. Vietnam and the Philippines have been less affected because of weaker growth and momentum before the crisis. By comparison, there has been less impact on Singapore so far, mainly because of the underlying strength of its economy. Japan will undoubtedly face problems because of the high level of Japanese banks' exposure to Southeast Asia. China's difficulties are due to the important role of Southeast Asian countries as a source of finance and market for exports. However, the sheer magnitude of the Japanese and Chinese economies has masked some of the negative impact, though few observers are sufficiently bold to predict an end to instability. As long as the banking sector in major economies, such as Japan, avoids serious reform, the region's economic future will remain unpredictable.

Yet the key question is how will the economic crisis affect the development of postcolonial space within Pacific Asia? Economic growth in the Asian Pacific region has resulted in models of a tripolar global economy, in which North America and Europe represent the two longstanding centres of economic activity, and Pacific Asia, anchored by Japan, the NIEs, and increasingly China, representing the third main pole. The devaluation of most regional currencies has reduced the prices of key assets throughout the region. This has attracted cash-rich North American and European investors wanting to buy up cheap, under-utilised productive assets, such as manufacturing plants, as a means of securing a significant export capacity able to capitalise on any future Asian economic recovery (Sender et al., 1998). Local Asian companies have been slower to respond (Elegant, 1998). Thus one outcome of the economic crisis may be a skewing of the globalisation process, with a strengthening of the North American and European poles at the expense of the Pacific Asian pole of the global economy.

The severity of the economic crisis has tested regional leadership, resulting in some loss of confidence in economic planning models and raising questions about leadership practices. In general, though, the major regional institutions, such as ASEAN and APEC, appear to have played a relatively minor role in managing the crisis (Hiebert et al., 1998). The incoming secretary-general of ASEAN, Rodolfo Severino, has admitted that insufficient frank consultation among ASEAN government heads exacerbated the financial crisis (Tesoro, 1998). However, he also added that ASEAN members have increased cooperation and consultation since the crisis began, and the group is intensifying its commitment to liberalisation through AFTA. Nevertheless, it is likely that a longer-term consequence of the crisis will be increased diversification of Pacific Asian economies in an attempt to spread economic risks.

Indonesia appears to have been the country most seriously affected by the region's economic crisis. In large part, this was due to the coincidence of economic and political crises, the failure of banks forcing a decline in the value of the rupiah, coinciding with the leadup to presidential and vice-presidential elections in which anti-Suharto sentiment was widespread, albeit repressed. There is widespread pessimism in Indonesia since the fall of President Suharto, on the ability of the new regime to exercise the discipline necessary to solve the financial crisis (Pangestu, 1998).

The social consequences of the crisis in Indonesia are severe, with huge rises in the price of food and essential goods, and an increase in social unrest and rioting. Changing patterns of population mobility reveal some of the key shifts in the space economy of Indonesia. Migration to the cities has begun to accelerate as rural folk leave in search of new sources of income. At times of economic crisis, the metropolis is erroneously perceived to offer better income prospects. In addition, the number of illegal labour migrants trying to enter Malaysia has escalated significantly.

Indonesia's six-million strong Chinese minority has, as in the past, been the target of much social unrest. Shops have been looted and burnt in towns throughout most parts of the archipelago. There have been few perceived safe havens in Indonesia; only Manado in North Sulawesi and the island of Bali were considered less risky. As a result, migrants departing Indonesia have increased significantly since the onset of the economic problem and increased social unrest. Moreover, while wealthy Indonesian Chinese have long had residences overseas in places such as Singapore and Sydney, it now appears that middle-class migrants have been emigrating, most of whom transferred all their assets with them. Indonesian immigration applications to Australia have risen 25 percent since the crisis began, while 35 percent of all Indonesian migrants to Australia locate in the city of Perth (Gilley et al., 1998:47). The Indonesian government was initially lethargic in its response to these occurrences.

Underpinning the rethinking of geographies is a questioning of the changing meanings of the nation-state. Is the nation-state weakening, its sovereignty undermined and replaced by a range of other political alliances? Macro-regional groups, such as ASEAN or APEC, are sometimes cited as evidence of another layer of political structures that erode some of the control functions of nations. However, as discussed above, neither institution has been able to make its mark on recent political events or the economic crisis. Both groups have struggled successfully to implement plans to reduce tariffs, finding that most member states have fallen behind their schedules.

Meanwhile the IMF has played an important role in providing financial support for beleaguered Asian economies (Thailand, South Korea and Indonesia), and at the same time setting down stringent guidelines for financial management. Indonesia, in particular, has responded with public concerns about the erosion of the rights of the sovereign state, though it appears that this has been intended to mask the regime's real concern to protect the wealth of the nation's former first family. The governance capacity of the state is also open to question as cities grow in economic strength and importance. At what point might the wealthy city challenge the nation by undermining its sovereignty? Parallels are occasionally drawn with the German Hanseatic League of centuries past.

In contrast, other interpretations return to the importance of the reinvention and reinforcement of the state, underscoring the point that the state's existence in its present form is more problematical than it has been. Throughout Asia, there is evidence of an accelerating search for identity which is interwoven with a more strident nationalism. Anderson (1991) has explored how historically, communities, and hence nations, are imagined. Maps have played an important part, along with the census and the museum, in forming ideas of nationalism. The rules by which government statistics are compiled, and the presence of contemporary lingua franca (e.g. Bahasa Indonesia) which correspond to national borders, continue to shape the mental boundaries of geographical investigation. Official boundaries, which evolved into national boundaries, have been crucial to the writing of the geography of Pacific Asia, whether during the colonial period or since. Contemporary Indonesian cinema, for instance, is an important shaper of nationalist sentiments (Heider, 1994).

Much of the imagining of new Pacific Asian geographies centres on economic integration and variations to the meaning of the nation-state, thus overlooking broader questions of emerging regional identities. Yet underpinning the expansion of ASEAN is a sense that Southeast Asia is a meaningful region, just as the putative formation of an East Asian Economic Caucus implies there is some coherence to this particular collection of countries. FitzGerald (1997:36) refers to the formation of stronger Asian political agendas, which is occurring in parallel with globalisation and cultural decolonisation, as the "Asianisation of Asia".

Yet clearly there are multiple identities embodied within the imagined region. Australia is presently excluded from this imaginative geography, but the way in which Australia deals with the present economic crisis, and the response of its neighbours, has the potential to be a new "defining moment" in the development of postcolonial space. Perhaps more profoundly, Australia's long-term enmeshment in Asia will revolve around questions of the kind of country it is to be. Australia's Asian future necessarily involves a greater understanding of culture, values and symbols, and in particular the embeddedness of Asia in Australian identity. The cutting edge of this debate in Australia will inevitably centre on the republican issue. It is in this debate that Australians will attempt to establish the symbols of a nation able to negotiate its own way in Asia. Thus the republican debate is a major part of the redefining/reinvention of Australia.

Conclusion

It is important to tackle the way in which the new postcolonial geographies of Pacific Asia are expressed. This does not mean the abandonment of the state as an important unit of analysis, but it does require a rethink of the metageographies and global regionalisations on which we depend, and it does require us to confront the new territorial arrangements which are active agents in changing the geography of the region. Institutions such as APEC and ASEAN, the regional economic zones, the regional network of world cities, and the rethinking of the previously excluded nations such as Australia, are part of the reinvention of the geography of Pacific Asia. The imaginative geographies currently emerging are strongly influenced by the politico-economic dimensions of globalisation. The postcolonial spaces of the next century will be more strongly identified with the postcolonial expressions of identity that are the inevitable, if discursive, outcome of the complexities of multifaceted globalisation.

ACKNOWLEDGEMENTS

I would like to thank Cecile Cutler for her assistance with the collection of information used in the preparation of this chapter.

Notes

1. Of the recent geographies of Southeast Asia, the book by Rigg (1997) makes the most substantial attempt thus far to look at what he calls "postdevelopmental" geographies. Essays in Yeung (1993) consider Pacific Asia's geography of the 21st century.

2. The term the "West" may, itself, "no longer be a geographical category but a state of mind" (Hutnyk, 1995:5). The same could be equally applied to the "East" (or the "Orient").

3. ASEAN commenced with five member states, Singapore, Malaysia, Indonesia, Thailand and the Philippines, later adding Brunei Darussalam, then Vietnam, Laos, Myanmar (Burma) and now Cambodia.

4. One of former Prime Minister Keating's last statements of his vision for Australia and Asia was delivered as the Singapore Lecture (Keating, 1996).

5. For similar reasons, FitzGerald rejects the use of the term "Asia–Pacific".

References

Alatas, A. (1997) "Remarks by H.E. Mr Ali Alatas Minister for Foreign Affairs Republic of Indonesia at the Seminar on the progress and challenges of the Indonesia–Northern Territory Memorandum of Understanding and the Australia–Indonesia Development Area (AIDA), Jakarta 3 April 1997". http://www.dfa-deplu.go.id/english2/aida.htm

Anderson, B. (1991) *Imagined Communities: Reflections on the Origin and Spread of Nationalism*. Revised edition. London: Verso.

Andressen, C. (1997) "Mental maps of Asia: The geographical knowledge of Australian university students". *Asian Studies Review*, 21:115–30.

Cumings, B. (1993) "Rimspeak; or, the discourse of the 'Pacific Rim'" In A. Dirlik (ed.), *What is in a Rim? Critical Perspectives on the Pacific Region Idea*. Boulder: Westview Press. pp. 29–47.

Dirlik, A. (1993) "Introducing the Pacific" In A. Dirlik (ed.), *What is in a Rim? Critical Perspectives on the Pacific Region Idea*. Boulder: Westview Press. pp. 3–12.

————. (1994) "The postcolonial aura: Third World criticism in the age of global capitalism". *Critical Inquiry*, 20:328–56.

EAGA. (1997a) "The BIMP EAGA Development Strategy". http://www.pugo.id/publik/kerjas~1/bimp-e~1

———. (1997b) "Brunei-Darussalam Indonesia Malaysia the Philippines — East ASEAN Growth Area (IMP–EAGA)". http://www.brunet.bn/org/bimpeabc/welcome.htm

Elegant, S. (1997) "Immigration: Southern comfort. Despite Pauline Hanson's outbursts, Australia has embraced Asian cultures". *Far Eastern Economic Review*, 160(43):77–80.

———. (1998) "Opportunity knocks". *Far Eastern Economic Review*, 161(11):10–14

FitzGerald, S. (1997) *Is Australia an Asian Country? Can Australia Survive in an East Asian Future?* Sydney: Allen and Unwin.

Forbes, D.K. (1996) A*sian Metropolis: Urbanisation and the Southeast Asian City.* Melbourne: Oxford University Press.

———. (1997a) "Metropolis and megaurban region in Pacific Asia". *Tijdschrift voor Economische en Sociale Geografie*, 88:457–68.

———. (1997b) "Regional integration, internationalisation and the new geographies of the Pacific". In R. Watters and T.G. McGee (eds.), *Asia Pacific: New Geographies of the Pacific Rim*. London: C. Hurst. pp. 13–28.

Gallant, N. & R. Stubbs. (1997) "APEC's dilemmas: Institution-building around the Pacific Rim". *Pacific Affairs*, 70:203–18.

Gilley, B., J. McBeth, B. Dolven & S. Tripathi. (1998) "Ready, set ..." *Far Eastern Economic Review*, 161(8):46–50.

Heider, K. (1994) "Indonesian cinema, national culture: The Indonesian case". In W. Dissanayake (ed.), *Colonialism and Nationalism in Asian Cinema*. Bloomington: Indiana University Press.

Hiebert, M., B. Dolven, M. Vatikiotis & S. Tripathi. (1998) "Out of its depth". *Far Eastern Economic Review*, 161(8):25–26.

Hutnyk, J. (1995) *The Rumour of Calcutta: Tourism, Charity and the Poverty of Representation*. London: Zed Books.

Keating, P. (1996) "The Singapore Lecture: Australia, Asia and the new regionalism". Institute of Southeast Asian Studies. Singapore, http://www.nla.gov.au/pmc/pjkspch170196.html

Lever-Tracy, C., D. Ip & N. Tracy. (1996) *The Chinese Diaspora and Mainland China: An Emerging Economic Synergy*. London: Macmillan.

Lewis, M.W. & K.E. Wigen. (1997) *The Myth of Continents: A Critique of Metageography*. Berkeley: University of California Press.

Linge, G. (ed.). (1997) *China's New Spatial Economy: Heading Towards 2020*. Hong Kong: Oxford University Press.

Lloyd, P.J. & L.S. Williams (eds.). (1996) *International Trade and Migration in the APEC Region*. Melbourne: Oxford University Press.

Lo, F.-c. & Y.-m. Yeung (eds.). (1996) *Emerging World Cities in Pacific Asia*. Tokyo: United Nations University Press.

McGee, T.G. (1995) "Eurocentrism and geography: Reflections on Asian urbanization". In J. Crush (ed.), *Power of Development*. London: Routledge. pp. 192–210.

Pangestu, M. (1998) "More misery ahead". *Far Eastern Economic Review*, 161(8):52–53.

Rigg, J. (1997) *Southeast Asia: The Human Landscapes of Modernization and Development*. London: Routledge.

Rimmer, P.J. (1995) "Moving goods, people, and information: Putting the ASEAN megaurban regions in context" In T.G. McGee and I.M. Robinson (eds.), *The Mega-urban Regions of Southeast Asia*. Vancouver: UBC Press. pp. 150–75.

———. (ed.). (1997) *Pacific Rim Development: Integration and Globalisation in the Asia-Pacific Economy*. Sydney: Allen and Unwin.

Said, E. (1978) *Orientalism: Western Conceptions of the Orient*. (1991 reprint). London: Penguin.

Sender, H., C.S. Lee, with M. Vatikiotis. (1998) "Few takers so far at Asia's great firesale". *Far Eastern Economic Review*, 161(10):52–54.

Tesoro, J.M. (1998) "Work together. ASEAN's secretary-general speaks". *Asiaweek*, 27 February.

Watters, R. & T.G. McGee (eds.). (1997) *Asia Pacific: New Geographies of the Pacific Rim*. London: C. Hurst.

Wilson, R. & A. Dirlik (eds.). (1995) *Asia/Pacific as Space of Cultural Production*. Durham: Duke University Press.

Yeung, Y.-M. (1985) "Geography and the developing world". Professorial Inaugural Lecture Series 10, Chinese University Bulletin Supplement, No. 17, Hong Kong. pp. 1–11.

———. (ed.). (1993) *Pacific Asia in the 21st Century: Geographical and Developmental Perspectives*. Hong Kong: Chinese University Press.

Chapter 2

IMPLICATIONS OF JOINING
ASEAN FOR MYANMAR

MYA THAN & TIN MAUNG MAUNG THAN

Introduction

At the special ASEAN Ministerial Meeting (AMM) in Kuala
Lumpur on 31 May 1997, it was decided that Myanmar would
be accepted as a full-fledged member of the Association of
Southeast Asian Nations (ASEAN) in July 1997, along with
Cambodia and Laos. Despite strong indications from the United
States and its allies to defer this decision on account of
Myanmar's alleged human rights violations, Myanmar was
formally admitted at a special ceremony held in Subang Jaya,
Malaysia, on 23 July and took part fully in the celebrations for
the 30th anniversary of ASEAN's founding.[1] This historic
decision by ASEAN was in line with the Bangkok Declaration
of 1995 which was issued after the 5th ASEAN Summit to
which Myanmar's Prime Minister Senior General Than Shwe
was invited by the host country for the first time.[2] Myanmar's
process of joining ASEAN was initiated by the country's
accession, in July 1995, to the Treaty of Amity and Cooperation
(TAC) at the 28th ASEAN AMM in Brunei. It was probably

triggered by political considerations but there are both political and economic dimensions to the benefits accruing from Myanmar's membership in ASEAN. However, before exploring and analysing the implications and impact of joining ASEAN, it may be worthwhile to consider whether Myanmar was really ready for joining ASEAN.

How Ready was Myanmar to Join ASEAN?

According to the ASEAN secretariat, the answer was a resounding "yes"; it was "technically ready" in terms of obligations for political, economic and functional cooperation. The conditions for "technical readiness" include acceding to basic agreements and declarations of ASEAN documents including the Bangkok Declaration of 1967, the Zone of Peace, Freedom and Neutrality (Zopfan), the TAC, the Southeast Asian Nuclear Weapons Free Zone (SEANWFZ), the ASEAN Free Trade Area (AFTA), and all other agreements that ASEAN has established. In this respect Myanmar would have no difficulty in acceding to all of them. In fact, Myanmar had already acceded to some of these including SEANWFZ. Myanmar could also meet the financial obligations for membership, such as equally sharing the cost of running the Secretariat, subscribing to various ASEAN funds and covering costs for attending some 300 ASEAN meetings a year. In addition, it had already met a few other conditions, like having embassies in all ASEAN capitals which Myanmar has had long before it even applied for membership, and having a large pool of government officials who can communicate in English. Myanmar's accounting system is also similar to many of the older member countries of ASEAN. Moreover, a national ASEAN secretariat and an AFTA unit had already been established in Yangon.

Furthermore, as a member of ASEAN, the country must become a member of AFTA with its attendant privileges as well as obligations. Also in this respect, Myanmar was in a far better position than other new members like Cambodia and Laos. There are English versions of all of Myanmar's economic laws and these are easily accessible. As a founding member of the General Agreement on Tariffs and Trade (GATT), granting the most favoured nation (MFN) status is not new to Myanmar, and ASEAN members are likely to receive such status from Myanmar. Myanmar is also prepared to give preferential treatment to ASEAN products on a reciprocal basis.

Obligatory to the AFTA membership, Myanmar has to bring down its tariffs to 5 percent or less by the year 2008. Unlike the other new members, more than half of Myanmar's current tariffs are already 5 percent or less. Cambodia's customs duties are mostly between 7 and 50 percent whereas those in the Lao PDR are mostly between 5 and 20 percent.

The impact of joining AFTA on the country's national budget is marginal compared to other new member countries. This is because Myanmar's customs duties make up only 16 per cent of total government revenues while those of Cambodia and the Lao PDR are 72 percent and 30 percent respectively. In this sense, Myanmar was more ready than the other new members. Moreover, Myanmar's dual exchange rate system seems to be a blessing in disguise as it will buffer the shock on the state budget, at least in the short term. However, in the long run, it may affect the balance of payments.

In short, Myanmar was more ready to join ASEAN than other new members like Cambodia and Laos, at least from the technical, economic and financial aspects. To achieve the goal of creating a free trade area, based on a 0 to 5 percent tariff range on trading with liberalisation of some goods, new members are given a grace period of 10 years, and for Myanmar the time frame appears to be more than adequate.

In fact, the latest tariff lists presented by the Myanmar delegation at the ASEAN Economic Ministers meeting in Kuala Lumpur in October 1997 confirmed Myanmar's readiness. According to a Myanmar delegate, some two-thirds of Myanmar's products fall already within the 0 to 5 percent tariff rate. Only 10 percent of products and services have a tariff rate of between 30 and 40 percent due to the government's intention to discourage certain activities. These include gambling businesses, and dealings in liquor, antiques, imported cars and others. "Of the 5400 tariff lines [in Myanmar's product list for the AFTA], about 2400 products are in the inclusion list. Over 2900 are in the temporary exclusion list, 108 in the general exception list and 21 in the sensitive list" (*The Star*, 14 October 1997). As such, the Secretary-General of ASEAN, Ajit Singh, was led to make a remark that Myanmar could enter the AFTA member group even before its stipulated deadline of 2008 (*The Nation*, 13 October 1997).

Political Implications

In Myanmar's state-owned newspapers, a series of boxed-inserts appearing in July and August 1997, entitled "Facts about ASEAN", highlighted the country's admission to the regional grouping. In one insert, it was stated that "Myanmar can now receive messages from ASEAN as a grouping, and she can make known to ASEAN her position in specific and precise terms." Obviously it was believed that new opportunities would be opened up to Myanmar with the help, understanding and sympathy of fellow ASEAN members.[3] Despite this, critics of the ruling State Law and Order Restoration Council (SLORC) maintained that by joining ASEAN, Myanmar's military junta hoped to gain legitimacy at home and abroad.[4] To some, joining ASEAN was seen as a calculated move by SLORC to counter Western sanctions, criticisms, and condemnations spearheaded by the US government as well as the pro-opposition lobbies and the so-called government-in-exile known as the National Coalition Government of the Union of Burma (NCGUB). In response to such reactions, Myanmar authorities adamantly insist that this is not a reactive process but a proactive one based on changing domestic and international circumstances. On the appeal of ASEAN to Myanmar, Foreign Minister U Ohn Gyaw alluded to the ending of the Cold War and the "shared destiny" of the 10 Southeast Asian nations. He added that Myanmar is "a Southeast Asian nation and we would like to aspire to the prosperity of Southeast Asian nations" and since "Asean is now very much solid in a leading role ... we would like to be part of it" (*The Nation*, 16 December 1995).

Now that Myanmar is part of ASEAN the political implications of its entry into the regional grouping may be identified in three areas: ASEAN's relations with the West; ASEAN organisational matters and intra-ASEAN relations; and Myanmar's domestic political development. Right from the beginning, Myanmar's ruling SLORC (reconstituted in November 1997 as the State Peace and Development Council or SPDC) has been ostracised by the Western powers, while the regional ASEAN states have cooperated with Myanmar in their efforts to end its economic and political isolation. The United States and its European allies persistently accused SLORC/SPDC of human rights violations and suppression of democracy activists while seeking punitive measures to advance their vision of democracy. Furthermore, the ASEAN member states have constructively engaged Myanmar in the belief that a gradual exposure to the market economy and regional cooperative efforts would be the best way to ensure regional security and socioeconomic development of Myanmar.

The stark contrast between these two approaches have never been clearer when in 1997, the US government imposed sanctions and together with its European allies tried to block Myanmar's early entry into ASEAN. Meanwhile, ASEAN decided to accord full membership to Myanmar in July, in time for the Association's 30th anniversary. In fact, on 22 April 1997, US President Bill Clinton announced a ban on new US investments in Myanmar citing "large-scale repression of the democratic opposition". This was followed on 20 May by an executive order "prohibiting United States persons from new investments in Burma" that formalised the earlier pronouncement (*Myanview,* July 1997:4). Despite efforts by the Clinton Administration to garner strong support from its allies, countries such as Japan, Australia, France and Germany did not join in the US censure. The US sanction came at a time when selected purchase laws and bans on companies doing business with Myanmar, by states such as California and Massachusetts as well as cities like New York, have become the bane of both US and foreign companies. The European Union (EU) had withdrawn the community's generalised system of preferences (GSP) benefits offered to Myanmar's industries and it had also imposed a ban on visas to SLORC members and senior military and government officials.[5]

Tensions between Myanmar and the United States as well as some Western developed nations suggest that discrimination against Myanmar would go against the grain of the group's stand on non-discriminatory treatment of its members. One example of a potential conflict is the current controversy over Myanmar's participation in the ASEAN–EU dialogue and the Asia–Europe Meeting (ASEM). The confrontational stage was set with the EU's statement on 26 June quoted as follows:

> ... the Council considers that the presence of Burma/ Myanmar at the forthcoming ARF/PMC Ministerial Meetings does not prejudice in any way its participation as observer at the upcoming EU–ASEAN Joint Cooperation Committee in November 1997 and other meetings in the institutional EU–ASEAN framework ... (*Myanview*, July 1997:5)

Moreover, British Foreign Secretary Robin Cook's remarks, during his recent Southeast Asian tour, that Myanmar would not be invited to attend the 2nd ASEM in London, elicited strong reactions from some ASEAN leaders. In particular, Prime Minister Mahathir Mohamad of Malaysia gave a "warning of a possible ASEAN boycott of the gathering" if the latter's members are discriminated against.[6] In another instance, a report from Manila indicated that ASEAN ask for a postponement of the 17–18 November meeting of the ASEAN–EU Joint Cooperative Committee (ASEAN–EU JCC) in Bangkok because Myanmar and Laos were unduly discriminated against.[7]

ASEAN was determined to pursue its constructive engagement strategy by welcoming Myanmar warmly and continuing to give a helping hand during the transition period, even to the extent of challenging its Western partners' decisions in intergroup relations. The impasse remained until mid-1999 but the hope is that in the long run, as Myanmar's membership of the regional grouping matures, there would be convergence between ASEAN and its Western partners over the Myanmar issue.

ASEAN, though not highly institutionalised as in the case of the European Union (EU), has its unique *modus operandi* known as the "ASEAN way". This has been characterised by informal interaction, quiet diplomacy, non-binding agreements, consensus-based decision-making, and non-interference of internal affairs of member states.[8] Indeed, it has been pointed out that the mindset of Myanmar would not allow for smooth integration with ASEAN.[9] More specifically, as Noordin Sopiee wrote:

> It is a different thing to generate consensus amongst a group of ten, many of whom have little experience in the Asean tradition of "agreeing to disagree without being disagreeable", while working very hard to secure the highest possible common denominator.[10]

Nevertheless, given Myanmar's past record in international relations and its political culture it seems unlikely that Myanmar would be out of its depth in adapting to the ASEAN way. Myanmar's comfort level with such an operational procedure is likely to be comparable to those of the older ASEAN members.

Moreover, Myanmar's bilateral relations with the other ASEAN member countries have been very good. Even though the lack of a comprehensive border demarcation between Myanmar and Thailand has given rise to some disagreement over territory along the Thaungyin/Moei River in southeastern Myanmar, it is not expected to escalate further and being members of the same regional grouping may eventually turn out to be quite helpful in resolving this problem amicably. ASEAN membership will probably strengthen Myanmar's bilateral relationship with other member countries through the diffusion of the ASEAN spirit; first among the ruling elites and then trickling down to the polities.

However, some suggestions have been made to change the way of engaging Myanmar as the latter becomes a full-fledged member of the grouping. The desire to deepen and extend the "constructive engagement" concept by introducing a proactive element of a more comprehensive "constructive intervention" was mooted by several regional thinkers including Malaysia's ex-Deputy Prime Minister Anwar Ibrahim.[11] The aim seems to be to help Myanmar achieve a more rapid transition towards internationally acceptable behaviour and norms not only in international relations but also in tackling national economic and political issues. It is too early to say what will come out of such ideas but one can be assured that any change would be made in a way that would not put undue pressure on Myanmar to accommodate them and that the grouping would not in any way jeopardise the cohesion and amity amongst its members by introducing changes that are not undergirded by consensus and practicality.

The implications of Myanmar's joining ASEAN on its domestic politics are clear. It was pointed out that the country's political temperature had been lowered by government conciliatory gestures towards the opposition National League for Democracy and its leader Daw Aung San Suu Kyi in September 1997.[12] Though cynics have commented that SLORC was introducing cosmetic changes and restoring some of the rights which should have been granted in the first place, one cannot deny that these were positive signs.[13] Although Myanmar authorities would most probably deny that such acts were the results of Myanmar's membership in ASEAN, there are evident grounds to believe that the timing was not entirely coincidental. One would tend to agree with the *Straits Times* editorial comment that "Yangon would not have gone even to this trouble [of allowing the NLD congress to convene] if it were not responsive to ASEAN expectations".[14]

Economic Implications

Joining ASEAN allows Myanmar to enjoy more trade and investment links within the region, increasing attractiveness to foreign direct investment (FDI) from outside the region. Membership will also secure Myanmar greater access to the ASEAN market; improve resource allocations through comparative advantage and economies of scale in an enlarged regional market; enhance industrialisation prospects of small and medium-sized enterprises, through spill-over effects and infant industry learning effects with improved quality control, design and marketing; and thus improve competitiveness in the world market.

More specifically, we will assess the impact of joining ASEAN/ AFTA in terms of international trade, government revenues, FDI and Myanmar's comparative advantage. Myanmar's trade with ASEAN has been growing since it opened up its economy. For Myanmar, ASEAN is one of its main export markets, comprising about one-quarter of the country's total exports in 1995 (Table 2.1). Export trade between 1985 and 1995, indeed, grew at an average annual rate of 18.1 percent. Most of these export items are agricultural products which are outside the Common Effective Preferential Tariff (CEPT) scheme[15] and they appear in either general or temporary exclusion lists. Therefore, the impact of reduction of tariffs (of CEPT scheme) on these products is unlikely to be significant. This means Myanmar's revenues from exports to ASEAN will not be significantly affected.

Table 2.1

Myanmar's Trade and FDI with ASEAN (in US$ million)

| | Trade* | | FDI** |
	Exports to	*Imports from*	*from*
Indonesia	20	51	236.4
Malaysia	63	255	524.2
Philippines	–	–	6.7
Singapore	192	701	1,223.8
Thailand	37	63	1,132.8
ASEAN Total	**312**	**1,070**	**3,123.9**
World Total	**1,214**	**1,589**	**6,361.3**
ASEAN/World (%)	**25.7**	**36.6**	**49.1**

Note: * 1995, ** as of 31 July 1997.

Source: IMF, DOTS 1996.

In parallel, Myanmar is an important importer from ASEAN, accounting for more than two-thirds of its total imports. The average annual growth rate was 45.3 percent between 1985 and 1995. Some 30 percent of the total imports are capital goods and about 40 percent consumer goods. Since most of the tariffs have been reduced to 20 percent or less, the impact of the CEPT scheme would have little effect on further tariff reduction. The scheme could boost imports and may reduce smuggling of consumer goods.

However, Myanmar's balance of payments after joining ASEAN may be affected. This is because, even with the various non-tariff barriers, the country's balance of trade has been in deficit of about Kyats 3.5 billion per year on average between 1990/91 and 1995/96 (equivalent to about US$600 million in official rate). Given the present situation, its exports cannot be expanded or diversified significantly. Therefore, with the removal of tariff and non-tariff barriers, the balance of payments may be in the red.

For Myanmar, the potential impact of AFTA is a cause of concern since customs duties form 16 percent of the total government revenue, though a small proportion compared with Cambodia (over 70 percent), Laos (31 percent) and Thailand (18 percent). Myanmar's dual exchange rate system may have an adverse effect on the balance of payments but it may work in the government's favour by bringing in more revenue from the tariff reduction process. In 1996, when the government changed the assessment of customs duties from the official rate of Kyat 6 per US dollar to a more realistic market-based effective rate of about Kyat 100 per US dollar thereby raising revenues (in Kyats per imported dollar terms) by about 16 times, while at the same time reducing the duty rate by 10 times. The net result was more revenues for the same quantum of imports (in dollar terms) in spite of tariffs reduction.

There will also be the indirect effect of joining AFTA on FDI. Since the promulgation of the Foreign Investment Law in 1998, FDI has been growing fast and it reached more than US$5 billion by the end of 1996. ASEAN's share in Myanmar's total FDI (approved) is significant accounting for more than

51 percent, with Singapore being the largest investor (Table 2.1). Since one of the main objectives of AFTA is establishing a unified market to attract foreign investment, multinational corporations will be encouraged to invest in ASEAN by taking advantage of low tariffs and an enlarged market. Moreover, ASEAN's reputation as a good place for investment will extend to all new members. These factors, along with the spill-over effect, will encourage foreign investors from inside and outside of ASEAN to invest more in Myanmar. The most significant impact of AFTA will be to enhance the ability of Myanmar to exploit its comparative advantage of abundant natural resources and cheap but literate labour, English-speaking urban populace, and a strategic location between India and China.

Conclusion: Issues and Challenges

There are many issues reflected in Myanmar's joining ASEAN/ AFTA. The first issue is whether Myanmar will once again become a supplier of raw materials as in the colonial period. Recurrence is unlikely to take place for the following two reasons. Due to rising wages and labour shortage, most ASEAN countries are moving from less capital-intensive to more capital-intensive manufacturing. In the case of Singapore, it is moving towards skill-intensive high-technology manufacturing. Myanmar is expected to fill in the vacuum left by more advanced ASEAN countries which are expected to invest, thus enhancing ASEAN economic cooperation.

Another key issue, among others, is that Myanmar, with its inefficient state-owned enterprises, will have to compete with ASEAN in the manufacturing sector. Currently, its small-scale enterprises in the private sector are facing a shortage of raw materials, power supply, capital and spare parts. Only with the government's further liberalisation of financial, banking and trade can Myanmar overcome the tough competition its state-owned and private enterprises are facing. Despite competition, there is ample room for cooperation between Myanmar and other ASEAN member states. It is important to note that even between similar economies, a complementary relationship can be achieved if members agree on the principles of free trade.

All in all, Myanmar will benefit from its membership in ASEAN/AFTA in the short to medium term regarding its economic development. The economic potential of ASEAN as a whole can be greater than the sum of the individual parts as AFTA is not a zero sum game. However, in the longer term, unless the government of Myanmar is committed to more economic reforms and will "carefully ascertain what is in her best interests in order to take advantage of flexibilities" accorded under AFTA regulations, the country will lose out in this competition. In the political sphere, as stated by Myanmar's Foreign Minister U Ohn Gyaw in his address at the admission ceremony at Subang Jaya on 23 July 1997, one hopes that Myanmar would be able to keep its "own house in order" with the support of ASEAN friends and "contributes towards order for the community" as well.

NOTES

1. Though Laos was admitted simultaneously with Myanmar, Cambodia's entry was "delayed until a later date" (*ASEAN Update*, February 1997, p. 1). Cambodia was finally admitted to ASEAN in April 1999.

2. It was stated that "ASEAN is committed to the establishment of an ASEAN comprising all countries in Southeast Asia" (*ASEAN Update*, January 1996, p. 1). The first meeting of the leaders of the 10 Southeast Asian countries took place during this summit.

3. See the highlighted box, "Facts about ASEAN-8", in *New Light of Myanmar*, 7 August 1997, p. 7.

4. A comment by James Guyot on the Voice of America (VOA) background report dated 7 July 1997 (Burmanet posting of 8 July 1997 on the internet).

5. *Myanview* (January 1997), p. 7 and *EIU Country Report Myanmar (Burma)*, 3rd quarter 1997, p. 21.

6. See "Its Our Party", *Far Eastern Economic Review*, 25 September 1997.

7. See "ASEAN lays down terms for EU", *Straits Times*, 24 October 1997, p. 41.

8. Personal communications with ASEAN scholars and officials from member states.

9. See "Retooling ASEAN", *Asiaweek*, 27 June 1997, p. 14.

10. See Noordin Sopiee, "Fulfilling dream of regional unity", *New Straits Times*, 6 June 1997.

11. See "The word is 'constructive intervention'", *Straits Times*, 15 July 1997; and Jusuf Wanandi, "Partners Should Nudge Burma", *International Herald Tribune*, 5 June 1997.

12. The government allowed the NLD to hold a congress at the premises of Daw Aung San Suu Kyi on 27–28 September and allowed her to travel to the suburbs of Yangon to address a party grouping. These were unprecedented moves, given that the government had prevented similar gatherings in the past two years and restricted the movement of Daw Aung San Suu Kyi as well.

13. For critical comments, see "Myanmar: A Glimmer of Hope?", *The Economist*, 4 October 1997, pp. 33–34; and Kavi Chongkittavorn, "Slorc under pressure to repay ASEAN's faith", *Nation*, 30 September 1997, p. 4. Even Daw Aung San Suu Kyi herself has acknowledged the government gestures and thanked the authorities expressing hope that "one day, the present authorities and members of the" NLD "will work hand in hand for the good of the country." (English translation of the transcript of Daw Aung San Suu Kyi's speech at the closing ceremony of the 9th NLD Party Congress, on 29 September 1997).

14. See "Signs of thaw in Myanmar", *Straits Times*, 13 October 1997, p. 38.

15. CEPT is the basis of AFTA with the goal of reducing tariffs and removing non-tariff barriers on all intra-ASEAN trade in manufactured and processed goods. It will be accomplished by two different tracks — a "fast track" and a "normal track". Under the "first track", the import tariffs for products with tariffs below 20 percent will be reduced to below 5 percent by 1 January 2000, and for other products by 1 January 2003. Under the "normal track", those with tariffs above 20 percent will be reduced to 20 percent within five to eight years in the first stage and reduced to below 5 percent in the following seven years.

REFERENCES

Baldwin, Peter. (1997) *Planning for ASEAN*. Hong Kong: Economic Intelligence Unit.

East Asia Analytical Unit (EAAU). (1997). *The New ASEANs: Vietnam, Burma, Cambodia & Laos*. Barton, Australia: Department of Foreign Affairs and Trade.

ISEAS. (1997) *Myanview,* July, 3(3). Singapore: Institute of Southeast Asian Studies.

Mya Than. (1997) "Six plus four: Economic cooperation in ASEAN". Paper presented at the conference on "ASEAN Today and Tomorrow". 16–17 September 1997. Hanoi.

Pham H.M. & D. Forbes. (1996) "The ASEAN Free Trade Area and its potential impact on Vietnam's economy". Paper presented at the workshop on "Development Dilemmas in the Mekong Subregion". 1–2 October 1996. Melbourne.

UN/ESCAP. (1997) Enhancement of trade and investment cooperation in Southeast Asia: Opportunities and challenges towards ASEAN 10 and Beyond". Mimeograph. Bangkok.

Chapter 3

ASEAN Economic Cooperation in the New Millennium

Linda Low

Introduction

Any institution which has survived the last three decades with tumultuous events ranging from two oil crises to the end of the Cold War would have been enriched by experiences and policy responses to challenges. The Association of Southeast Asian Nations (ASEAN) was born in 1967 out of security concern as the Americans wound down their activities after the Vietnam War and the British were withdrawing their military presence east of the Suez. The new sovereign ASEAN states wanted security and stability to ensure that economic growth and development can take place.

A full circle is reached as ASEAN enters its 30th year since its inception in 1967 when it started as a security pact. Despite the end of the Cold War by 1991, the formation of the ASEAN Regional Forum (ARF) in 1994 was only different in terms of ASEAN states now having more progress and wealth to protect.

Again, US foreign policy of disengagement in Asia, pressured as much by its domestic issues looming large, has given ASEAN states cause for concern. A stocktaking by ASEAN is timely as the new millennium draws near. It has to consider the new geopolitical paradigm in tandem with the throes of expansion as Cambodia joined ASEAN as the tenth member[1] and the slowing economic boom in Asia Pacific which had superseded transatlanticism.

Technology, capital and labour flows in an increasingly borderless economic global framework, globalisation and growing regionalism are the external drivers for change (Cleaver, 1997). Internally, ASEAN states have restructured and diversified their economies with parallel changes in labour and employment patterns and composition. Demographic, sociopolitical and growing competitive pressures confront policy-makers at both the national and regional levels. As a relatively successful grouping of developing countries, ASEAN states have to carefully synthesise these external and internal forces as its membership widens beyond market economies. No less worrisome are systemic problems erupted ranging from the currency crisis a month before the 30th anniversary of ASEAN and the worsening forest fires and haze in Indonesia engulfing the whole of Southeast Asia.

Founding fathers of ASEAN may have been prescient as ASEAN10 is now a truly Southeast Asian group. This chapter will review the last 30 years of economic cooperation in ASEAN and the next phase of ASEAN efforts in the context of a new world order and global economy. It will analyse the challenges and issues that have arisen and some policy implications.

The Heritage in Economic Cooperation

In reviewing the three decades of ASEAN economic cooperation,[2] the chapter will focus on changes in principles and *modus operandi* in ASEAN, identifying and analysing conditioning factors within and outside of ASEAN to learn its weaknesses and difficulties. A more mature set of economic, sociopolitical and personality factors awaits ASEAN in the 2000s.

The Early Phase

The early phase of economic cooperation was characterised by political and bureaucratic schemes and committees. In 1969, ASEAN foreign ministers had requested technical assistance from the United Nations to investigate areas of ASEAN economic cooperation. The Kansu Report[3] studied comprehensively major areas covering trade and industry, monetary and financial matters, agriculture, forestry and shipping between 1970 and 1972. With trade liberalisation put under the ASEAN Preferential Trading Arrangement (PTA) in 1977, specific economic projects included the ASEAN Industrial Project (AIP) in 1976, the ASEAN Industrial Complementation Scheme (AIC) in 1981 and ASEAN Industrial Joint Venture (AIJV) in 1983.

Thus, ASEAN's focus moved from security to economic cooperation which gained ascendancy in the 1976 Bali Summit. In the 1977 Kuala Lumpur meeting of ASEAN Economic Ministers (AEM), five economic committees were formed, namely, the Committee on Trade and Tourism (COTT), the Committee on Industry, Minerals and Energy (COIME), the Committee on Food, Agriculture and Forestry (COFAF), the Committee on Transportation and Communication (COTAC) and the Committee on Finance and Banking (COFAB). There was, however, many layers of rivalry between the Annual Ministerial Meeting (AMM) of Foreign Ministers and the AEM on one hand, and between them and the five committees on the other (Luhulima, 1990).

Institutionally, the formation and subsequent restructuring of the ASEAN Secretariat and the streamlining of ASEAN committees to more action-oriented bodies involving private sector more intimately was a positive development. Prior to the institutional revamp, the ASEAN Secretariat had no direct role either in identifying or approving products for various ASEAN industrial cooperation schemes. Instead, this was done through the Federation of ASEAN Chambers of Commerce and Industry (ASEAN–CCI) with policy-making and approval exercised solely by government institutions. Moreover, there was little cooperation or interaction between the government and private-sector institutions in formulating policies and guidelines.

In those years, there were regular ASEAN committee meetings involving discussions of national interests while ASEAN–CCI represented interests of the private sector. But none was concerned with ASEAN's broader interests or those of small and medium enterprises. These gaps in representation, institutional weaknesses and bureaucratic delay led to a suggestion that there was minimal government intervention and simplified procedures (Chee & Suh, 1988). The government should only provide a conducive environment to facilitate economic cooperation. Reducing politicisation and bureaucratisation was necessary to get projects moving.

The principle of economic cooperation was reshaped after the failure of various ASEAN projects under the AIPs and AIC. They include emphasising cooperation rather than integration or resource pooling, market sharing, encouraging investors to look beyond the ASEAN market, a more meaningful role for the private sector in formulating policies and reducing intervention by both the government and bureaucracy.

The achievements of these cooperative efforts had been rather dismal. The share of intra-ASEAN trade to total ASEAN trade reached only 5 percent although it grew by 1.8 times over the 1980s. In contrast, the shares of intraregional trade among the newly industrialising economies (NIEs) and the Asia Pacific were 28.8 percent and 77.6 percent respectively, growing by 1.9 and 2.3 times respectively over the same period. The extraregional orientation of all ASEAN countries cannot be denied. In fact, that brought the needed capital and technological infusions which sustained every ASEAN state's industrial restructuring and growth. Japan is the most significant trading partner in both extra and intraregional dimensions of ASEAN trade (Tambunlertchai & Samad, 1996).

The Next Phase

By the early1990s, all ASEAN economies except the Indochinese states have diversified their industrial structures and they have become more complementary (Masuyama et al., 1997; Chia et al., 1997). While the role of the state and implicit industrial policy remain dominant in all ASEAN states (Naya & Tan, 1995; Ng et al., 1996), the private sector has grown. Some alliance between state-owned enterprises (SOEs) and indigenous enterprises on the one hand, and foreign firms on the other is common. Depending on nationalistic sentiments and ownership concerns, ASEAN's private sector modalities range from a high dependence on foreign multinational corporations (MNCs) and government-linked companies (GLCs), such as those in Singapore, to carefully nurtured indigenous entities to protect local interests, such as those in Indonesia and Malaysia.

A greater degree of confidence and leadership is displayed by local entrepreneurship (Brown, 1994) in areas such as savings, technology transfer and acquisition accumulation. In particular, a comfortable level of public-private sector collaboration and cooperation has been demonstrated in a more market-based framework as in various ASEAN growth triangles (Lim, 1996; East Asia Analytical Unit, 1995). The pioneer southern growth triangle has expanded to the Indonesia–Malaysia–Singapore Growth Triangle (IMS–GT) (Low, 1996a) incorporating more Malaysian states (Malacca, Negri Sembilan and southern Pahang) and more Indonesian provinces (West Sumatra).[4] Up north, the Asian Development Bank (ADB) sponsored the Indonesia–Malaysia–Thailand Growth Triangle (IMT–GT) (ADB, 1994) and the East ASEAN Growth Area involving Brunei–Indonesia–Malaysia–Philippines (BIMP) (ADB, 1996; Mijares, 1996) but all growth triangles are dependent on private-sector participation. They have responded to government facilitation in infrastructural, fiscal and monetary incentives.

However, networking and bonding among politicians, bureaucrats, business stewards and chambers of commerce and industry cannot be discounted. Though ASEAN meetings may seem rhetorical and social in function, they provide occasions and structures for nuances of culture and alchemy of power play and negotiations to be acted out. There is no explicit hierarchy in ASEAN politics and economics but an implicit understanding exists where even richer but smaller states concede to "big brother" dynamics which buttress the region's centre of gravity. Many personal relationships at the highest political level cannot be underscored. More importantly, the ASEAN framework projected the determination of a group of successful developing countries to spread more of the East Asian "miracle" around them (Campos et al., 1996).

By the 1990s, a multi-layered collaboration has evolved with much regional and global changes which affected the next phase of ASEAN economic cooperation (Kimura, 1995; Chia et al., 1997; Chan, 1997). The North American Free Trade Agreement (NAFTA) was conceptualised around the same time in 1991 as the Single European Market (SEM) to lead to a full European Union (EU). With the completion of the Uruguay Round which nearly stalled under the General Agreement on Tariffs and Trade (GATT), Malaysia mooted the idea of an East Asian Economic Grouping (EAEG) in 1991, evolving to East Asian Economic Caucus (EAEC) (Low, 1991) as an ASEAN project in 1993. The EAEC remains in limbo with US opposition and Japanese ambivalence despite Malaysia's hope that it would represent a much bigger voice than ASEAN.

By then, the Asia Pacific Economic Cooperation (APEC), formed in 1989, has expanded to 18 members amidst growing regionalism and protectionism. The 6 ASEAN states were among the 12 founding members of APEC and ASEAN is looked upon as an important core group representing Southeast Asia and developing countries in general. While APEC hopes to promote freer trade and liberalisation in investment, short of forming a free trade area, it is congruent with ASEAN in aims and motivations. With no real conflict of interests, possible areas of collaboration should spawn. As regional groups, both ASEAN and APEC operate in the wider context of multilateralism under the World Trade Organisation (WTO). While APEC aspires to practise open regionalism, however defined (van Dijk et al., 1996), ASEAN is more traditional in adopting a free trade area approach.

ASEAN's flagship, the ASEAN Free Trade Area (AFTA), was proposed in 1993 and was targeted to be completed by 2008. However, this has been brought forward to 2003 (Low, 1996b). A determined progression from the PTA to AFTA recognises that intraregional trade must accelerate. With industrial restructuring, greater complementation in trade and investment is possible. There is strong political commitment and a message, which should not be dismissed too lightly, that economic integration must be more concrete with AFTA.

There is overlapping membership of ASEAN in these various blocs. Apart from established dialogues with the United States, Canada, Japan, European Union, Australia and New Zealand, ASEAN initiated the Asia–Europe Meeting (ASEM) in March 1996 involving China, Taiwan, Japan and South Korea with the European Union on the other side. Such summit-level meetings have value in paving the way and breaking the ice on more practical schemes and projects. The arithmetics are convincing to suggest that regionalism as building blocks should be pursued with ASEAN7 accounting for 6.8 percent of total world trade in 1996, APEC 45.0 percent, EU 37.4 percent and NAFTA 18.7 percent. The Mercusor group comprising Argentina, Brazil, Paraguay and Uruguay accounted for only 1.5 percent of total world trade but if the Free Trade Area of the Americas (FTAA) materialises to join 34 countries in North and South America, the effects would be substantial.

The ASEM summit in Singapore in 1997 wisely avoided potential conflagrations of human rights issues in East Timor and Myanmar, championed by the Europeans (*Far Eastern Economic Review*, 13 February 1997). Closer ASEM relations require innovative bureaucratic engineering to avert conflict with the sentiments of Portugal, the European Commission, the European Council of Ministers and the United Nations Commission on Human Rights. ASEAN, for instance, did not demur on Myanmar's membership much as its human rights record was criticised by the West.

From a global perspective, strengthening ASEAN–EU ties creates a more stable system (Chia & Tan, 1997). Among the triad, the Asia–Europe leg is weaker than the US–EU and US–Asia sections. If the third leg between Asia and Europe is reinforced, the triad structure could be more reassuring as a check and balance of political and economic power in the global equation. Based on geography, *APEC sans Europe* is uncomfortable for Europe as well as Asia as both have a certain fear of US hegemony.

Asia also has fears of the gargantuan alliance in the proposed Transatlantic Free Trade Agreement (TAFTA) (*Economist*, 27 May 1995). In turn, TAFTA may be borne as much out of a mutual fear of Asia by the Atlantic partners. Unfortunately, such regional groupings heighten the cultural aspects of trade disputes already manifest in US–Japan discords in semiconductors and automobiles. Taken to its logical conclusion, the clash of civilisations is propounded by Huntington (1996) as the basis of potential global conflicts rather than pure political or ideological wars.

Enlarging Membership

As part of the next phase of economic integration and to revive the geographical value of Southeast Asia, ASEAN10 was mooted as the transitional economies emerged following the economic reforms in both China and Russia. The reasons were simple and clear. A stable and peaceful Southeast Asia means more resources and market potential. Greater economic interdependence in the region is also superior to fragmented and isolated development when regionalism is growing unabated elsewhere. Very obvious too is that the transitional economies would need technical as well as financial assistance. This translates to business opportunities as well as challenges for ASEAN. Many ASEAN economies are already diversifying and investing in and around the region.

Strategically, ASEAN10 is significant in that it represents an autonomous regional order which will not accept any external pressure with regard to membership. Given Myanmar's initial self-imposed isolation and consequent economic stagnation, ASEAN felt it timely to extend assistance and influence to accelerate its transition to a global economy. More Western sanctions will only harden its resolve and will not speed up political reforms. Economic cooperation is the preferred and proven ASEAN approach.

There have been suggestions, however, to delay Myanmar's membership even before Cambodia's membership became an issue. Myanmar's attitude towards ASEAN seemed divided with the opposition under Aung San Suu Kyi not in favour of joining ASEAN as it feared that membership may legitimise the ruling government. As Myanmar is attacked for its political and human rights issues, ASEAN's dealings with Western dialogue partners may be affected. But this problem paled by comparison to Hun Sen's coup which ousted his rival and First Prime Minister Prince Ranariddh in early July 1997. The fall of the Khmer Rouge's Pol Pot, just as the ARF meeting concluded in Kuala Lumpur, was another real test for ASEAN after it decided to delay Cambodia's membership. The Indochinese states are also infamous for illegal drug trafficking, prostitution and other vices which may upset both internal and external relations for ASEAN.

With the appropriate extension in dates for the four new ASEAN states to join AFTA — Vietnam in 2006, Laos and Myanmar in 2008 and Cambodia in 2009 — the final outcome is still perplexing. There were initial claims that Indonesia and the Philippines, two older ASEAN states, have asked that the Common Effective Preferential Tariff (CEPT) be pushed back from 2003 to 2010 for integrating sensitive items like sugar and rice. However, both will begin phasing in these products by 1 January 2003 till 1 January 2010, with flexibility on ending tariff rates and safeguards.

Sheer political will will ensure that timetables are honoured as ASEAN realises that the whole world is watching the progress of ASEAN10 and AFTA. Its own seriousness and commitment would increase its regional and international profile and give ASEAN a distinctive voice and credibility. Hiccups and problems are not unexpected but probably not with the urgency and severity posed by the Indochinese states and the currency crisis following the floating of the baht in early July 1997. All ASEAN currencies dipped under a speculative assault escalating into a full-scale recession which occurred probably a bit too soon after many economies were recovering from a downturn due in part to the electronic cycle in 1996. To add to the economic upsets, the haze which started in the Indonesian Kalimantan forest fires and blanketed Southeast Asia, affecting tourism and other activities in August 1997, was malingering. The apparent lack of concern and capability of the ASEAN countries to protect the environment gave cause for anxiety.

Beyond a Free Trade Area

Unlike the European Union, there is no incentive nor need for AFTA to move beyond a free trade area into customs union, common market or economic union as the final steps towards economic integration. A customs union requires a common external tariff which is unfeasible given the extreme disparity in ASEAN tariff structures. Singapore and Brunei are virtual free ports at one end. A common market means further liberalisation in movement of capital and labour, another sensitive problem in ASEAN where immigration is held as a sovereign right. Neither would fiscal and monetary harmonisation as in an economic union be appealing implying a surrender of national sovereignty to supranational bodies. Economic integration would entail some political integration which is not ASEAN's goal. If ASEAN10 and AFTA can work well, they would suffice.

Even fulfilling AFTA is not an easy task. Covering only 15 product groups, AFTA is not yet a total free trade area. For all items traded in ASEAN, dismantling non-tariff barriers (NTBs) and implementing an effective trade dispute settlement body are formidable tasks which will occupy ASEAN for at least another decade. For ASEAN10 to undertake similar tasks, it may take another decade. On a parallel plane, furthering sociocultural ties is an important adjunct to cross-cultural management. This is important for business relations and political understanding as more intra-ASEAN corporations grow.

Amidst the political and security challenges, ASEAN economic cooperation schemes, especially for post-2003, must be planned ahead. There is a Loosely United ASEAN Economic Entity (LUAEE) in context of AFTA to move beyond trade to pull together cooperation and liberalisation in investment, industry and services. An ASEAN Investment Area (AIA) has been agreed upon to attract more foreign direct investments and promote greater intra-ASEAN investment. It aims to make investment rules and regulations more transparent. The ASEAN Industrial Cooperation (AICO) scheme, organised for to attract more investments, allows participating companies to enjoy preferential tariff rates of 0–5 percent immediately upon approval for the export of products within the region.

The various ASEAN growth triangles would dovetail to concretise these framework agreements. More strategic and innovative thinking in economics, politics, geopolitics, demography and technology are the wherewithals to promote change. Financial support in infrastructure projects in the IMT–GT, BIMP, as well as the Greater Mekong Scheme, must be garnered. Collaborative human resource development and management (ADB, 1990) is a logical and feasible approach to meet the challenges of new technology and globalisation (ADB, 1995).

Even the Hashimoto principle where Japan wanted to elevate ASEAN–Japan relations to a summit-level like ASEM which had been rebuffed earlier in 1997, may be worth a rethink. The US–Japan collaboration in post-Cold War plans revealed in September 1997 is a thin disguise of China's wariness, ignoring or distrusting the Chinese reorientation towards commerce and growth. Rather than dismiss the Hashimoto principle as being out of turn, ASEAN should play a buffer role before US–Japan belligerence sparks off another Cold War, this time with China as the Russian ghost. Political leaders in ASEAN have been twinning economics with political imperatives long enough to realise the affinity of Japanese investment with ASEAN. The technology windows it offers constitute a much needed catalyst.

Currency Crisis

The currency crisis sweeping across ASEAN since July 1997 reminds ASEAN that growth and prosperity cannot be taken for granted if basic macroeconomic fundamentals are ignored. Despite the financial reforms undertaken since the late 1980s which exposed Thai domestic banks to competition from foreign institutions and developed other financial markets to mobilise financial resources, Thailand was ill-equipped to face a global financial system with mobile capital and volatile exchange rates (Fujita, 1996). The Thai financial system before the reform was under relatively strict government control. Market segmentation separated the domestic banking sector and other domestic financial institutions from competition with foreign financial markets and foreign banks. Shielded from competition, Thai domestic banks which monopolised household savings as deposits formed the most important financial asset. As Thai domestic companies with weak creditworthiness have difficulty accessing financial resources of foreign sources, corporations borrowed mainly from domestic banks as the capital market is undeveloped and loans from financial companies are regulated.

The fast pace of growth meant that growth tended to be indiscriminate, as it happens in speculative investment in real estate, leading to partial or complete loss of control manifested as run-away inflation. Thailand had the initial economic conditions which, on hindsight, should have been strengthened and reinforced. It neglected prudence in fiscal and monetary policies, infrastructural development and investment in highways, sea and air transportation, telecommunications and human resource development. At the other extreme, Malaysia probably overdid this. The net result was the same in debt and current account deficits to finance such growth.

Thailand's successive government changes, peaceful coups and cavalier attitude about financial shortcomings, balance of payments deficits, traffic congestion and environmental problems may be part of its sociopolitical culture. A state of denial in soothing values and traditions like the monarchy, fatalism of Buddhism and the mannerisms of polite Thais gloss over impending structural issues. Malfeasance in self-serving interest groups and corruption stretching into the government and military were rife. One study by Thammasat University estimated that as much as 14–19 percent of Thai gross domestic product is supported by the illegal underground economy which keeps unemployment down (*Asian Wall Street Journal*, 5 December 1995).

While financial and foreign exchange liberalisation in the 1980s and 1990s was a step in the right direction, the financial structure was rudimentary. Central banking, notably the supervisory skills of the Bank of Thailand, was as inadequate to the task (Maxfield, 1997). Fanned by real resource bottlenecks and speculation, inflation rose. The impotent government and cumulative virulence brewed a self-inflicted crisis waiting to happen. Such is the background of the day the economy buckled when the central bank could no longer keep the exchange rate within the acceptable peg.

Cut from its peg to a basket of currencies dominated by the US dollar, the baht was devalued *de facto* by about 30 percent. Other Asian currencies plunged as aftershocks sailed across the region. Indonesia immediately widened the rupiah's trading band, already significantly loosened the previous year. The rupiah had held steady despite both the May disturbances following the elections and rumours of President Suharto's health. Malaysia held its ringgit firm but had to give way to market forces later.

No Asian currency was immune and it was a new era where every currency in the region needed to weaken if only to restore the *status quo ante*. Otherwise, the Thai devaluation will make its exports cheaper and worsen current account deficits already prevalent in many Asian countries like Hong Kong, the Philippines and South Korea. By early 1997, Malaysia had improved somewhat from a deficit in 1996.

The seismic importance of 2 July 1997 marks the birth of a new currency environment in the region's changing economic landscape. With a global economy and fluid capital flows, beating off speculative attacks to maintain an exchange rate becomes harder. A messier and more volatile period of adjustment and slower economic growth amidst more fluid global exchange rates means central banks obsessed with currency stability will have to rethink and retool their objectives and monetary management skills. Even well-behaved Singapore was not spared as much as it was a victim of the circumstances in the other countries.

A number of implications and rethinking in ASEAN have been prompted by the regional financial crisis. Asian currencies are linked to the US dollar for various reasons including giving their exporters and foreign investors currency stability. Such stability entails a price which included tying domestic monetary policy to some extent to the United States and encouraging huge inflows of foreign capital suddenly freed of foreign exchange risk.

Real costs to the region include inflation, which hurts every country particularly those newly recovering from the 1997 crisis. Interest rates will rise with anti-inflationary monetary policy just as investors would demand a greater risk premium from a more uncertain and volatile region. They may not just avoid Thailand but shun the region altogether.

Asian governments including Thailand, the Philippines and Malaysia, blame foreigners for the pressure on their currencies instead of recognising that the underlying weakness of their economies cast further doubts on misdiagnosis or the possibility of more astute macroeconomic management. Many sellers of Asian currencies are Asian players themselves, either banks or corporations, some betting against their home currency to make a quick profit.

The hands of central banks are tied as interest rates cannot be raised too much without hurting stock prices as there is a growing class of shareholders in the region. Whatever the charges and counter-charges, the first priority of central banks is to shore up their financial systems. But clearly, liberalisation becomes uncontrollable when short-term and capital markets are underdeveloped and immature.

The simultaneous speculative attack on the Malaysian ringgit and the devaluation of the Philippine peso did put the rupiah under some downward pressure but Indonesia appeared better prepared having learnt from previous crises. In a preemptive strike, Bank Indonesia widened the band from 8 to 12 percent. More confident with a higher 8-percent gross domestic product growth, higher trade surplus and falling inflation, the rupiah strengthened. Prodded by foreign donors concerned with Indonesia's large debt, the central bank was forced to cut domestic interest rates and had to liberalise the currency regime. Unlike Thailand, it does not suffer as badly in an ailing property sector. But it took the toll in some rupiah devaluation from both the baht and peso devaluation which made exports from the respective countries cheaper.

Probably, ASEAN states should have heeded the financial meltdown in Mexico in 1995 when the peso was devalued, the effects of which were felt by the neighbouring countries around. That was already a signal of the new era of flexible and liberalised financial markets and foreign exchange regimes. Instead, ASEAN states including Thailand, Malaysia, Indonesia and the Philippines, were trying hard to prove how dissimilar their economies and conditions were from Mexico. But after two years of unchecked overindulgence, history repeated itself in Thailand as it too liberalised too fast before its financial and capital markets were ready and monetary supervision and other institutions adequate to the task. The cavalier omission may support the infamous Krugman's thesis that Asia is growing by perspiration and not inspiration or by a sausage model depicting more inputs to generate more output and greater credence. As Krugman concludes, the Mexican and ASEAN cases are qualitatively though not quantitatively similar (*Far Eastern Economic Review*, 25 September 1997).

ASEAN Monetary Union

The possibility of a monetary union as a single currency unit after the attainment of AFTA seems a logical sequence. Increasingly, ASEAN states are trying to wean themselves from the traditional dependence on the triad of the United States, Japan and Europe. Greater intra-Asian economic relations would begin to integrate the economies with China and weave the greater China concept with Japan. However, like the appeal of a yen bloc (Okuda & Mieno, 1996), there are more odds than plausibility of an ASEAN monetary union even if it is targeted for the distant 2020. Thus economic integration in ASEAN is unlikely to go beyond a free trade area.

Some lessons from Europe are germane. Like ASEAN, the European Community (EC) debated between deeper integration and a push for monetary union or widening membership at the expense of closer monetary and economic cooperation. The Maastricht Treaty appeared to have cast the die and set the timetable for a monetary union by the end of the decade. The two criteria to be satisfied, fiscal stability and nominal convergence, are already causing problems as many current EU members are unable to qualify with even Germany failing to meet the budget deficit criterion.

Like ASEAN, the European Union (EU) today comprises a number of countries (Gayno & Karakitsos, 1996). They are categorised as the core group (similar inflation and interest rate performance), median group (inflation differential from the core average, less credible exchange rate target and some debt and deficit problems reflected in higher nominal interest rates) and peripheral group (relatively large inflation and interest differential, weak currencies, high deficits and debts). The Werner Report in 1970 proposed a three-stage plan to achieve monetary union under, the first of which was to reduce exchange rate fluctuations and begin the process of monetary and fiscal policy coordination. The second stage would be to consolidate once inflation differential and exchange rate variance have declined further. In the third stage, the irrevocable fixing of exchange rates, removal of capital controls, emergence of European central banks to operate monetary policy and closer coordination of fiscal policy would complete the exercise. Events overtaking this ambitious plan as benign neglect of both its fiscal and trade deficits led the United States to float its dollar first in 1971 and again in 1973 despite the Smithsonian Agreement to shore up the crumbling Bretton Woods system. As the gold window remained closed with the dollar devalued against gold, the new official gold price became one at which the United States would not buy or sell.

A "snake in the tunnel" or a regional bloc of exchange rate stability was created in 1972 in the European Community. Member currencies were to have a fluctuation band of 2.25 percent against each other while as a whole, they would move within the 2.25 percent band against the dollar. The latter formed the tunnel, the former the snake. The tunnel lasted until 1973 when generalised floating began. Part of the failure may be explained by German domination and unilateral decisions on parity settings. The golden era before the oil crisis has gone and the monetary union died with it. There is a seeming inconsistent quartet of free trade, full capital mobility, fixed exchange rates and national monetary policy autonomy envisioned by the European Monetary System (EMS). Others paid the price of the German reunification as the German hegemony began to diverge from the average with serious consequences for other members. Increased fiscal deficits and a tight monetary policy increased German interest rates, changing them from being "locomotive" to "brakesmen".

Noting the difficulties and the nature of the European integration process, ASEAN may wonder at the wisdom of going further than liberalising trade, which in itself is a very demanding task. However, the European experience does provide some lessons. The rational expectation theory postulates that people have economic knowledge and information and use them systematically to make rational choices. In the Mexican case, investors had panicked as they had little or no information as to what was going on and reacted less than rationally and more speculatively. Governments, learning from this experience, should release and disseminate information more frequently, promptly and be more transparent. Understanding and knowing fundamental economic conditions should arm people against responding to herd instincts, minimising if not truly able to avert the damage.

For instance, if serious speculative attacks on local currencies do occur, more information by the government on how it would counter these problems would prepare people on what to expect and do. Uncertainty will certainly invite fear and miscalculations. Paradoxically, protecting individual interests first often hurts the macroeconomy. Better information would also prevent the panic from spreading. ASEAN governments, however, are not inclined towards open information especially with regard to what is deemed state confidential matters and are not too transparent in its thinking and policy deliberations.

Another lesson is the importance of international or regional cooperation by other countries to shore up a financial crisis. Several Asian central banks have made arrangements to deal with speculative attacks on each other's currencies.

But as events proved themselves, the bilateral repurchase agreements among ASEAN central banks were ineffective. While such a joint action cannot avert a financial collapse, it can delay or postpone it and meanwhile alert the afflicted nations to be more circumspect. What central banks can best do in speculative attacks, if a prolonged defence is too costly, is to try to restore calm as quickly as possible while waiting for some financial rescue package. The International Monetary Fund (IMF) which came to Thailand's rescue has instituted new procedures to help restore the financial stability of the country more quickly.

More fundamental lessons concern macroeconomic housekeeping and management. Asian states have to steadfastly maintain rather than blatantly ignore their economic fundamentals and economic health. They have to be vigilant for signs of a bubble economy, chronic deficits in balance of payments or spiralling debts, all of which would seem no more than basic logic and common sense. Self-serving interest groups and political interests, including blatant malfeasance, may be difficult to clean up but credibility and confidence have to be restored. Recognising that the global economy and financial environment have fundamentally changed with greater mobility of capital, following liberalisation and deregulation of capital means a rethink of conventional monetary macroeconomic management is called for. The rules of the game have irrevocably changed. Governments have to see policies (like macroeconomic and exchange rate targets) through consistently and not liberalise some sectors and still expect the general order to be the same.

Once an economy has opened up, the rules of macroeconomic policy change. In an open economy under floating exchange rates, if the government tries to increase its budget deficit as a fiscal policy, the effect is ineffective in the short term because capital flows in from abroad and the currency appreciates. This reduces aggregate demand, offsetting the initial fiscal expansion through government borrowing with crowding-out of private spending. In the long term, if government borrowing remains too high for too long, a debt problem would develop. On the other hand, monetary policy is powerful in the short term as money supply is increased. Capital flows in from abroad and the currency depreciates increasing aggregate demand, output and employment. In the long term, prices rise to neutralise the effect of currency depreciation. As output and employment return to trend, nothing "real" has changed.

If the government chooses to fix exchange rate in an open economy, the reverse results occur with fiscal policy being powerful in the short run as interest rates rise, less than in a closed economy and not at all if there is perfect market mobility. The international capital market finances government borrowing and less crowding-out occurs. In the long term, prices rise as in the case of the open economy with floating exchange rate and a debt burden arises. For an expansionary monetary policy, interest rates rise in the short term influenced by the global capital market. Capital flows out, neutralising the increase in money supply and making monetary policy ineffective.

Only in a closed economy would both fiscal and monetary policies be effective in the short term. Neither works in the long term. The conclusion is that if a government pursues a fixed exchange rate policy, fiscal policy is effective and monetary policy ineffective. If it chooses to let the exchange rate float, it has to rely less on fiscal policy, more on monetary policy. Free international capital flows have narrowed the government's choice over macroeconomic policy, no less in ASEAN.

In reality, when the government tries to maintain a semi-fixed exchange rate regime as a compromise without giving up the monetary policy, awkward as it is, the lessons of the Mexico peso and the Thai baht crises in 1995 and 1997 respectively remain true. Where there are strong capital controls, it is sometimes possible to share attempts at macroeconomic stabilisation between fiscal and monetary policies. Where control is weak or non-existent, a sharper choice must be made between fixing the currency and fiscal policy and the floating rate and monetary policy. By implication, capital mobility has lessened the government's power unless financial repression is resorted to. Policy mistakes are also more likely with their due punishment.

A more careful watch over possible stagnation in leading industries, declining exports, slowing down of economic growth, increasing current account deficits and currency instability has to be institutionalised. Rising corporate indebtedness and excessive investment in real estate, particularly by financial institutions, leading to an asset value bubble, which is waiting to implode, have been noted. Investments should be returned to productive sectors. Current account deficits have been tolerated in pursuit of export-oriented industrialisation much as even that did not really occur. More fundamentally, as dependence on imported capital goods grows, it could deprive domestic manufacturers of opportunities to sell producer goods, the usual "bypass" effect of export industries. This is another aspect of the failure of the NIEs to transform from externally dependent to internally demand-led development. Demand for imported luxury goods inevitably rises with growing affluence.

All NIEs and more ASEAN economies are facing high-cost structures and a decline in international competitiveness. This can be attributed as much to domestic causes as to the fightback by industrial countries as their deindustrialisation and long-term unemployment reach sociopolitical levels of concern. International division of labour and globalisation have quickened the pace of reorganising competition all round. Appreciation of the yen and other Asian NIE currencies have prompted regionalisation and the relocation of activities abroad and increased intra-firm division of labour. These structural checks have been seeping through even before the currency crisis. The episode would undoubtedly fuel pessimism further and longer. On the positive side, it may strengthen the resolve of ASEAN states to pay more attention to its industrial structures and make the needed and overdue correction.

The Changing Global Context
New Growth Models

Over the last three decades, both the theoretical and environmental contexts in which ASEAN economies operated have altered drastically. Theories of economic growth and development have mutated and hybridised with the East Asian miracle (World Bank, 1993; Campos & Hilton, 1996) and new growth theories (Scott, 1989) in their attempts to explain the phenomenon. Already in the backwaters were theories like the Rostovian stage of development approach, the structuralist and dependency schools.

Even neo-classical theory and the "market-friendly" approach (World Bank, 1991) as well as new institutional economics (Samuels, 1988; Williamson et al., 1989; Alston et al., 1996) or the "market-enhancing" approach, were deemed unsatisfactory as Japanese economists proposed the economic systems approach to move thinking away from the "framework" mode of neo-classical economics and the World Bank to "ingredients" thinking as in organisational capabilities of firms and deepening interfirm relationships (Yanagihara & Sambommatsu, 1997). They advocate an economic systems approach which focuses on intra and interfirm relations at the level of an industry or an industry cluster and relate such industry level analysis to macro-level performance. As the second generation NIEs or "tiger cub" economies, ASEAN states have more models to apply. They also offer the empirical evidence for studies which would substantiate these theories and models.

The economic takeoff of many ASEAN economies is and will continue to happen in a new world order or disorder (Shirk & Twomey, 1996; Vatikiotis, 1996). Geopolitics encompass profound sociopolitical changes. Even the cultural topography (Fukuyama, 1992; 1995; Huntington, 1996) is changing with Asia reawakening. The economics of comparative advantage has given way to competitive advantage, borderless economics, globalisation and technology in the postindustrial age and knowledge economy.

Technology and Globalisation

A third industrial revolution started with automation and knowledge industries. New management theories and practices following reengineering and downsizing have moved away from Adam Smith's division of labour, Taylorism and Fordism. The impact on future work is of tectonic dimension. The nature and scope of work have changed. Atypical work, as in part-time and temporary work and portfolio work, together with outsourcing has become typical as a just-in-time or contingent workforce evolves. In one fell swoop, blue-collar workers as well as the bureaucratic professionals are redundant. Entrepreneurial professionalism and the right kind of education and skills confer a property right for such workers.

Greater job insecurity and long-term unemployment tend to discourage workers or push them into the third informal sector, widening class inequities. Winners and losers in the era of high technology and information technology go global as national borders become porous and seamless. In turn, heightened anxieties and tensions from migration and export of employment add to cultural-political clashes of civilisations. Cultivating a learning organisation and adapting the ageing demographic structure to multi-skill and multi-dimensional jobs require continuous education and retraining.

Globalisation is not new but is now intensified by the changing character of international investment and changes in the form of corporate activity, organisation and relationships, transport and communication technologies, technical advances in production, processing methods and adoption of market liberalisation and deregulation policies (UNIDO, 1996). The emergence of generic technology as in microelectronics, information technology, biotechnology and new materials have a profound effect on industrial development in developing countries like ASEAN. Three major characteristics which distinguish them from conventional technologies (UNIDO, 1996:47).

• They have the power to transform conditions of production and properties of materials to give rise to a variety of new products as in consumer electronics, to induce a dramatic change in industrial production reflected in automation, flexibility and mass customisation.

- The pervasive, multisectoral scope with which new technologies can be applied to many branches of manufacturing result in a blurring of conventional classifications and activities. For instance, machine tool industry, which includes as much electrical and non-electrical engineering, and food processing and pharmaceutical industries employ similar forms of new biotechnologies.

- The tendency to promote increasingly homogeneous processes of industrial production especially through growing standardisation of components, such as control units and design systems in production equipment which have significant implications for human resource development and vocational training.

New generic technology affects competitiveness in several ways, first, by prompting a shift in the determinants of global competition. Developing countries depending on the comparative advantage of low-cost labour find that this is being eroded by automation, e.g. in textile and clothing industry using computer-aided design (CAD), computer-aided manufacturing (CAM) and computerised numerical control (CNC) systems. Similarly, more efficient use of materials partly through CAD/CAM and partly through substitution of new biotechnology products and other advanced materials will affect exporters of raw materials. As these changes are not likely to bring about massive relocation, developing countries have the opportunity to adapt.

Second, generic technology enhances product quality and flexibility of production. Many new materials in aerospace and military applications, for instance, have demonstrated superior performance. New precision tools and professional instruments have lowered rejection rates and loss of competitiveness. Small batch production of garments made possible by new equipment of this type allows quick and flexible responses to frequent changes in fashion demands.

Third, generic technology allows for organisational innovations designed to maximise the advantages of flexibility and quality. Production systems based on mass customisation, new management styles and use of multi-skilled workers have occurred.

Fourth, with growing flexibility in the process of production, economies of scale is eclipsed by economies of scope. The move from single-product to multiple-product manufacturing reduces the need for large production runs to recover high investment cost and thus increases efficiency.

Fifth, the emergence of new technology is accompanied by increased entry barriers for new companies, in the form of access to new technology and skills required, as well as additional capital requirements as in research and development (R&D) and marketing which has led to corporate concentration at both the national and international levels. Only biotechnology, which is research intensive but not capital intensive, may be more accessible to developing countries with core scientific capabilities and supportive infrastructure.

Sixth, with increasing trade in high technology products on an intraindustry basis, comparative cost advantages are no longer the primary determinants of competitiveness. Neither availability of natural resources nor relative factor endowment determines high technology products. Instead, arbitrary or acquired comparative advantage with government intervention allows the choice of specific lines of technological development which can be promoted and subsidised. Educational, social infrastructure and conducive public policies translate into competitive advantage.

Finally, new technology is changing cost structures in all industries, especially in information technology. Falling unit costs together with alternative communication options reduce the relative cost of processing and transmitting information. Telematics can be extended to many areas in merchandising by integrating point-of-sale systems with inventory and purchasing; in manufacturing, through integration of production with inventory and orders and centralised CAD; and in transport, with the ability to coordinate and optimise worldwide despatch and centralised control systems.

Competition through innovation intensifies with new generic technology which may revive and resuscitate stagnant and declining industries. Labour intensive textiles, clothing, furniture and food processing may regain competitiveness through adjustment and adoption of new technology. Terms of entry for industrial development have changed and the inferior status of developing countries in technological capability may weaken their competitiveness further. Export orientation is still superior to import substitution industrialisation to acquire technology and raise productivity.

Clustering based on flexible specialisation is concerted industrial intervention which enables collective efficiency and reduces transaction costs as buyers, intermediaries and suppliers are brought together at the same time. Acquiring foreign technology can be divided into formal and informal channels. The formal methods include imports of capital goods, non-equity licensing and other contractual modes, foreign direct investment, strategic alliances and outward foreign direct investment. The informal channels include exchange of views, information through published literature and communication networks, migration of skilled workers, official government assistance and cooperation and demonstrations.

The changing comparative advantage, competitive advantage and complementarity of trade and investment are observed. In particular, Japan's policy of moving labour-intensive exports to lower wage countries in the NIEs, the ASEAN and China is replicated by the NIEs themselves (Bettignies, 1997). Comparative advantage indices for imports and exports computed show the relocation of industries from Japan and the NIEs to other ASEAN countries as having expedited the industrialisation process under the wild flying geese pattern (Tambunlertchai & Samad, 1996). Even Australia and New Zealand are integrating increasingly with East Asia and ASEAN economies.

Issues and Challenges in the Next Millennium

Against the internal and global developments and dynamics of the last two sections, several issues and challenges await ASEAN in the next millennium.

Domestic Challenges

Starting from within ASEAN, three decades of collaboration and economic cooperation among existing ASEAN members still produce the occasional bilateral hiccup. Nothwithstanding the unique historical context between Singapore and Malaysia, rivalry persists because they have adopted the same growth strategies. Except for Singapore's nominal status, all ASEAN states are still developing economies grappling with structural and cyclical upheavals punctuated with as much sociopolitical problems, notably, rural poverty and inequitable income distribution.

Malaysia and Thailand have incurred rising current account deficits with rapid growth and need for capital and technological imports. These precipitated the 1997 Thai financial crisis and drew comparisons with Mexico's peso devaluation in 1995. Neither are Indonesia and the Philippines spared from the same brush given their large external borrowings. While Singapore has excelled itself as an NIE and near developed industrial economy, its small size and economic vulnerability draw perpetual doubts about its viability and sustainability. But difficult and tumultuous as economic growth and development have been, together with oil-rich but no less small and undiversified Brunei, ASEAN has succeeded more than other developing groups.

When bilateral repurchase agreements among ASEAN central banks proved ineffective during the currency crisis (*Straits Times*, 6 August 1997; *Business Times*, 7 August 1997), monetary union and a single currency unit seemed a logical sequence after the completion of AFTA. Increasingly, ASEAN states are establishing their economic independence from the United States, Japan and Western Europe. Greater intra-Asian economic relations would include the NIEs, Japan, China and the participation of the overseas Chinese.

However, even if the target is set for 2020, there seems to be more odds than plausibility of a monetary union for a number of reasons. Economic integration in ASEAN is unlikely to go beyond free trade as argued. Progressing from the ASEAN preferential trading area (formed in 1977) to even thinking about AFTA (initiated in 1993) took about two decades. By the time AFTA is concluded in 2003, it is still not a true free trade area with only 15 manufacturing groups free from tariffs, not to mention the complexities posed by non-tariff barriers (NTBs). However, should ASEAN progress beyond a free trade area, it would lead to higher and higher levels of economic integration which must inevitably imply a political union.

Even the European Union with its supposedly stronger historical and cultural ties is struggling with its European Monetary System recast as the European Monetary Union after the Maastricht Treaty. More than economic integration is implied once an economic grouping exceeds a common market though it is inconceivable that ASEAN states would ever venture into a political union. Supranational bodies, like the European Commission or European Parliament, must be established to make regional policies which entail the surrender of national sovereignty. Such an idea is still inconceivable for ASEAN states even if this is targeted for the year 2020.

By 1999, ASEAN is projecting its ambition and image as a power to be reckoned with. The timing is right with the end of the Cold War and economies in transition poised to enter the capitalist world. The opportunity to make ASEAN truly Southeast Asian cannot be postponed, ignored or denied without ignominy and loss of "face" being the long-term consequences.

ASEAN10 was deemed necessary on the supposition that left to their own, the Indochinese states may be forced to turn to other neighbours like China, South Asia or Russia. These countries do not present a natural setting themselves based on geographical propinquity. With the ASEAN Regional Forum (ARF) set up, the imperative to extend membership is made even more urgent. If a few successful ASEAN states are willing to pick up the mantle to inspire and assist others in the belief that a more positive sum game will be gained by all, the chances for ASEAN10 to achieve its objectives would be greater. Singapore and Malaysia, for instance, could contribute in information technology and put the whole of ASEAN on the electronic highways of the new era for production, distribution, telecommunications and so forth.[5]

Rightly or wrongly, the original ASEAN6 felt that extending membership to the rest of Indochina would oblige them to try harder with both political and economic reforms. It is unfortunate that the West considers this stance as ASEAN legitimising or recognising their regimes. Like the gradual, evolutionary approach in China in developing processes and market institutions (McMillan & Naughton, 1996), ASEAN6 can assist the new members particularly in the entry of new firms, creation of market institutions and restructuring state-owned enterprises. New challenges lie in new organisational forms, property rights, a market-oriented financial system, and legal and regulatory frameworks which must be transparent.

The enlarged body of ASEAN is as much as what the EAEC proposal can attain at this stage and it is not surprising that Malaysia is a strong champion. On its own, Malaysia is forging bilateral relations with African states in its own version of south–south economic cooperation which is probably what ASEAN10 would mean. More economies of scale and economies of scope can be created together with resource pooling and improved market potential. The older ASEAN6 probably feel confident that its state dominant and interventionist industrial policies would fit the transitional economies very well.

An expanded ASEAN will address the problem of ageing demographic trends critical in some ASEAN states especially Singapore. While migration and foreign labour policies remain sacrosanct within each ASEAN state, the vibrancy and dynamism of a younger population in a new ASEAN composition will be useful. By the same token, more cultural and ethnic differences should add to variety and foster a richer, more multi-ethnic mosaic of cultures for exploitation in the arts, cultural tourism and educational services.

External Environment

These standard economic arguments for greater ASEAN economic cooperation are further reinforced by more competitive pressures culminating in regionalism, globalisation and technology. Greater synergy among the members of an enlarged ASEAN seems to be the most viable option to face each of these three challenges. While still smaller than NAFTA or the European Union in per capita income, ASEAN10 eventually ensures that some bloc-to-bloc collaboration would not pass it by as it may if ASEAN regionalism is not sufficiently assertive. The true benefits and costs of globalisation are arguable and can vary from country to country.

Plausibly, ASEAN10 should manoeuvre and steer the effects of globalisation more steadily as a group than each economy could on its own. With new technology changing the paradigm of competitiveness and efficiency, uplifting ASEAN science and technology on a common platform is again more feasible and more effective than individual efforts. More than in other areas, in information technology, competition defined as cooperating with a business competitor in an attempt to improve both parties' performances is the new term in friendly competition.

After the Cold War, a multi-layer of mechanisms for regional cooperation, with economics and security equally emphasised, now operates (Kimura, 1995). ASEAN comprises no less than half a dozen groups, including its own ASEAN bodies like AFTA and ARF as well as ASEM, APEC, WTO and other UN-sponsored groups. There are more informal groupings in the growth triangles and other private-sector driven schemes. Multiple membership should be positive rather than conflicting in interests as these bodies have deliberately organised themselves on consistency principles. Properly managed, these multiple memberships and associations should contribute to multilateralism as subregional groups enable smaller experiments with a greater tendency towards centrifugal rather than centripedal forces.

In the next millennium, ASEAN has not only to play a more proactive role in regional and global affairs, it will be sought in terms of its leadership and experience (Low, 1997). Following the Cambodian coup in 1997, the world at large including the United States, was watching ASEAN's response and action before entering the foray. This is an eminent recognition of its efforts in the region and in handling "domestic" ASEAN matters. Taken to its logical conclusion, ASEAN can wield considerable influence and opinion on almost all matters ranging from trade and investment to more seamless and borderless environmental issues.

One lesson learnt from the 1997 baht devaluation which led to some speculative attacks on all ASEAN currencies is that despite the group's seeming economic robustness, there still exists an inherent vulnerability.[6] Some ASEAN economies have weak current accounts which run into chronic deficits and possibly some macroeconomic mismanagement may have also opened them to financial crises. Some rethinking on fast rates of infrastructure development and expansion into certain areas which accounted for huge capital imports and hence current account deficits, more conservative fiscal policies and borrowing may be in order.

No matter how far and fast ASEAN economic cooperation can proceed with AFTA and other projects, the outward orientation of all ASEAN economies will increase rather than decrease. All ASEAN economies remain dependent on the developed industrial economies for trade, capital, technology and other factor flows. Greater intra-ASEAN economic interdependence notwithstanding, globalisation has made all outward-oriented economies global economies as well.

The cast of the more experienced and older ASEAN6 represents a formidable assembly of experienced politicians, able technocrats and entrepreneurial business leaders. By 1997, each national team has had at least three or more decades of blending national interests with ASEAN strategies. In many ASEAN states including Indonesia, Malaysia and Singapore, the stable political structure and style of administration have pervaded under very developmentalist governments despite what may be criticised as less democratic regimes. With the end results tangible in altered physical and infrastructural landscapes, home ownership, education and health improvement and others as well as non-material aspects of better welfare and standards of living, mass contentment counts more than any ideological abstractions.

Beyond ASEAN10 and AFTA, the Southeast Asian concept may reach a glass ceiling. In 1993, Thailand proposed that Australia join ASEAN but Malaysia felt that Australia was not even in Asia (Edwards & Skully, 1996:339). Even Sri Lanka was rebuffed as otherwise ASEAN would be overwhelmed by the rest of South Asia and others. Malaysia, however, proposed that realising ASEAN10 and AFTA10 should do rather nicely without ASEAN losing its intrinsic value. It must realise its ambitions without any external pressures and be as efficient and effective as possible.

Conclusion and Policy Implications

As the world gets paradoxically bigger and smaller, the same is happening in ASEAN. Transition economies moving from extremely centrally planned economies into capitalism have created more economic space and latitude which enables ASEAN10 eventually to be more formidable and resilient. With new transport, communication and telecommunication technologies, more and better infrastructure and facilities, spatial distance is being conquered as unit costs fall progressively.

A reinforced ASEAN attracts more trade, investment and business opportunities, especially if the ASEAN framework acts as an implicit guarantee to average and even out the odds in some countries with the proven records of others. In this regard, Singapore leading or pacing other members, would invoke greater investor confidence and stability than one member ASEAN state going solo.

With industrial restructuring and diversification, an enlarged ASEAN offers greater complementarity and deeper and more economic interdependence. If these are the objectives of economic cooperation, then ASEAN is on the right path into the next century. A multi-layered economic and political platform has evolved not just within ASEAN but throughout the Asia-Pacific region and beyond. These developments actually give ASEAN a more focused and direct role to play in creating and sustaining the synergies within various fora. The Southeast Asian model of development is gaining acceptance (Masuyama et al., 1997). If the three strong trends towards liberalisation, industrial upgrading and regional networking continue, optimism abounds for sustained industrial development in East Asia as a whole.

As the Malaysian proposal of an EAEC is not taking off yet, growing and strengthening ASEAN10 and achieving AFTA's objectives constitute an immense challenge which can make or break the grouping. Neither would the transitional economies be easy to assimilate and integrate. The traditional formula of personal friendship among ASEAN statesmen and personalities performing the bridging or intermediary roles cannot easily apply when dealing with the Indochinese states. It will be the consensus of the people, who desire economic growth, higher standards of living and a better quality of life as attained in many present ASEAN states, which will forge the integrative and cooperative efforts. The usual sensitivity and ASEAN principle of no direct force and intervention will continue to serve well though with much more patience and perseverance.

The ASEAN sense of solidarity should be more restorative and engender a greater sense of confidence. As events proved, it was not Myanmar's membership based on its human rights record which was delayed but Cambodia's in July 1997. The ASEAN10 concept was severely tested following the Cambodian coup when co-Premier Hun Sen ousted the First Prime Minister Prince Ranariddh. The coup tested ASEAN's diplomatic resilience as well as its principle of consensus decision-making and non-interference in members' domestic affairs. But the case was deemed a clear-cut violation of ASEAN's legal requirements which include non-violence and observance of constitutional formalities.

During the same period, ASEAN solidarity was rallied on a separate matter following the *de facto* devaluation of the Thai baht. Both events occurring within days of each other in early July 1997 may have marred ASEAN's 30th anniversary but they make the group more resolute in its objectives in terms of regional stability and progress. In truth, ASEAN has expected difficulties, though not with such intensity, so soon and at so fast a pace. But that is the reality check for ASEAN as the new century unfolds. To continue as a credible successful group, ASEAN has to rethink and evaluate its cooperative efforts more seriously as witnessed in the rhetorical rather than more critical assessment of the currency crisis and haze.

Both can be attributed to an abject lack of discipline within national ASEAN economies. A role exists for more ASEAN-wide studies and research, possibly at the ASEAN secretariat level where deeper cross-national and ASEAN studies should be promoted. Current research tends to be focused on individual economies in respective states and even ASEAN research projects cannot be but superficial. A more open attitude where problems and issues, as perceived by other ASEAN states, should be more openly discussed or at least transmitted to others, without raising hackles of pride and sensitivity should be adopted.

While supranational bodies may have such authority and legitimacy to caution members, the ASEAN Secretariat is unfortunately powerless and lacks the resources to be backed up by robust policy-oriented research. Research institutes and universities in ASEAN should seriously offer their facilities and resources and not be remiss in putting ASEAN economic cooperation on needful and solid areas to chase away the overhang of crisis surrounding the 30th anniversary.

The road ahead will be a rough one as more economies in Asia and the rest of the world follow the good macroeconomics of market opening, liberalisation, deregulation and focusing on efficiency and competitiveness. In many areas, friendly competition or competition may generally prevail which makes regionalism more meaningful and relevant. As the ASEAN identity gains recognition and legitimacy on a global basis, membership in it should become as much sought after by the new members as by the rest of ASEAN. A sense of mutual benefit and gain should prevail. Having learnt the lesson that such benefits and gains should be assessed on a long-term basis and not through bureaucratic formulae, ASEAN states should have a more mature vision into even longer term challenges, especially in terms of sustainable growth.

NOTES

1. Brunei joined the founding ASEAN states comprising Indonesia, Malaysia, the Philippines, Singapore and Thailand in 1984 while Vietnam joined in 1996. ASEAN10 would have materialised in

1997 with Cambodia, Laos and Myanmar in ahead of the dawning of the new millennium. Cambodia's membership was delayed following its political turmoil though ASEAN overlooked Western protestations over Myanmar's record of human rights. ASEAN10 was completed by 1999 with Cambodia's entry into the group.

2. More comprehensive reviews of ASEAN economic cooperation exist in the following literature like Sopiee et als. (1990) and Sandhu et als. (1992).

3. Gunal Kansu headed the team of experts from the UN Department of Economic and Social Affairs, UN Conference on Trade and Development (UNCTAD), Economic Commission for Asia and the Far East (ECAFE) and the Food and Agriculture Organisation (FAO).

4. By a presidential decree of 4 May 1995, Keppres No. 27/95, Batam was administratively taken out of the IMS–GT while the rest of the Riau Province is still in it. This administrative move may have more to do with personality and political conflicts in Indonesia than with the IMS–GT. The economic impact on investment and economic cooperation is also not apparent as for most intents and purposes, the separation seems like a non-event and very little publicity is made of the matter.

5. Seen in this view, Singapore ONE Network and Malaysia's Multimedia Supercorridor working in cooperation rather than competition should be more beneficial to all concerned. Thailand has its Information Technology 2000 (IT2000), Indonesia, its National Policy in Science and Technology for Industrial Development and the Philippines, its Science and Technology Agenda for National Development (STAND). But currently, these appear vague and less formalised and some shared experience with Singapore and Malaysia may be useful.

6. George Soros, the billionaire financier, with an estimated fortune of US$12 billion, has been blamed by Malaysian Prime Minister Mahathir Mohamad for running down Asian currencies as punishment for admitting Myanmar into ASEAN (*Straits Times*, 28 July and 4 August 1997; *Economist*, 2 August 1997). Mahathir condemned currency trading as "unnecessary, unproductive and immoral" ("Soros/sorrows", *Economist*, 27 September 1997).

REFERENCES

Alston, Lee J., Thrainn Eggertson & Douglass North (eds.). (1996) *Empirical Studies in Institutional Change*. Cambridge, New York: Cambridge University Press.

Anwar, Ibrahim. (1997) *The Asian Renaissance*. Singapore: Times Books International.

Aranal-Sereno, Maria Lourdes & Joseph Sedfrey Santiago (eds.). (1997) *The ASEAN: Thirty Years and Beyond*. Quezon City: Institute of International Legal Studies, University of the Philippines Law Center.

Asian Development Bank. (1990) *Human Resource Policy and Economic Development: Selected Country Studies*. Manila: Economics and Resource Center, ADB.

————. (1994) "Indonesia–Malaysia–Thailand Growth Triangle Regional Technical Assistance". TA 5550. Volumes I and II. December.

————. (1995) "Technology Transfer and Development: Implications for Developing Asia". Manila: ADB.

————. (1996) "Brunei–Indonesia–Malaysia–Philippines East Asia Growth Area Regional Technical Assistance". TA 5625. February.

Bell, Daniel. (1973) *The Coming of Post-Industrial Society: A Venture in Social Forecasting*. New York: Basic Books.

Bettignies, Henri-Claude (ed.). (1997) *Trends and Investment in the Asia-Pacific Region*. London: INSEAD Euro-Asia Centre.

Bora, Bijit & Christopher Findlay (eds.). (1996) *Regional Integration and the Asia-Pacific*. Melbourne: Oxford University Press.

Brown, Rajeswary Ampalavanar. (1994) *Capital and Entrepreneurship in South-East Asia*. London: St Martin's Press.

Campos, Edgardo & Hilton L. Root. (1996) *The Key to the East Asian Miracle: Making Shared Growth Credible*. Washington DC: Brookings Institution.

Chan Heng Chee (ed.). (1997) *The New Asia-Pacific Order*. Singapore: Institute of Southeast Asian Studies.

Chee Peng Lim & Jang-Won Suh (eds.). (1988) *ASEAN Industrial Co-operation: Future Perspectives and An Alternative Scheme*. Kuala Lumpur: Asian & Pacific Development Centre.

Chia Siow Yue & Wendy Dobson (eds.). (1997) *Multinationals and East Asian Integration*. Singapore: Institute of Southeast Asian Studies.

Chia Siow Yue & Marcello Pacini (eds.). (1997) *ASEAN in the New Asia*. Singapore: Institute of Southeast Asian Studies.

Chia Siow Yue & Joseph L.H. Tan (eds.). (1997) *ASEAN & EU: Forging New Linkages and Strategic Alliances*. Singapore: Institute of Southeast Asian Studies.

Cleaver, Tony. (1997) *Understanding the World Economy: Global Issues Shaping the Future*. London and New York: Routledge.

East Asia Analytical Unit, Department of Foreign Affairs and Trade, Commonwealth of Australia. (1995) *Growth Triangles of Southeast Asia*. Canberra: Commonwealth of Australia.

Edwards, Ron & Michael Skully (eds.). (1996) *ASEAN Business, Trade and Development*. Singapore: Butterworth–Heineman Asia.

Fukuyama, Francis. (1992) *The End of History and the Last Man*. New York: Free Press.

————. (1995) *Trust: The Social Virtues and the Creation of Prosperity*. New York: Free Press.

Fujita, Seiichi. (1996) "Yen Area in Asia? An Analytical Framework". Discussion Paper Series, APEC/SC/Kobe, No 7. APEC Study Center, Kobe University and Institute of Developing Economies. March.

Gaynor, K.B. & E. Karakitsos. (1996) *Economic Convergence in a Multispeed Europe*. London: Macmillan Press.

Higginson-Dobbs, M.S. (1995) *Asia Pacific: Its Role in the New World Order*. London: Mandarin.

Huntington, Samuel. (1996) *Clash of Civilisations and Remaking of World Order*. New York: Simon & Schuster.

Kimura, Michio (ed.). (1995) *Multi-Layered Regional Cooperation in Southeast Asia after the Cold War*. Tokyo: Institute of Developing Economies.

Lim, Imran (ed.). (1996) *Growth Triangles in Southeast Asia*. Kuala Lumpur: Institute for Strategic International Studies.

Low, Linda. (1991) "The East Asian Economic Grouping". *Pacific Review*. Oxford University Press. 4(4):375–82.

————. (1996a) "Government Approaches to Growth Triangle". *Asia-Pacific Development Journal*, 3(1):1–19.

————. (1996b) "The ASEAN Free Trade Area". In Bijit Bora and Christopher Findlay (eds.), *Regional Integration and the Asia-Pacific.* Melbourne: Oxford University Press. pp. 197–206.

————. (1997) "ASEAN Economic Cooperation in the New World Order". In Maria Lourdes Aranal-Sereno & Joseph Sedfrey Santiago (eds.), *The ASEAN: Thirty Years and Beyond.* Quezon City: Institute of International Legal Studies, University of the Philippines Law Center. pp. 245–70.

Luhulima, C.P.F. (1990) "ASEAN Institutions and Modus Operandi: Looking Backward and Looking Forward". In Noordin Sopiee, Chew Lay See & Lim Siang Jin (eds.), *ASEAN at the Crossroads.* Kuala Lumpur: Institute of Strategic and International Studies. pp. 161–82.

Masuyama, Seiichi, Donna Vandenbrink & Chia Siow Yue (eds.). (1997) *Industrial Policies in East Asia.* Singapore: Institute of Southeast Asian Studies.

Maxfield, Sylvia. (1997) *Gatekeepers of Growth: The International Political Economy of Central Banking in Developing Countries.* Princeton: Princeton University Press.

McMillan, John & Barry Naughton (eds.). (1996) *Reforming Asian Socialism: The Growth of Market Institutions.* Ann Arbor: University of Michigan Press.

Mijares, Roy. (1996) "The BIMP–East ASEAN Growth Area". *RIM Pacific Business and Industries,* IV(34):41–56.

Naya, Seiji, F. & Joseph L.H. Tan (eds.). (1995) *Asian Transitional Economies: Challenges and Prospects for Reform and Transformation.* Singapore: Institute of Southeast Asian Studies.

Ng Chee Yuen, Nick J. Freeman & Frank H. Huynh (eds.). (1996) *State-owned Enterprise Reform in Vietnam.* Singapore: Institute of Southeast Asian Studies.

Okuda, Hidenobu & Fumiharu Mieno. (1996) "The Impact of Financial Liberalization Policy on ASEAN Commercial Banks: A Case Study of Thai Commercial Banks". Discussion Paper Series, APEC/SC/HIT DP, No. 3. APEC Study Center, Hitotsubashi University and Institute of Developing Economies. March.

Robison, Richard (ed.). (1996) *Pathways to Asia: The Politics of Engagement.* Sydney: Allen & Unwin.

Samuels, Warren, J. (ed.). (1988) *Institutional Economics.* Vol. I. Aldershot: Edward Elgar.

Sandhu, K.S., Sharon Siddique, Chandran Jeshurun, Ananda Rajah, Joseph L.H. Tan & Thambipillai (comp.). (1992) *The ASEAN Reader*. Singapore: Institute of Southeast Asian Studies.

Scott, Maurice. (1989) *A New Theory of Economic Growth*. Oxford: Oxford University Press.

Shirk, Susan L. & Christopher P. Twomey (eds.). (1996) *Power and Prosperity: Economics and Security in the Asia-Pacific*. New Brunswick and London: Transaction Publishers.

Sopiee, Noordin, Chew Lay See & Lim Siang Jin (eds.). (1990) *ASEAN at the Crossroads*. Kuala Lumpur: Institute of Strategic and International Studies.

Tambunlertchai, Somsak &Syed Abdus Samad (eds.). (1996) *Flying Wild Geese Pattern of Development: Changing Comparative Advantage and the Pacific*. Kuala Lumpur: Asian & Pacific Development Centre.

United Nations Industrial Development Organization. (1996) *Industrial Development Global Report 1996*. New York: Oxford University Press for UNIDO.

van Dijk, Meine Peter & Sandr Sideri (eds.). (1996) *Multilateralism versus Regionalism: Trade Issues After the Uruguay Round*. London: Casson.

Vatikiotis, Michael R.J. (1996) *Political Change in Southeast Asia: Trimming the Banyan Tree*. London: Routledge.

Williamson, Oliver E., Sven-Erik Sjostrand & Jon Johanson. (1989) "Perspectives on the Economics of Organisation". Lund University, Institute of Economic Research, Crawford Lecture 1.

World Bank. (1991) *World Development Report 1991*. New York: Oxford University Press for the World Bank.

————. (1993) *The East Asian Miracle*. New York: Oxford University Press for the World Bank.

Yanagihara Toru & Sambommatsu, Susumu. (1977) *East Asian Development Experience: Economic System Approach and Its Applicability*. Tokyo: Institute of Developing Economies.

Chapter 4

Whither ASEAN? Convergence and Divergence of the Region's Socioeconomic Dynamics

Mohan Singh

Introduction

One of the most dominant features of modern economic, social and demographic history is the study of regional dynamics and its associated changes. Such an understanding can be used to increase cooperation and, thereby, pave the way for greater interaction between the various countries (Hagedoorn, 1995). The Association of Southeast Asian Nations (ASEAN) provides, for instance, a unique platform to measure the convergence and divergence of per capita income, improvement in the quality of life and regulation in demographic behaviour between member countries (World Bank, 1995). Although ASEAN was created for greater political stability and cooperation, it has since been moving into other areas of welfare and development of the region.

The concept of convergence and divergence has initially been used to analyse the pathway of economies such as the transition of Soviet-style economies into mixed economies. The use of the concept in analysing social and demographic situations is new. This, however, is becoming important as regionalisation and globalisation gather further momentum and more regional groupings emerge to achieve greater levels of development and prosperity. The study of convergence and divergence of socioeconomic and demographic dynamics is of special significance for ASEAN which continues to work on enhancing harmony among the member states and helping each other to achieve much needed progress by reducing disparities among the member countries so that they not only achieve political but socioeconomic and demographic objectives.as well.

Over the years, particularly after the 1970s, the ASEAN countries have experienced rapid changes in demographic dynamics, health status of populations, literacy and education, and economic development. However, the speed of change and the reduction in disparities between the ASEAN countries are two phenomena that have challenged social scientists. While there is evidence of a general upward social mobility, the speed of mobility and the narrowing of gaps between the ASEAN countries remain less understood.

The ASEAN regional grouping came into effect some 30 years ago. The grouping now comprises 10 Southeast Asian countries with Myanmar, Vietnam and Cambodia being the most recent members of ASEAN. All 10 Southeast Asian countries that fall within the region are included in the analysis except Brunei for which there is a paucity of data.

This chapter explores changes in educational attainments, health conditions, and the demographic and economic situation in the ASEAN countries. The main issues to be addressed are:

- The socioeconomic and demographic trends in the last 20 years.

- Causes for gap widening and narrowing within the ASEAN member countries.
- Future directions that ASEAN will be heading for, especially during the early 21st century.

The main aim of this chapter is to identify whether convergence or divergence is taking place in socioeconomic and demographic situations in ASEAN countries. This aim is realised by analysing changes in educational levels, fertility and mortality rates and economic progress. The chapter will also identify whether the changes in various countries have brought them closer to each other or have taken them apart.

Socioeconomic and Demographic Change: An Overview

In 1996, ASEAN accounted for a total population of 490 million. Between 1995 and 1996, the grouping's population grew by 1.7 percent. The annual growth rate of population varied from 1.1 percent in Thailand to 2.8 percent in Laos. These countries have experienced a reduction in fertility and mortality levels. But the average total fertility rate remains high enough (3.0) to allow population to continue to grow. Although the average mortality rates have fallen in the region, people are living much longer than their ancestors (see United Nations, 1994): less than 65 years for men and 68 years for women.[1] The infant mortality rate has remained considerably high at 49 per 1,000 live births.

There have been improvements in education and literacy levels (Jones, 1989), but average school enrolment rate for the whole region stood at 59 percent (Table 4.1). Such a low school enrolment rate falls short of achieving the targets of universal literacy in the near future.

Economic growth is recorded throughout ASEAN. Despite this, the region's average per capita income is much lower than that of the whole Asia-Pacific region (United Nations, 1996).

Table 4.1

Summary Statistics for Southeast Asian Countries, 1996

Population	490.4 (million)
Annual growth rate of population	1.7 percent
Total fertility rate	3.0 per woman
Life expectancy at birth: Males	64 years
Females	67 years
Infant mortality rate	49 per 1000 live births
Population aged 60+ years	7 percent
Density of population	109 per square km
Gross school enrolment rate	59

Source: United Nations, 1996

What has thus become apparent is that although there have been improvements in the socioeconomic and demographic situations in ASEAN, the overall outcome is less satisfactory as compared to the Asia-Pacific region as a whole. Elaboration on the development trends in ASEAN will throw light on whether convergence or divergence is predominant in the region.

Advances in Education

Education is one of the main social indicators which reflects change in the quality of human resources in a country. More specifically, it provides a yardstick of measurement in terms of high literacy rates linked with a high level of child survival and low levels of infant and child mortality (Caldwell, 1979). A relatively high secondary school enrolment ratio would suggest that a greater proportion of children that completes primary school enter secondary school. This means that education is being given considerable priority to create an educated and trained workforce. Thus, where primary education provides basic literacy, secondary school education provides functional and skilled literacy.

The advancement in education has been noticeable in ASEAN. The period between 1975 and 1991 saw improvement in both adult literacy rates and secondary school enrolment ratios. Data given in Table 4.2 show a considerable improvement in literacy rates for both males and females in all the ASEAN countries. Countries such as Indonesia and Malaysia with low literacy rates in 1975 had improved, approaching closer to those with higher rates. The latter countries (i.e. the Philippines, Thailand and Singapore) improved even further during the period 1975–91, and came closer to attaining universal literacy.

Table 4.2

Adult Literacy Rates by Sex in ASEAN, 1975–91

Countries	Adult Literacy Rate					
	Male			Female		
	1975[a]	1985[b]	1991[c]	1975[a]	1985[b]	1991[c]
Cambodia	n.a.	n.a.	48.2	n.a.	n.a.	22.4
Indonesia	69.5	77.5	88.3	44.6	57.7	75.3
Laos	n.a.	92.0	69.0	n.a.	75.8	75.8
Malaysia	69.1	79.6	86.5	46.8	59.7	70.4
Myanmar	84.1	85.8	89.1	58.3	71.7	72.3
Philippines	84.3	83.9	93.7	80.9	82.8	93.4
Singapore	83.0	91.6	n.a.	54.3	74.0	n.a.
Thailand	87.2	92.3	94.8	70.3	84.0	91.3
Vietnam	91.0	90.5	92.0	78.0	78.3	83.6

Source: United Nations, 1994

Notes: a Data relate to years 1970 through 1979.

b Data relate to years 1980 through 1987.

c Data relate to 1990 estimates for adult literacy rate and years 1987 through 1991 for gross primary and secondary enrolment ratios. n.a.: data not available.

Plotting of the above data on literacy rates in Figures 4.1 and 4.2 suggest that the gaps in literacy rates among the ASEAN countries have narrowed considerably between 1975 and 1991. This shows that not only is there a trend to improve on the literacy situation but also to achieve universal literacy for both males and females. Therefore, a convergence in male and female literacy rates is obvious.

Secondary school enrolment ratio largely depends on the availability of schools, cost of education and government legislation on education. In developing countries, many children do not enrol in the secondary schools because there are either no schools in their residential vicinities or schooling is far too expensive. Children either have to travel a considerable distance to attend school or make arrangements to live in the student hostel or in private accommodation close by. This can be expensive and not all parents can afford to do so. Elementary education in many countries is compulsory. Nonetheless, secondary education is optional and accessible to children from well-to-do families.

Table 4.3 also shows that secondary school enrolment ratios have improved in ASEAN for both males and females, a general phenomenon of the rise in universality and affordability of the secondary school education. Effective comparison is somehow hindered because not all data are available for every country. It is apparent that, despite a general improvement, the gap in secondary school enrolment rates between the ASEAN countries has widened over the years, as shown in Figures 4.3 and 4.4. Indeed, between 1975 and 1991, those countries with higher ratios have improved much faster than the other countries with lower ratios, thereby contributing to divergence, in both male and female ratios.

Access to Health Facilities

Health conditions are a major concern in the ASEAN countries. Access to health care is important to maintain a healthy population, as in many developing countries health care facilities are not easily accessible nor adequate. In this chapter,

Table 4.3

Gross Secondary School Enrolment Ratios in ASEAN Countries, 1975–91

	Enrolment Ratios					
Countries	Male			Female		
	1975	1985	1991ᶜ	1975	1985	1991ᶜ
Cambodia	n.a.	n.a.	n.a.	n.a.	n.a.	n.a.
Indonesia	25	53	49	15	43	41
Laos	n.a.	27	31	n.a.	19	19
Malaysia	53	53	57	39	53	59
Myanmar	24	n.a.	25	20	n.a.	23
Philippines	n.a.	62	71	n.a.	65	75
Singapore	51	61	70	52	64	71
Thailand	28	30	34	22	28	32
Vietnam	38	44	43	41	41	

Source: United Nations, 1994.

Notes: c Data relate to 1990 estimates for adult literacy rate and years 1987 through 1991 for gross primary and secondary enrolment ratios.
n.a. = data not available.

the quality of health conditions is measured in terms of number of persons per hospital bed and number of persons per physician, a standard which has been frequently used by epidemiologists and health care planners to measure health status of the population (Singh, 1996).

In general, the population in ASEAN has greater access to health facilities than most other developing countries. Variation among the ASEAN member states, however, is great (United Nations Children Fund, 1994). Singh (1996) observes that while all Singaporeans have access to health centres, as many as 25 percent of the Filipinos, and 20 percent of the Indonesians do not have such access.

The ratios of persons per hospital bed and persons per physician seems to have improved in most ASEAN countries but the improvement is inconsistent, as shown by Table 4.4. For example, between 1975 and 1991, the ratio of persons to hospital beds declined from 283 to 277 in Singapore whereas it increased in Indonesia from 1,222 to 1,476. Similarly, the ratio of persons to physicians have declined in Singapore from 1,395 in 1975 to 757 in 1991 whereas it increased in the Philippines from 3,150 to 8,120 during the same period.

To measure whether there is a convergence or divergence in these areas, the above data are plotted in Figures 4.5 and 4.6. These figures suggest that while there is clear evidence of divergence in the ratio of persons to hospital beds, a weak convergence is evident in the ratios of persons to physicians. These results suggest that while most of the ASEAN countries

Table 4.4

Health Status in the ASEAN Countries, 1975–90

Countries	Persons Per Hospital Bed			Persons Per Physician		
	1975[a]	1985	1990[c]	1975[c]	1985	1990[b]
Cambodia	925	n.a.	491	16,248	16,489	9,727
Indonesia	1,222	1,484	1,476	16,430	8,122	6,786
Laos	1,078	n.a.	405	15,156	1,362	4,446
Malaysia	409[f]	408	466	4,480	3,175	2,533
Myanmar	n.a.	1,506	1,607	5,410	3,861	3,365
Philippines	606	645	714	3,150	6,570	8,120
Singapore	283[e]	256	277	1,395	972	757
Thailand	899	614	618	8,460	5,975	4,479
Vietnam	336	284	365	5,668	3,135	2,491

Source: United Nations, 1994

Notes: a Refers to the period centring on 1975.

b Data refers to the most recent year prior to the captioned year.

c In most cases, data refers to 1976.

d Refers to the period 1985–91.

e Government hospital beds only.

f Government hospital beds only; Figure is for Peninsular Malaysia only. n.a. = data not available.

might have been trying to improve the health status of their population, the influence of other factors might be making it difficult for these countries to achieve the desired results.

Demographic Change

Demographic variables used in this study are fertility and mortality. Fertility is measured in terms of total fertility rate per woman whereas mortality is measured in terms of expectation of life at birth. Total fertility rate is the sum of age specific fertility rates over the whole range of reproductive ages for a particular period (usually a year). It can be interpreted as the number of children a woman would have during her life time if she were to experience the fertility rates of the period at each age (see Pressat & Wilson, 1985).

According to the demographic transition theory, a high total fertility rate is associated with the primitive, traditional and agrarian societies where there is a low cost of child-bearing and child-rearing as compared to the benefits they bring to their parents. A low total fertility rate is, however, associated with urbanised, modern industrial societies where there is high cost of child-bearing and child-rearing. Children in the latter category of society are considered economic burdens and the cost of bringing them up heavily outweighs the benefits to be obtained from having them (Caldwell, 1976).

One of the most noticeable changes in the ASEAN region has been the change in fertility rates. Total fertility rate (TFR) has declined rapidly in most countries but in a few countries, the decline either has been much slower than elsewhere, and in a few cases, it has actually increased. For example, in Thailand, the total fertility rate declined from 6.3 in 1975 to 2.3 in 1991 whereas in Laos, it rose from 6.2 to 6.6 during the same period (see Table 4.5).

These data are further presented in Figure 4.7 so as to discern whether divergence or convergence is taking place. Figure 4.7 confirms a decline in fertility rates in most countries but fails to provide a clear conclusive indication. A further

Table 4.5

Total Fertility Rates, ASEAN Countries, 1975–91

Countries	Total Fertility Rate (Births Per Woman)		
	1975	1985	1991
Cambodia	5.5	5.1	5.1
Indonesia	5.5	4.1	3.0
Laos	6.2	6.4	6.6
Malaysia	5.7	3.7	3.7
Myanmar	5.5	3.9	4.2
Philippines	6.4	4.3	3.6
Singapore	2.8	1.7	1.8
Thailand	6.3	3.2	2.3
Vietnam	6.2	4.6	3.8

Source: United Nations, 1994

analysis of data from Table 4.5 suggests that the difference between the countries with the highest TFR and the lowest TFR increased from 3.6 in 1975 to 4.8 in 1991. This means that while the fertility rate has fallen across the countries, it has fallen far too much in some of them and far too little in others. This is therefore an indication of divergence rather than convergence.

Another demographic variable under consideration is expectation of life at birth. This is an indicator of mortality and refers to the number of years a new-born infant would live if the mortality conditions implied by a particular life table applies. The calculation of the expectation of life at birth is based on the mortality experience of the population of various ages at a point in time. A high life expectancy suggests a low level of mortality, better health conditions, higher level of economic development and an affluent modern society, whereas a low life expectancy at the time of birth is associated with high mortality level, poor health conditions, low level of economic development and a primitive traditional society.

Table 4.6

Expectation of Life at Birth by Sex, ASEAN Countries, 1975–91

	Expectation of Life at Birth					
	Males			Females		
Countries	1975[a]	1985	1991	1975	1985	1991
Cambodia	39	45	50	41	47	54
Indonesia	50	53	58	53	57	61
Laos	39	45	50	41	48	53
Malaysia	63	66	68	66	70	73
Myanmar	52	57	55	56	61	63
Philippines	57	61	63	60	65	66
Singapore	67	70	72	72	75	77
Thailand	59	62	66	63	66	72
Vietnam	56	62	63	60	66	68

Source: United Nations, 1994

Notes: a   Refers to period centring on 1975.

The expectation of life at birth has increased in all countries between 1975 and 1991 (Table 4.6), but the most interesting feature is the reduction in the difference between the countries with the highest and lowest values (Figure 4.8). The observed pattern remains similar for both males and females but the gap narrows far more significantly for males than females.

Economic Performance

The most important measure of economic performance of a country is the per capita gross national product (GNP per capita) often expressed in US dollars. This measure, however, provides a misleading picture if cross-country comparison is made because of the differences in local purchase power. A better measure of the income thus requires the variable purchasing power of a currency to be taken into consideration. This concept is known as purchasing power parity (PPP). Because of the paucity of data on the PPP, the GNP per capita is still used. Where possible, the real gross domestic product (GDP) and percentage of population in absolute poverty are also included to reflect changes in economic performance more effectively.

Some of the ASEAN countries, known as the "tiger economies", have recently achieved high growth rates. The most notable is Singapore where the per capita income (PCI) increased from US$12,400 in 1990 to US$15,750 in 1992. The situation in other countries has been drastically different from Singapore, as can be seen in Table 4.7. Nonetheless, a general upward trend has been observed between 1990 and 1992. Figure 4.9 confirms this pattern graphically. It also

Table 4.7

Per Capita GNP[a] in ASEAN Countries, 1990–92

	Per Capita GNP (US$)		
Countries	**1990[b]**	**1991[c]**	**1992[d]**
Cambodia	170	200	n.a
Indonesia	560	610	670
Laos	200	230	250
Malaysia	2,360	2,520	2,790
Myanmar	n.a.	n.a.	n.a.
Philippines	730	740	770
Singapore	12,400	14,140	15,750
Thailand	1,470	1,650	1,840
Vietnam	150	110	n.a.

Source: United Nations, 1994.
   All figures are rounded to the nearest 10.

Notes: a Per capita GNP are estimated according to World Bank Atlas method of converting data in national currency to current US dollars.
   b In 1988–90 base.
   c In 1989–91 base.
   d In 1990–92 base. n.a. = data not available.

shows that the gap between the PCI in Singapore and other countries have widened over the years. Furthermore, the increase in PCI in other high performers, such as Malaysia and Thailand, has outpaced the increase in PCI in low performers, such as Cambodia and Laos. Therefore, there is an overall divergence rather than convergence in the PCI of ASEAN countries.

During the period 1981 to 1993, the rate of per capita income as measured in terms of real GDP increased in most ASEAN countries except Laos, Myanmar and the Philippines where it decreased at various times (Table 4.8). However, the period after 1991 has shown a continuous increase for all countries.

Malaysia and Thailand have made significant achievements in their overall PCI and have moved closer to Singapore. Indonesia, Vietnam and Cambodia have registered an annual growth rate exceeding 5 percent but they have so far failed to narrow the gap with the high achievers. Figure 4.10 gives a complex picture in this regard, suggesting that the per capita income among the ASEAN countries move somehow towards a convergence.

Economic performance is further examined by looking at the income ratio of the population between the highest earning 20 percent and the lowest earning 20 percent, as well as the percentage of population living in absolute poverty. Comparing the highest earning 20 percent with the lowest 20 percent shows that Indonesia and Myanmar have experienced a relatively low income disparity while income disparity within Malaysia is high (Table 4.9).

Furthermore, the percentage of population in absolute poverty varies in various countries. Between 1980 and 1990, 85 percent of the Laotians, 60 percent of the Vietnamese, Filipinos and Indonesians, some one-third of the Thais and Burmese, and one-seventh of the Malaysians were living in absolute poverty. Rural poverty throughout was more acute than urban poverty. Singapore was the only country where no one was recorded as living in absolute poverty.

Table 4.8

Average Annual Growth Rate of Real GDP[a] (Percent), ASEAN Countries, 1980–93

| | Percentage Growth | | | | | | | | | | | | | |
Countries	1980	1981	1982	1983	1984	1985	1986	1987	1988	1989	1990	1991	1992	1993
Cambodia	n.a.	n.a.	n.a.	n.a.	n.a.	n.a.	n.a.	n.a.	9.8	3.5	1.2	7.6	7	4.1
Indonesia	9.9	7.9	2.2	4.2	7	2.5	5.9	4.9	5.8	7.5	7.2	6.9	6.4	6.5
Laos	n.a.	n.a.	7.1	4.7	7.2	n.a.	4.8	-1.1	-1.8	13.4	6.7	4	7	5.9
Malaysia	7.4	6.9	5.9	6.3	7.8	-1.1	1.2	5.4	8.9	9.2	9.7	8.7	7.8	8
Myanmar	7.9	6.3	5.4	4.4	4.9	2.9	-1.1	-4	-11.4	3.7	2.8	-1	10.9	5.8
Philippines	5.1	3.4	3.6	1.9	-7.3	-7.3	3.4	4.3	6.8	6.2	2.7	-0.5	0.6	2
Singapore	9.7	9.6	6.9	8.2	8.3	-1.6	1.8	9.4	11.1	9.2	8.8	6.7	6	9.9
Thailand	4.8	5.9	5.4	5.6	5.8	4.6	5.5	9.5	13.3	12.2	11.6	8.1	7.6	7.8[d]
Vietnam	-1.3	2.2	8.9	7.2	8.3	n.a.	6.5	3.3	4.6	2.7	2.3	4.8	7.5	8

Source: United Nations, 1994

Notes: a Unless otherwise indicated, growth rates are based on GDP at constant market prices in national currency.

      d Preliminary figure based on the ADB Annual Report 1993.

Table 4.9

Poverty Indicators in ASEAN Countries, 1985–90

Countries	Income Ratio of Highest 20% to lowest 20% 1985–89 Ave.	Gini Coefficient 1975–88 Ave.	Population in Absolute Poverty (%)[a] Total 1980–90 Ave.	Population in Absolute Poverty (%)[a] Rural 1980–90 Ave.
Cambodia	n.a.	n.a.	n.a.	n.a.
Indonesia	4.9	0.31	25	27
Laos	n.a.	n.a.	n.a.	85
Malaysia	11.7	0.48	16	22
Myanmar	5.0[b]	n.a.	35[c]	40
Philippines	7.4	0.45	54	64
Singapore	9.6	0.42	n.a.	n.a.
Thailand	8.3	0.47	30	34
Vietnam	n.a.	n.a.	54	60

Source: United Nations, 1994

Notes: a People in absolute poverty are those living below poverty line. Poverty line refers to income level below which a minimum nutritionally adequate diet plus essential non-food requirements are not affordable.

b Centring on 1975.

c Average for 1980–89.

Conclusion

Thus far, it has become clear that both divergence and convergence of income levels, quality of life and demographic behaviour are operational in the ASEAN region. In some respects, such as the advancement of education and mortality reduction, there is a clear indication of convergence. However, there is divergence in terms of total fertility rate, health status and economic performance. What has been phenomenal in most ASEAN countries is that a series of programmes has been initiated to improve education and health care, especially towards mortality reduction. These efforts have made it possible to reduce the gap between countries in terms of literacy rates and expectation of life at birth. The gap is expected to narrow down further in future. Literacy rates and mortality rates in countries such as Vietnam, Laos and Indonesia may soon converge with other ASEAN countries.

Nonetheless, divergence is a common feature with regard to hospital beds and physician population ratios as well as per capita income. Although the number of hospital beds and physician population ratio have increased in all countries, the improvement in population hospital bed ratio and population physician ratio has lagged behind the growth of population. A reduction in these ratios will require far greater improvements in the supply of hospital beds and physicians and greater efforts to reduce fertility.

The PCI gap between the ASEAN countries has widened, and this trend continues between the low-income and high-income countries. Over the past 20 years, countries with relatively higher income have been able to improve more on their PCI than those with lower income. Furthermore, even a relatively low annual growth rate has made it possible for the higher income countries to gain much more on gross total addition in PCI than the lower income countries with a relatively higher growth rate. Therefore, countries with a lower income will need to attain a much higher PCI growth rate if they are to narrow the gap with their higher income counterparts. What is visible at present is a divergence in certain socioeconomic trends in the ASEAN region especially when indicators of social and economic advancement are taken into consideration. Although the less developed economies in ASEAN are catching up with their more advanced counterparts, they have still some way to go to narrow the gap as more advanced countries have grown as well. Furthermore, the persistently high rates of fertility in these economies counter the effects of the progress they make.

A Prognosis for the Future

The patterns in divergence and convergence of socioeconomic dynamics suggest that the ASEAN countries have improved in the areas of education, health and income. Some areas, however, will remain largely uncertain in the 21st century. For example, the narrowing of the gap in education suggests that further improvement is required in low performer countries such as Vietnam, Cambodia and Myanmar. These countries have a long way to go in order to achieve universal education. A greater dialogue and closer cooperation between the ASEAN countries will help to pave the way for further improvement in education towards convergence in the early 21st century.

Health conditions is another common issue among members of ASEAN. There is a strong correlation between education and health, which is more or less well documented (see Caldwell & Santow, 1989). Rising educational levels will arouse greater awareness among people, especially women in Vietnam, Laos, Myanmar and Cambodia, about their own and their children's health. With greater input in education in these less developed countries, health conditions will improve so that all the ASEAN countries will have a relatively high standard of health.

In the study of demographic rates in the ASEAN countries, certain trends have been observed. Fertility and mortality rates are on their downward path and further decline will be inevitable when the educational levels as well as health conditions improve. While the already low rates of fertility and mortality in high performers, such as Singapore and Thailand, remain constant, lower performers will eventually catch up with them, thereby paving the way for convergence.

Although most of the ASEAN countries have focused on increasing economic development and thereby income levels, an analysis of per capita GNP and growth rate of per capita GDP has revealed that the gap between various countries has either remained unchanged or has increased over the years. Going by the past performance of these countries would suggest that the situation will continue in the future especially in the early part of the 21st century. However, the countries with low-income levels will make greater progress, thereby narrowing the gap with the high-income countries such as Singapore. Such a possibility may arise with the opening of economies and a greater movement of goods and services between these countries. Possible changes in the health conditions of the population and a reduction in the fertility and mortality levels will also create a more constructive environment for further improvement in income in countries such as Cambodia, Vietnam, Myanmar, Indonesia and the Philippines. Such a possibility has been strengthened by the recent spurt in direct foreign investment in these countries.

Finally, the ASEAN countries are heading for a certain convergence in socioeconomic and demographic dynamics. This may pave the way for greater integration in ASEAN which will contribute to the development of closer ties and cooperation in the 21st century.

NOTES

1. This is far too low as compared to the low mortality in countries such as Japan, Sweden, Australia and even poor countries such as Sri Lanka and Jamaica.

APPENDIX

Figure 4.1

Adult Literacy Rates, ASEAN Countries, Males, 1975–91

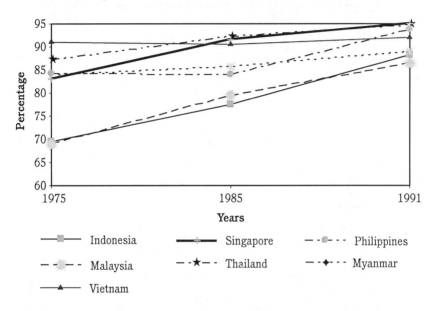

Figure 4.2

Adult Literacy Rates, ASEAN Countries, Females, 1975–91

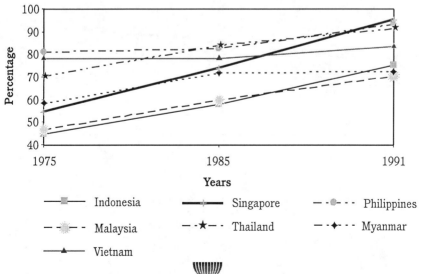

Figure 4.3

Gross Secondary School Enrolment Ratios in ASEAN Countries, Males, 1975–91

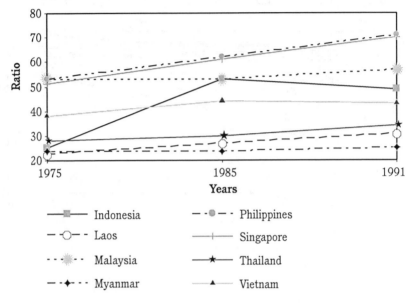

Figure 4.4

Gross Secondary School Enrolment Ratios in ASEAN Countries, Females, 1975–91

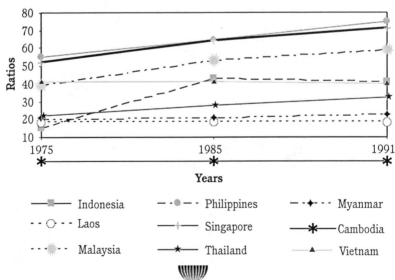

Figure 4.5

Number of Persons Per Hospital Bed, ASEAN Countries, 1975–90

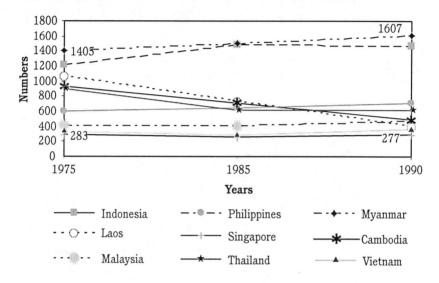

Figure 4.6

Number of Persons Per Physician, ASEAN Countries, 1975–91

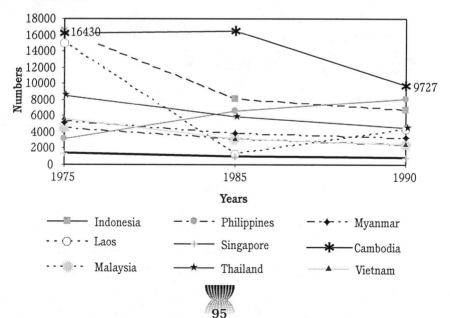

Figure 4.7

Total Fertility Rates, ASEAN Countries, 1975–91

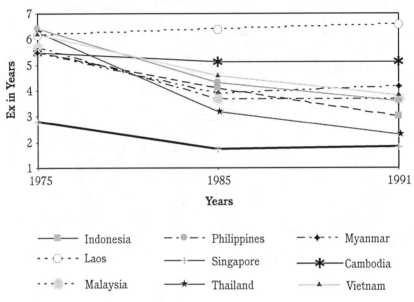

Figure 4.8

Expectation of Life at Birth, Males, ASEAN Countries, 1971–91

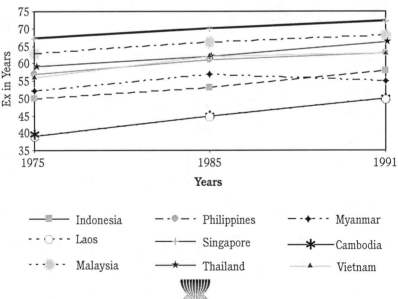

Figure 4.9

Per Capita GNP, ASEAN Countries, 1990–92

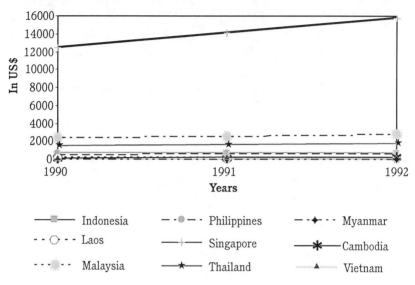

Figure 4.10

Growth Rate of GDP, ASEAN Countries, 1980–93

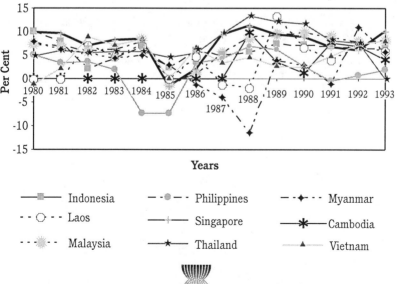

REFERENCES

Caldwell, J.C. (1976) "Towards a restatement of demographic transition theory". *Population and Development Review*, 2:321–66.

———— (1979) "Education as a factor in mortality decline: An explanation of Nigerian data". *Population Studies*, 33:395–411.

Caldwell, J.C. & P.F. McDonald. (1984) "Influence of maternal education on infant and child mortality: Levels and causes". *Health Policy and Education*, 2:251–67.

Caldwell, J.C. & G. Santow. (1989) *Selected Readings in Cultural, Social and Behavioural Determinants of Health*. Canberra: The Australian National University.

Hagedoorn, J. (1995) *Convergence and Divergence in Technology Strategies*. Vermont: Edward Elgar.

Jones, G.W. (1989) "Expansions of secondary and tertiary education in South East Asia: Some implications for Australia". *Journal of the Australian Population Association*, 6:57–72.

Pressat, R. & C. Wilson. (1985) "Total fertility rate". In C. Wilson (ed.), *The Dictionary of Demography*. Oxford: Blackwell Reference.

Singh, M. (1996) "Socio-economic and demographic indicators: A comparison of ASEAN countries".*Teaching and Learning*, 16:95–106.

United Nations. (1994) *Socio-Economic and Demographic Indicators for Asia and Pacific Countries*. New York: The United Nations.

————. (1996) *Demographic Estimates for Asian and Pacific Countries, 1996*. New York: The United Nations.

United Nations Children's Fund. (1994) *The State of World's Children 1994*. New York: Oxford University Press.

World Bank. (1995) *World Development Report 1995*. New York: Oxford University Press.

Chapter 5

Climbing up the Technological Ladder: Some Issues and Problems in ASEAN

Goh Chor Boon

Introduction

Paul Kennedy (1993) has argued that, in broad terms, the world is now divided into technological "haves" and "have-nots". Technological advances determine to a large degree who has power, how much and for how long. Industrialised nations with their powerful multinational corporations (MNCs) are now shaping the globalisation process. Markets are becoming more global due to the vast progress made in leading-edge technologies, especially in the power of the computer, computer software, satellites, fibre-optic cables, and high-speed electronic transfers. In the global market, high value-added activities include the export and import of goods and services, outward and inward flows of direct investment, embodied and disembodied technology, and movements of skilled personnel, and other transborder information flows. Consequently, many successful companies are internationalising their roles by setting up research and development (R&D) facilities, production plants and even retail outlets in all major economic regions of the world.

Globalisation, according to Robert Reich (1991), also affected the career expectations of individuals and the structure of employment generally in the developed world and the newly industrialising countries (NIEs) in Asia. The key players are now lawyers, biotechnology engineers, economic editors, software engineers and strategic brokers. These are the creators and conveyors of high value-added information whose knowledge, skills and inventiveness are eagerly sought after by consumers.

In Asia, globalisation in the 1980s was marked by very rapid infusion of Japanese capital into China, the East Asian newly industrialised economies (NIEs) and countries in ASEAN. This sharp rise in Japanese foreign direct investments (FDIs) was chiefly attributed to the high value of the yen, the need to re-invest trade surpluses, and the increasing threat of protectionism in foreign markets. In the process, a number of large Japanese MNCs — and small- and medium-sized companies, what Mitsuhiro (1994) termed as "migratory birds" — set up plants *en masse* in China, South Korea, Taiwan, Singapore, Thailand, Malaysia and Indonesia. According to Mitsuhiro (1994:18 & 32), this thrust into East Asia and ASEAN "extend[s] beyond the traditional simple assembly industries to those involving fundamental technologies" and that "technical transfer and mutual interdependence are discussed with the total development of East Asia in mind". Hatch and Yamamura (1996) suggest further that "Japanese high-technology industry is building a production alliance in Asia" to the extent that, in order to sustain their high growth rates, countries in Southeast Asia have "become embraced by, or dependent on, Japanese capital and technology".

There are favourable traits in ASEAN countries which contributed to a favourable climate for investments by MNCs. These comprise abundant natural resources in countries like Malaysia, Indonesia and Thailand, and their common economic philosophies, albeit some differences in approaches and techniques, and the practice of pragmatic, market-oriented, economic systems, with minimum governmental interference in the private sector. Lacking in largely home-based, internationally competitive technology, the task of the ASEAN governments is to provide a stable, predictable set of investment regulations and policies. The third common factor is the young, forward-looking population of the ASEAN countries.

Technological Dependency and Upgrading in ASEAN

Simply stated, the dependency theory maintains that growth and development in the developing countries (the "periphery") is hampered by structural dependence on the advanced, industrialised countries (the "core"), although the degree of such constraints varies widely. The dependency theory was made popular during the 1970s by the pessimistic views of Gunder Frank (1967) and Samir Amin (1973), both of whom asserted the virtual impossibility of take-off development in the peripheral Third World because of the exploitative ways in which capitalist industrialised core countries developed by "underdeveloping" the Third World. In a later work and in response to the emergence of newly industrialising countries, Frank (1983:323–46) argues that the popular strategy of export-led growth adopted by these countries did not create genuine development because it was largely dependent on the flow of international capitalism and foreign technology.

Some proponents, while claiming that peripheral capitalist development is possible, are "hard" or "rigid" on the concept of technological dependence. As stated by Cardoso and Faletto (1979), "[b]asically the dependence situation is maintained because, in addition to the already stated factors of direct control by the multinationals and dependence on the external markets, the industrial sector develops in an incomplete form". Cardoso argues that "dependent-associated" development of the Third World countries was not merely constrained by the structure of unequal exchange imposed by the advanced countries; their growth paths were also determined by their domestic circumstances, such as the low levels of indigenous technological capabilities.

Writing some 25 years later and when the world economy is becoming more competitive, more global, and increasingly controlled by information and communication technology, Cardoso and his colleagues (Carnoy et al., 1993) reaffirm the dependency position of many Third World countries. But they now face "a crueller phenomenon: either the South (or a portion of it) enters the democratic-technological-scientific race, invests heavily in R&D, and endures the 'information economy' metamorphosis, or it becomes unimportant, unexploited and unexploitable". They further state that even for those former Third World countries, such as the Asian NIEs, India, China and Chile, which have been incorporated in the global economy, there is an urgent task to introduce changes. These changes include an appropriate industrial policy, an educational policy to upgrade human resources and to integrate the masses into contemporary culture, a science and technology policy capable of producing a technological leap forward in information technology, new materials and new modes of organisation, and social reforms to produce an "atmosphere of freedom which is conducive to organisational and technological innovation" (Carnoy et al., 1993:156). Hence, under certain circumstances, "dependent development" in Third World countries was possible. A similar view on technological dependency was expressed by a historian of technological change, Nathan Rosenberg. He maintained that, because they lack "organised domestic capital goods sector", developing countries generally do not possess the indigenous capabilities to make capital-saving innovations (Rosenberg, 1976:146–47). Thus, they have to import their capital goods — at the expense of not being able to develop their own technological base of skills, knowledge and infrastructure which are the key elements for further technical progress.

In the late 1970s, the dependency perspective came under criticism largely due to a changing relationship between global capitalism and Third World economic development. By the mid-1970s, it was evident that a number of East Asian countries were experiencing a process of "late industrialisation". Beginning with Japan in the 1950s, Hong Kong in the 1960s, and South Korea, Taiwan and Singapore in the 1970s and 1980s, and possibly Malaysia, Thailand, and Indonesia today, these countries confirmed that successful capitalist accumulation and growth, albeit slow, of indigenous technological effort in innovation and research and development was possible in "the periphery". More importantly, the dynamic role of the state, especially in the Asian NIEs, in promoting industrialisation and technological change exposed the structural determinism of the dependency theory as its fundamental flaw. In the wake of this development, a somewhat "softer" view of technological dependence became popular. Consequently, research interest on the "late industrialisation" of the Asian NIEs shifted from issues relating to the costs and benefits of technology transfer to the ways in which these countries adapted and mastered imported technology. In the process, theoretical considerations of the relationship between technological progress and economic development in the Third World gravitated towards explanations of why some nations, like the Asian NIEs, were able to catch up and leapfrog technologically while the majority of the Third World countries is still struggling to achieve industrial and economic success.

Unlike the technological structures of Taiwan and South Korea (which are now gaining strengths in "high-technology"), countries in ASEAN, including Singapore, have developed competencies in intermediate technologies but with a weak base in fundamental technologies.[1] Colonialism in Southeast Asia had failed to create the foundation of an indigenous industrial base. Rapid industrialisation only took place with the arrival of foreign manufacturing companies which provided opportunities for local firms to acquire established assembly and production technologies. As shown in Table 5.1, some progress has been made in strengthening science and technology (S&T) as a factor of competitiveness:

To leapfrog into large-scale manufacturing of high-tech products and, given time, to become innovators of new

Table 5.1

Science and Technology as a Factor of Competitiveness (ranking among 46 Countries)

	1996	1997
ASEAN		
Singapore	12	8
Thailand	44	23
Malaysia	29	25
Philippines	26	29
Indonesia	40	41
East Asian NIEs		
Taiwan	17	10
Hong Kong	20	18
South Korea	25	22

Source: *World Competitiveness Yearbook*, 1997:29

products and processes, the ASEAN countries have adopted S&T policies which, essentially, have three main features: (a) creation of an S&T infrastructure; (b) support for strategic industries; and (c) scientific and technical manpower development. However, at this stage, technology upgrading is still very dependent on the willingness and cooperation of MNCs to transfer and diffuse advance technologies to indigenous firms.

The Singapore Model

The Singapore model takes into account a two-stage developmental strategy adopted by the government. The first stage is seen as an off-shoot of its Export-Orientation Industrialisation (EOI) strategy implemented by the Economic Development Board (EDB) since the 1970s. The EOI strategy was founded on the attraction of foreign investments in order to create jobs for the masses in the manufacturing sector. As full employment was reached in the 1970s and as the labour market tightened in the early 1980s, EDB shifted its emphasis to capital-intensive manufacturing of higher value-added products. This policy was successful in creating a manufacturing sector that boasted many big foreign multinationals, producing high value-added products ranging from precision tools to pharmaceuticals.

As in the other ASEAN countries, Singapore's strategy to catch up with technological advances depends much on technology transfers by multinationals, especially those technological leaders in respective fields. The EOI strategy had allowed Singapore to move into areas of production and standardised technologies that were no longer economically viable in the industrialised countries. The assumption here is that, given the conducive environment, foreign investment and technological-manufacturing packages would continue to flow into Singapore so long as multinationals, in order to stay competitive, are prepared to escape the profit squeeze at the maturity stage of the product life-cycle. Multinationals were urged to transmit technology and skills through their in-house training and joint-venture or licensing agreement with local manufacturers. By doing so, multinationals could provide exposure in the latest technologies to local managers and workers in their specialised fields. This would help to upgrade the country's technological competence. This traditional pathway to technological development was seen as highly effective for a trading country like Singapore to close the technological gap. On the surface, importing foreign technology may be an appealing shortcut. However, this pathway is often fraught with uncertainties and successful transfer and diffusion of foreign technology really depends on the manner and terms of its acquisition.

In the late 1980s, in order to emerge from the embryonic stages of multinational-based technology transfer and dependency and to achieve technological self-reliance, the model was refined to provide greater emphasis on sophisticated research and development (R&D) work in a few selected niche or strategic areas. The primary objective was to build up local technological capability. A government agency, the National Science and Technology Board (NSTB) was formed in 1991 to spearhead the challenge. The eventual goal was to transform the engine of growth of the Singapore economy from factor-driven to innovation-driven. In this respect, what can be termed as the NSTB model aims to foster the growth and development of two important areas: first, a pool of "technopreneurs" and, second, indigenous scientific and technological innovations. The model, shown in Figure 5.1, is operated by four main mechanisms:

- **Monetary support**. A S$2-billion[2] fund for the period 1990–95 was set aside for the promotion of high-level R&D, "Silicon Valley" type of technology and scientific projects. There is also the "buying" of imported talents in science and technology and up-to-date technologies embodied in machinery to enhance productivity and quality. A budget of S$4 billion has been approved for the period 1996–2000.

- **Technology management**. In 1991, the National Technology Plan was launched and administered by technocrats in the newly formed National Science and Technology Board. They are responsible for charting the course of technological upgrading in Singapore.

- **Science and Technology Park**. The country's quest for technological excellence and self-reliance is represented by the functions of the Science and Technology Park. It hopes to provide the environment conducive for scientific and technological innovations to flourish.

- **Manpower development of scientists and engineers**. The country's two universities and four polytechnics were given the important task of producing a pool of scientists, engineers and technologists. Foreign researchers were also actively recruited. This is intended to help to alleviate the problems posed by the lack of a critical mass of scientific and professional engineers.

Figure 5.1

A Conceptual Model of Singapore's Strategy in Technology Leapfrogging

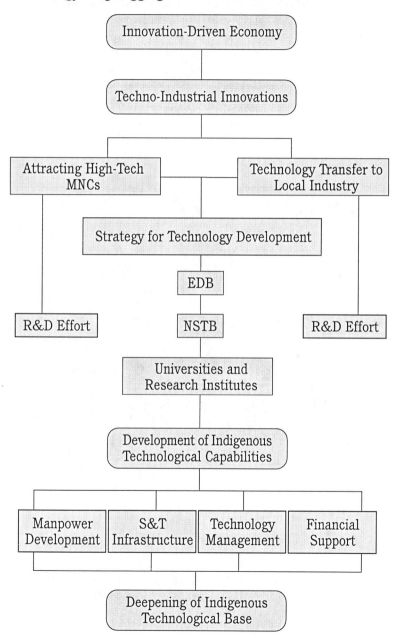

One significant result of Singapore's proactive science and technology policy is that the small city-state has not only become the world's largest producer of hard disk drives, but also plays an integral role in the product development and manufacturing processes. In most cases, MNCs will embark on first-generation production (including the critical ramping-up process), immediately after the completion of the design and prototype stage in the United States. Once manufacturing becomes standardised, production is moved to low-wage assembly sites in Indonesia, Malaysia or Thailand. In the meantime, Singapore starts work on the fundamental technologies related to the next generation of hard disk.

Other ASEAN Member States

Efforts were also undertaken in Indonesia, Malaysia and Thailand to upgrade technologically. In Indonesia, the target of the Sixth Five-Year Development Plan (1994–2000) is to enhance the capabilities to utilise, expand and master science and technology. This implies technology transfer, supported by the development of human resources, and facilities and infrastructure for research. As in the case of Singapore's NSTB, the system for R&D coordination in Indonesia is monitored under the Interdisciplinary Competitive Research (RUT) programme. The products of this programme are in the form of new materials, processes, and software which can be patented or commercialised. Like Indonesia, Thailand is also a latecomer in transforming its agriculture-based economy to a manufacturing-based, export-oriented economy. The role of technology, as a factor determining international competitiveness and sustainable development, has been given serious attention since the implementation of the country's Fifth National Development Plan (1982–86). Its main strategy is to import foreign technology and, at the same time, to build up the country's capacity to select, absorb, and adapt the imported technology in order to deepen its indigenous technological base. However, like the rest of the ASEAN countries, Thailand is still predominantly labour-intensive in sustaining its economic activities and lacks the quality and quantity in terms of manpower development in science and technology.

Malaysia is rapidly joining the rank-and-file of Asian NIEs and intends to become a developed nation by the year 2020. The launching of the Industrial Master Plan 1986–1995 marked the start of a national effort to accelerate the growth of the manufacturing sector by upgrading the country's indigenous technological capability. Science and technology policies and strategies are implemented by the National Council for Scientific Research and Development (NCSRD), its secretariat being the Ministry of Science, Technology and the Environment (MOSTE). As seen by the country's prime minister, Mahathir Mohamad, one of the central challenges which Malaysia has to overcome is the "challenge of establishing a scientific and progressive society, a society that is innovative and forward-looking, one that is not only a consumer of technology but also a contributor to the scientific and technological civilisation of the future" (Aziz & Pillai, 1996:26). The country has launched a series of measures to leapfrog the technological ladder. These include the formation of the Multimedia Super Corridor (MSC) and the Kulim Hi-Tech Park. The MSC is geared to become the centre for state-of-the-art products, such as wafer fabrication, electronic publishing and intelligent information kiosks. It has already attracted some of the world's leading information technology companies, such as Microsoft and Nippon Telegraph and the Telephone Corporation of Japan, which would form joint ventures with local firms. The Malaysian government has also engaged Kenichi Ohmae and Bill Gates as advisors to ensure the success of its MSC project. By the third quarter of 1997, the visionary project had attracted S$1.3 billion of approved investment commitments from 63 companies, with 10 additional companies expected by the end of the year (*Straits Times*, 23 October 1997). The Kulim Hi-Tech Park is modelled after the Silicon Valley in the United States and planned as a science city of the future, comprising a self-contained environment for high technology, research and development, and design and engineering. It caters to industries in advanced electronics, biotechnology, medical and scientific instrumentation, opto-electronics, process control and automation equipment.

However, the real challenge of Malaysia's "tropical Silicon Valley" is to match the top-down developmental approach with the technological culture and creativity of its people.

In short, to remain competitive, countries in ASEAN must innovate. As manufacturing technology moves more and more freely across borders, it will become more difficult for any one country to gain a competitive advantage over the other just by making things. The thrust of ASEAN's science and technology development for the years 1996–2000 is to promote technology transfer and commercialisation, networking of centres of excellence and SCIENCE AND TECHNOLOGY awareness among members. However, despite the recent shift of emphasis towards the enlargement of the indigenous technological base, ASEAN's leapfrogging effort in science and technology is still very much dependent on the traditional pathway — the inducement of advanced technology by encouraging foreign investment. Singapore, for example, pursued an open-door policy with regard to multinational computer firms. To gain that extra edge, the ASEAN countries must restructure its industrial sector and innovate, especially in designing and marketing of products which are not easily copied by competitors. The Singapore government recognises that its manufacturing sector must not be just a production base. The country must develop a strong foundation in the design and marketing of new products. However, it would be a long road for the ASEAN countries, including Singapore, to achieve technological self-reliance or autonomy and to invent, commercialise and market new, high-tech products.

Whither the Research Engineers?

Undoubtedly, globalisation and rapid technological advances have motivated governments to create conditions which allow them to compete more effectively. As manifested in South Korea and Taiwan, the key elements are a national system of innovation, a well-educated workforce, lots of engineers, designers and professional managers, a sophisticated financial structure, "super-information" communication highways, availability of venture capital, risk-taking entrepreneurs, and a few home-grown multinational corporations (Woronoff, 1992; Vogel, 1992; Campos & Root, 1996). In his well documented research on Japan's technological transformation, Hayashi (1990) and his researchers stressed the importance of native scientists and engineers. They are seen as the key factors in a country's attempt at achieving technological self-reliance and, consequently, becoming a creator of technological innovations. Similarly, Amsden (1989) argues that South Korea's rise to become a world player in the microchip industry was due no less to the rise of what she termed as "salaried engineers". Between 1960 and 1980, the number of South Korean engineers increased tenfold, from 4,430 to 45,000 and this large number of engineers has meant "competition among them for the best jobs and the fastest promotions, thereby driving up productivity" (Amsden 1989:9). Like his Japanese counterpart, the Korean engineer, with his vast exposure to shop floor management, is now seen not just as learner of new technologies but also as a technological innovator. In their case study of South Korea's Samsung, Dodgson and Kim (1997) conclude that "[f]rom a company dependent upon overseas technology and licenses, Samsung has developed advanced R&D capabilities and is developing the innovation management skills needed to compete as a technological leader". From a country that registered only a few international patents in the early 1980s, South Korea's engineers (similarly, Taiwan's engineers) have placed the country into the top 20 ranking of nations in terms of securing international patents (*World Competitiveness Yearbook*, 1997:444).

One difficult problem facing all ASEAN countries is the supply of indigenous engineers, especially those willing to take up R&D activities. Table 5.2 shows the number of scientists and engineers engaged in R&D in the East Asian economies. Clearly, Thailand, Malaysia, Indonesia and the Philippines are experiencing a severe shortage of engineers. A Thai official of the Technological Promotion Association lamented that the country only "produced about 3,000 new engineers a year, and we needed about 5,000 to 6,000 a year" (Hatch & Yamamura, 1996:84). In the case of Malaysia, to attain the

Table 5.2

Scientists and Technologists in R&D (per 1,000 people)

ASEAN	
Singapore	1.8
Malaysia	0.4
Indonesia	0.2
Thailand	0.2
Philippines	0.1
East Asian NIEs	
Taiwan	3.3
South Korea	2.2

Source: *UN Statistical Yearbook 1993*, Table5-4
Note: Figure for Indonesia includes only scientists, not technicians, in R&D.

status of a developed nation by 2020, the country would need 1,000 scientists and researchers per million people by the year 2000 — way above its current ratio of about 400 scientists and researchers per million people (*Straits Times,* 19 March 1997). Although Singapore is far ahead of its ASEAN neighbours in terms of the manpower engaged in R&D, its government is equally concerned about the supply of engineers who are committed to long-term industrial research. The strength of Singapore's manufacturing sector is based on an "entrepreneurial state" economic model. Essentially, it hinges on the government technocrats' abilities for picking "winners" and encouraging technology transfer through the continued involvement of foreign MNCs. As in the case of Japan and the Asian NIEs, the economy has already priced itself out of low-cost, labour-intensive manufacturing operations and shifted towards high-skill and technology-driven operations, as exemplified by the government's investment in wafer fabrication plants. This industrial restructuring requires the growth of a new breed of engineers — local R&D engineers in design, product and process developments. However, the city-state faces a major problem in her quest for the creation and commercialisation of indigenous technological innovations: a shortage of native scientists and engineers. Singapore's Finance Minister Richard Hu expressed in 1994 the concern of the government in his budget speech:

> Manufacturing is a cornerstone of our economy. Our education system must produce sufficient numbers of computer scientists, engineers, technicians and skilled workers to support the manufacturing sector and to attract high technology companies to locate in Singapore. Many Singaporeans may find it interesting and rewarding to pursue a career in medicine or law. But, if too many of our best and brightest gravitate towards these disciplines, not enough will become engineers and computer scientists. The viability of our economy will be at risk (*Straits Times*, 24 February 1994).

After its overwhelming success at the General Election in January 1997, the Singapore government, through the People's Action Party, launched a series of measures to emphasise the importance of the "human capital" component of national wealth. This stock of intangible human wealth comprises education, training and health care embodied in the labour force. As Singapore (and the other Asian NIEs) become more knowledge-intensive, human resources become central to economic progress. Productivity will increasingly be determined by the knowledge and skills workers put in their tasks. The requisite human resource development involves investment principally in education and training. This is clearly illustrated in the Singapore government's policy to motivate the young to take up science and technology studies so as to produce a large pool of native research engineers.

Despite the government's attempt to generate an interest in science and technology, young Singaporeans still have to be motivated to take up science and engineering courses in tertiary institutions, especially in the universities. In March 1997, the government announced new, attractive university course fees for laboratory-based disciplines and an increase in the fees for non-laboratory based areas — much to the chagrin of those who wish to pursue law, business and the humanities. The objective is to encourage higher enrolments in science and engineering courses. The assumption is that Singapore would then possess a large pool of scientists and engineers to support the manufacturing sector and attract high technology companies to locate in Singapore.

While attractive "carrots" are offered for prospective science and engineering students, the reality is that research engineering is still not a common or popular profession in Singapore. In 1995, in terms of the number of research scientists and engineers (RSEs) per 10,000 labour force, Singapore has 47.7 RSEs per 10,000 labour force, as compared to 57.2 RSEs per 10,000 labour force (in 1994) for South Korea and 61.0 per 10,000 labour force (in 1994) for Taiwan (National Science and Technology Board, 1996:5). It is also true that official statistics do indicate an annual increase in the number of RSEs since 1991, increasing from 33.6 RSEs per 10,000 labour force in 1991 to 47.7 in 1995, but what is more important is the possession of a correct mindset, attributes and commitment to R&D work. Although empirical research in this area is scarce, fieldwork carried out since 1994 suggests that the mindset and work culture of young engineers is not compatible with the long-term commitment required for successful industrial R&D.

Characteristics of Singapore Scientists and Research Engineers

From 1994 to 1996, in-depth interviews with scientists and research engineers in the public and private sectors were conducted by the author. The survey results provide useful insights on the interests of young engineers in R&D.[3] Some generalisations that emerged from the case-interviews are listed below:

• Young engineers leaving the local universities have a vague idea of the nature of R&D. This is due in part to the lack of a deliberate effort to provide effective communication between university researchers and the student population in science and technology disciplines.

- While it is not difficult to recruit fresh engineering graduates, companies do face problems in employing experienced and committed engineers, especially those with the inclination for research work. Usually, the "shelf-life" of engineers within a manufacturing or research environment is about three years, after which many would venture into "non-engineering" fields.

- Local engineers have a weak attitude and aptitude towards sustaining their interests in science and technology, and R&D work. They lack qualities, such as patience, creativity, interest and motivation, essential for a long-term commitment in research activities. Many strictly observe the nine-to-five work schedule. They prefer to work behind computers in air-conditioned offices and do not wish to have "dirty-hands" as result of handling machinery at floor level.

- Economic and social objectives strongly influence the career paths of young engineers, and science and engineering undergraduates. These objectives also influence the decisions of potential candidates to forego postgraduate studies in science and technology. A related point is that academic science is not fully appreciated by school students and undergraduates.

- Although foreign scientists and research engineers play an important role in helping the country to leapfrog technologically, it is important that Singapore relies on its own critical mass of indigenous scientists and engineers to create a self-reliant technology base.

All the interviewees in the manufacturing sector agreed that Singapore engineers have an aversion to R&D work. The main factors cited were the lack of personal interest in R&D, inadequate knowledge of the nature of R&D, the lack of monetary rewards and poor promotion prospects, and the long hours of work which also create undue stress and disrupt social lives. A senior researcher in semiconductor, an adjunct professor who supervises engineering undergraduates on industrial attachment, attributed the lack of interest in R&D and the lack of patience to learn and master specialised technical knowledge and skills among young engineers to complacency, reinforced by an equally apathetic attitude on the part of the management. The interviewees acknowledged that it is not difficult to fill up job vacancies (with new engineering graduates) and that the young engineer possesses good theoretical knowledge and diligence, and performs well if he has been assigned specific tasks and provided with proper instructions. However, when left alone to finish a research project, little initiative is being exercised to explore ways of getting the desirable or more innovative results.

Interviews with four recent science and engineering graduates also revealed an aversion towards R&D work. One of the interviewees, with an honours (second class upper) degree in engineering, related how his enjoyment of science slackened. His industrial attachment at one of Singapore's foremost high-tech multinational corporations convinced him that a career in R&D is not for him to pursue. He commented that "the thought of looking and handling machinery everyday is really boring". Peer pressure also played a part in his decision to forego an engineering career. Within his group of 30 classmates, discussion on R&D hardly surfaced. According to him, 10 of his classmates had accepted jobs in the financial and business sector even before their graduation. The interviewee himself became a forex trader because "the prospect of earning more money is good". Another honours graduate in biotechnology (who has applied to join the teaching profession) felt that there is a lot of uncertainty in R&D and "nobody knows how much effort you put in the research". Hence, some of his course mates who were employed as industrial researchers quit their posts after two years. As another science graduate commented, R&D involves "doing something over and over again". Although perceptions of R&D for these young science and engineering graduates are limited and perhaps skewed, the situation reflects the prevalence of a mindset which does not match the Singapore government's desire to entice more young graduates into R&D activities.

Two other salient points need to be noted here. Although no statistics are available, it is not surprising that increasingly more university graduates (including engineers and science graduates) are involved in brokering activities because of the chances of "making it" in a relatively short time than, say, working in the civil service or in an MNC. Science and engineering graduates are also willing to forego careers in science and engineering and take up jobs in the service sectors. In a survey conducted in 1994 with 347 engineering undergraduates at the Nanyang Technological University, 54 per cent said that they would take up non-engineering related jobs upon graduation (Goh, 1998). Better monetary rewards, personal interests in other fields, and the desire to acquire knowledge and skills in other fields made up slightly over 70 per cent of the reasons cited by the students. Some specific jobs in the sales, marketing and banking sector for example, presumably offer higher monetary gains, a higher status, and better promotion prospects to managerial ranks than the engineering sector.

A significant trend that is likely to raise the profile of the service broker is the growing importance of simple and direct face-to-face services, especially in the field of education, health and lifestyle services. Like other developed and mature economies with an ageing population, Singapore's consumption pattern is likely to shift from material to personal quality services. But these service areas require the acquisition of new knowledge and skills in order to increase efficiency and improve the quality of services. It is likely that an intensive application of information technology by the service broker would certainly raise the quality of services and improve productivity.

In view of Singapore's aggressive efforts in promoting the application of information technology in the workplace and at home, the traditional role of a middleman is likely to take a different form in time to come. Through the Internet and other forms of electronic sales and marketing, the trend is for companies and consumers to source directly from manufacturers. But Singaporeans are perceptive of money-making opportunities. It is not surprising that, in the near future, and with adequate exposure to knowledge and skills in information technology, the "cyber-merchant" or "entrepreneur" — in services such as book-selling, publishing, advertising, and food catering — would surface as a prominent player, creating virtual or Web "communities" of clients and customers. The implication for the computer and information technology engineers is significant. They would no longer be just programmers. They have to acquire the "soft skills" of the system analyst who brokers his knowledge and skills on computer systems to solve problems and troubleshoots for his clients. This approaching scenario is well understood by the Singapore government, as seen by its national programme to transform Singapore into an intelligent island by the turn of the century. In the midst of this technological change, the service broker remains a key economic player. This is because Singapore's economic life-line lies in its role as the region's most advanced trading, servicing and brokerage centre. Indeed, the country's historical role has not changed drastically; only now, technology is used to give it a new and uplifted dimension and project the image that the small island is one of the most thriving R&D hubs in the Asia-Pacific region. The creation of the Science Park exemplifies this vision.

Science Parks: A Communicative Hub?

Historically, great metropolitan cities in the world (such as Manchester, Milan, Rome and Helsinki) have manifested their greatness through the concept of the "creative city", both as a global publicity showpiece and a mechanism for cultural, technological and economic development (Castells & Hall, 1994). Contemporarily, Silicon Valley has been seen as the archetype of the innovative milieu. In her comparative study of Silicon Valley and Route 128, Saxenian (1994) emphasises the importance of "social contacts and socialisation processes inherent not only in the industries themselves but also in the broader local communities" — as the distinctive feature between the two technopoles. Similarly, Castells and Hall stress that "social networks are indeed essential elements in the generation of technological innovation" (1994:234). Thus, Japan too, is at the forefront of technology creation because social networking takes place between scientists and engineers, especially in sushi bars. In his study of Japan's Tsukuba Science City, Dearing (1995) has identified three interactive processes which would lead directly to the generation of technological innovations: researchers communicate with each other, collaborate on research projects together, and work creatively. These processes thrive within an "ecology of innovation". Other empirical studies have indicated that the level of interaction between firms located on science parks and local universities is generally low and that their locations are not a strong determinant of the level of innovativeness (Massey et al., 1992; Joseph, 1989; Felsenstein, 1994). Partly in response to global competitive pressure and partly motivated by the success stories of technopreneurs in United States' Silicon Valley, the creation of science and technology parks or technopoles is one popular strategy adopted by ASEAN members. It was envisaged by the policy-makers that science parks, due to their strategic locations with local universities, would encourage the development of seedbeds of innovation. However, little research has been done on the "innovativeness" and "culture" of these parks in Southeast Asia which were designed to provide the environment for the spawning of indigenous technological innovations.

The 30-hectare Singapore Science Park, situated in the southwestern part of the island and in close proximity to the National University of Singapore, was built in 1984. Modelled along the lines of British science parks, such as the Heriot-Watt research park in Edinburgh, the Science Park is the focal point of all industrial R&D activities and "brain services" in Singapore. Phase Two of its development, covering 20 hectares and costing S$300 million, was started in 1993 and is now fully operational. Eventually, the Singapore Science Park will extend over 110 hectares by 2005.[4] Within and in the vicinity of the Science Park, are 13 national research centres and institutes. Indeed, one could safely say that Singapore has the best technology infrastructure amongst ASEAN members. However, to what degree is interdisciplinary and inter-organisational communication in evidence in the Science Park? Though based on interviews and observation, the discussion on Singapore's Science Park as a case example is both exploratory and deductive.

My findings, based on preliminary fieldwork conducted in June 1997. have shown that there is limited communication among scientists and engineers. A retired US scientist (recruited by the Singapore government to spearhead the use of supercomputers in manufacturing) commented that he did not feel the vibrancy of a technology climate usually associated with a science park. There was hardly any informal interaction between his researchers and those situated on the same floor. In his words: "Everyone seems to tend to his own business in the Science Park". A similar view was also expressed by a director of a research institute situated within the university campus. He felt strongly that more activities could be planned to increase social networking and communication between staff of research firms. Indeed, such a call for a more interactive R&D community was inevitably brought up by three other researchers interviewed. During one of these interviews with a US-trained, Taiwanese scientist recruited by the Singapore government to strengthen the country's R&D in advanced semiconductor, research engineers were seen trooping out of the building. This provoked the scientist to comment that such work culture is a mismatch with the innovative dynamics of a research community. He added that even his expatriate researchers were gradually influenced by this "nine-to-five" attitude of Singaporeans. Another interesting observation commented by most interviewees is that generally, engineers have little knowledge of the production shop floor. They prefer to stay behind their computers in air-conditioned comfort. Unlike Japanese engineers, Singapore engineering graduates have limited hands-on experience at the production line; they are, in the words of an R&D manager with Singapore's Creative Technology, "very good at the theoretical level but not at the application level ... many have difficulties in rectifying faults in production machinery".

Another noteworthy point was made by an expatriate scientist heading Singapore's first commercial R&D company. He argued that Singapore's science and technology development is more "economic focus" rather than "technology focus". The government, through infrastructures such as the Science Park and the government research institutes, aims to project a high-technology environment so that more foreign investments can be attracted to sustain the country's manufacturing sector. The bottomline, he added, is profit-making and that means minimal risks and low tolerance of failures. He reiterated that it is only with failures and a good amount of risk-taking that innovators are able to reap the fruit of their labour. A well-known Singaporean researcher who played a major role in the creation of the country's manpower and infrastructure in information technology offered his explanation to the constraints in producing technological entrepreneurs within the Science Park:

> In Silicon Valley, a prospective entrepreneur would trigger off a supplier-chain effect, that is, he is supported by a network of people and technology. In Singapore, this symbiosis is missing; the supplier-chain effect is absent. This is because Singaporeans tend to work on an individual basis. He is left very much on his own. Perhaps this is a reflection of the migrant heritage which is symbolised by the constant struggle of the individual to survive and succeed.

My survey has included observations of social networking within the lounges and recreational facilities of the Science Park. Apart from the lunch-time crowd, these spots were hardly visited by the "research community" of the Science Park, especially during the evenings. Indeed, the Science Park, which houses more than 100 local and international companies and employing some 6,000 of Singapore's core of R&D personnel, does not exude the image of an "innovative hotbed" — on weekends (and even during week-nights). The technological nerve centre appears to be nothing more than blocks of building with empty car-parks. A system analyst in the Defence Science Organisation described the Science Park as a place possessing an "uncanny quietness" in the evenings and at weekends. She attributed the situation to the total lack of public transportation and food within the complex during those times. Studies done by Herbig and Golden (1993) on the evolution of innovative hot spots in the United States have shown that an innovative hot spot, once developed, is not necessarily a permanent entity and care must be given to maintain it. Close proximity to prestigious universities is not enough. Elements that propelled it to grow, such as economic policies towards technological entrepreneurship and a minimum level of physical attractiveness and available infrastructure must be maintained and improved. In collaboration with NSTB, attempts were made by Arcasia Land (the company that operated the Science Park) to create opportunities for more interactive activities amongst those involved in R&D. An administrator of the company agreed that, unlike expatriates, local scientists and engineers are less inclined to participate. Perhaps this less proactive stance reflects the researchers' loyalty to their company and, in some cases, corporate policies required them to remain "inactive" for fear of divulging classified information.

In summary, feedback from interviewees do point to a weak interactive research community within the Singapore Science Park, but this does not mean that there is a lack of intra-organisation networking and quality R&D work. The argument is that the capacity of a science park or region to successfully innovate and compete is crucially linked to its social and cultural context. Although well supported by professional organisations and public institutions, R&D companies in the Singapore Science Park should learn from one another about changing markets and technologies and, in the process, encourage experimentation and entrepreneurship. The challenge for the administrative bureaucrats in ASEAN, therefore, lies in the development of policy tools that will encourage science parks to develop into more than just a "collection of firms".

Conclusion

The year 1997 will be remembered for its economic pain that forced policy-makers of ASEAN to ponder whether the region's fast growth is all a mirage or, indeed, a sustainable miracle. Corruption, unscrupulous spending, self-indulgence, over-ambitiousness and even communal tension have all contributed to the squandering of wealth. Inevitably, ASEAN's vision of a high-tech region, capable of commercialising its own technological innovations, is severely dented. Nevertheless, in good or bad times, Singapore and the rest of ASEAN have to reckon with the heavy constraints of what it takes to develop a high-tech, knowledge-driven economy. The two issues discussed in this chapter — the aversion of Singapore's engineers to R&D activities and the lacklustre research community of the Singapore Science Park — indicate a basic policy conclusion. Technological change takes place within a cultural context. Hence, the establishment of an excellent technology infrastructure and other institutional changes to promote R&D and technological innovation must be matched by appropriate sociocultural attributes of the people. But attitudes can only be bred slowly and with the support of the right institutional framework. In short, for ASEAN countries to become technological innovators, governments must exercise patience in implementing their science and technology policies and in creating a technological culture in a region which, historically, was (and is) the mercantile centre of trading and brokerage activities.

NOTES

1. "Fundamental technologies" refer to industries that have developed a high mastery of casting, forging, plastic moulding, pressing and other process technologies; "intermediate technologies" refer to the production and assembly technologies, low-transistor integrated circuits, and other formerly advanced technologies that are commonplace today; "high or advanced technologies" refer to generic and proprietary or prototype technologies which eventually lead to product commercialisation.

2. US$1 = S$1.6 (March 1998)

3. The fieldwork was carried out from 1994 to 1996. Thirty-two R&D personnel and administrators were interviewed and a survey was conducted on computer and applied engineering undergraduates at Nanyang Technological University. See my article, "Science and Technology in Singapore: The Mindset of the Engineering Undergraduate". *Asia Pacific Journal of Education*, 1998, 18(1):7–24.

4. The Singapore government is also planning a two-year feasibility study on an underground science city to provide the supporting infrastructure for research activities.

REFERENCES

Amin, S. (1973) *Neocolonialism in West Africa*. Harmondsworth: Penguin.

Amsden, A. (1989) *Asia's Next Giant: South Korea and Late Industrialization*. Oxford: Oxford University Press.

Aziz, A. & G. Pillai. (1996) *Mahathir: Leadership and Vision in Science and Technology*. Malaysia: Universiti Pertanian Malaysia Press.

Campos, J.E. & H. Root. (1996) *The Key to the Asian Miracle: Making Shared Growth Credible*. Washington DC: The Brookings Institution.

Cardoso, F.H. & E. Faletto. (1979) *Dependency and Development in Latin America*. Berkeley: University of California Press.

Carnoy, M., M. Castello, S. Cohen & F.H. Cardoso. (1993) *The New Global Economy in the Information Age: Reflections on our Changing World*. Pennsylvania: Pennsylvania State University Press.

Castells, M. & P. Hall. (1994) *Technopoles of the World*. London: Routledge.

Dearing, J.W. (1995) *Growing a Japanese Science City: Communication in Scientific Research*. New York: Routledge.

Dodgson, M. & Y. Kim. (1997) "Learning to Innovate — Korean Style: The Case of Samsung". *International Journal of Innovation Management*, 1(1):53–71.

Felsenstein, D. (1994) "University-related Science Parks — 'Seedbeds' or 'Enclaves' of Innovation?" *Technovation*, 14(2):93–110.

Frank, A.G. (1967) *Capitalism and Underdevelopment in Latin America*. New York: Monthly Press Review.

———— (1983) "Global Crisis and Transformation". *Development and Change*, 14:323–46.

Goh, C.B. (1998) "Science and Technology in Singapore: The Mindset of the Engineering Undergraduate". *Asia Pacific Journal of Education*, 18(1):7–24.

Hatch, W. & K. Yamamura. (1996) *Asia in Japan's Embrace: Building a Regional Production Alliance*. Cambridge: Cambridge University Press.

Hayashi, T. (1990) *The Japanese Experience in Technology: From Transfer to Self-Reliance*. Tokyo: The United Nations University Press.

Herbig, P. & J.E. Golden. (1993) "How to Keep that Innovative Spirit Alive: An Examination of Evolving Innovative Hot Spots". *Technological Forecasting and Social Change*, 43:75–90.

Joseph, R.A. (1989) "Technology Parks and their Contributions to the Development of Technology Oriented Complexes in Australia". *Environment and Planning*, 7:173–92.

Kennedy, P. (1993) *Preparing for the Twenty-First Century*. London: Harper Collins.

Massey, D., P. Quintas & D. Wield. (1992) *High Tech Fantasies: Science Parks in Society, Science and Space*. London: Routledge.

McRae, H. (1994) *The World in 2020: Power, Culture and Prosperity*. London: Harper Collins.

Mitsuhiro, S. (1994) *Beyond the Full-Set Industrial Structure: Japanese Industry in the New Age of East Asia*. Tokyo: LTCB International Library Foundation.

National Science & Technology Board. (1996) *National Survey of R&D in Singapore 1995*. Singapore.

Reich, R. (1991) *The Work of Nations: Preparing Ourselves for the 21st Century Capitalism*. New York: Vintage Books.

Rosenberg, N. (1976) *Perspective on Technology*. Cambridge: Cambridge University Press.

Saxenian, A. (1994) "Lessons from Silicon Valley". *Technology Review*, (July), 97(5):42–51.

Straits Times. (1997) "Blueprint for More Scientists being Drawn Up". 19 March and 23 October.

Vogel, E. (1992) *The Four Little Dragons: The Spread of Industrialization in East Asia*. Cambridge: Harvard University Press.

World Competitiveness Report 1997. Lausanne: International Institute for Management Development. (1997) June.

Woronoff, J. (1992) *Asia's "Miracle" Economies*. New York: M.E. Sharpe.

Chapter 6

TRADE AND THE ENVIRONMENT IN SOUTHEAST ASIA

OOI GIOK-LING

Introduction

Discussions which have focused on trade and the environment in ASEAN in the 1990s add what can be considered as one of the more recent and urgent dimensions to the environmental debate. Environmental concerns among ASEAN member countries, we are reminded, date from 1977 (ASEAN Secretariat, 1994). In much of the discourse on issues centred on environment and development in ASEAN countries, the tendency has been to view one as being balanced against the other rather than the balance that needs to be struck between both development and environment. While the effects of trade and trade liberalisation have until recently been neglected in the ASEAN region, there is increasing recognition by the governments of the member states that more attention has to be paid to the reconciliation of international trade and environmental policies. Many of these policies are being put in place as much by external and international pressure as by growing recognition of the need to manage the impact on the environment of rapid industrialisation and urbanisation.

Regional Cooperation on the Environment and Economic Growth

The earliest effort at securing regional cooperation on environmental management in ASEAN was in 1977 when the ASEAN Sub-Regional Environment Programme (ASEP) was drafted with the help of the United Nations Environment Programme (UNEP). This early initiative was followed by the First ASEAN Ministerial Meeting on the Environment in Manila in 1981. The outcome was the first ASEAN declaration on cooperation on the environment which is now known as the "Manila Declaration on the ASEAN Environment of 1981". Cooperation was then defined very broadly as "[ensuring] the protection of the ASEAN environment and the sustainability of its natural resources so that it can sustain continued development with the aim of eradicating poverty and attaining the highest possible quality of life for the people of the ASEAN countries" (ibid.:14). Broad policy guidelines were laid down in the declaration, urging member states to enact and enforce environmental protection measures as well as promote environmental education programmes.

A series of declarations followed the first made in Manila. The second Bangkok Declaration of 1984 adopted guidelines on environmental management, nature conservation, marine environment, urban environment, environmental education and training, environmental information systems, involvement of non-governmental organisations (NGOs) and international cooperation (ibid.:15). In the Jakarta Resolution on Sustainable Development which followed in 1987, the Ministers recognised that the need for a strong link between availability of natural resources and the sustainability of developmental processes.

More progress towards closer cooperation in environmental management appeared to have been made with the last two declarations, an earlier one in 1990 in Kuala Lumpur and later in 1992 in Singapore. The Kuala Lumpur Accord on Environment and Development was issued by the ASEAN Ministers for the Environment in 1990 with one of the aims being to formulate an ASEAN strategy and action plan for sustainable development. The strategy and plan would incorporate environmental quality standards, transboundary pollution prevention and abatement practices together with the promotion of the use of clean technologies.

In the Singapore Resolution on Environment and Development of 1992, the link between environment and trade was a major concern in the deliberations for regional cooperation. One of the policy guidelines underscored the necessity for joint regional action to respond to the anti-tropical timber campaign being organised by the environmental NGOs and governments in developed countries because the success of the campaign would seriously affect the timber and wood industries in the ASEAN region (ibid.:16).

If the dilemma facing ASEAN countries *vis-à-vis* the balance between environment and development in recent years have been resolved, clearly the effort being made to strike this balance has had little impact on economic growth in the region. Between 1980 and 1992, Indonesia's average annual real gross domestic product growth rate was 5.7 percent compared to Thailand's 8.2 percent, Malaysia's 5.9 percent and Singapore's 6.7 percent (Spofford, 1995:7).

ASEAN, until its fiscal and currency crisis in 1997, was considered among the world's most dynamic regions, with a gross domestic product growth rate (excluding Vietnam) averaging 6.1 percent a year in 1980 to 1993 (Chia & Tan, 1996:1). There has been economic growth in ASEAN countries on the one hand, and on the other, the lengthening list of problems arising from the impact of such growth — natural resource exploitation, industrialisation and urbanisation.

This chapter discusses the developments in the link being drawn between ASEAN's trade and its environment in the last three decades. During this period, there has increasingly been international pressure imposed on ASEAN member states to reconcile the needs of both trade and environmental management. In the discussion, the evolution of the regional cooperation agenda will be studied alongside the effort of individual member states to respond to the challenge of reconciling trade with environmental protection needs.

Environmental Issues in ASEAN and International Environmental Agreements

Trade and environment have gained prominence as areas of concern in agendas of regional cooperative organisations from NAFTA to ASEAN (Tay & Esty, 1996). While it is not clear whether the incorporation of environmental concerns in trade negotiations has more to do with trade concerns than environmental issues, generally the indications are that the environment has been seriously affected by trade in ASEAN countries.

A state of the environment report on Malaysia (Douglas, 1984; Goh, 1991) strongly suggests that the overall situation is unsatisfactory. Goh's (1991:12) observation reflects thus:

> The downstream portions of all the rivers in Penang Island are badly polluted and ... sedimentation in the Klang Valley has caused inconvenience to tens of thousands, misery to hundreds and has far reaching effects for the whole community.

While environmental problems present a major problem not only in Malaysia but among other ASEAN countries, the greatest source of concern is how trade will be affected if trade measures are used to achieve environmental management objectives by ASEAN's major trading partners.

International trade agreements have used trade measures to secure international environmental objectives. Such agreements include the Montreal Protocol, the Basel Convention on trade in hazardous wastes and the Convention on International Trade in Endangered Species (CITES). "By one estimate, of 170 international agreements to protect natural resources, wildlife, and cultural and historical property, 19 employ trade restrictions" (UNCTAD, 1991).

International environmental agreements potentially have as important an impact as trade agreements on ASEAN because of the significance of foreign investment in the member countries and the markets for their products. To assess the importance of trade to the economies of ASEAN, the indicators in Table 6.1 compares the value of total trade of individual Southeast Asian nations with China and Japan. In 1994, Singapore's total trade alone, was more than half of China's in value. Through mechanisms such as eco-labelling and ISO14000, developed countries can wield considerable influence on the trade and environmental policies of developing countries.

This link between trade and environment provides the context for the many conflicts and controversies in the on-going discussion. Much of the discussion is concerned equally with the north–south differences in development as with what appears to be wide gaps in views on the importance of environmental management between developed and developing countries.

Literature on the subject tends to have focused on either environment or trade in ASEAN countries. But the research which has focused on the relationship between both areas have tended to be biased towards trade even when written by scholars concerned about environmentally sustainable development. This chapter studies the relationship between trade and environment in ASEAN member countries without focusing on the multilateral trade negotiations which have incorporated environmental concerns. Instead the discussion will be centred on the impact and implications of the relationship between trade and the environment in ASEAN countries. Indeed, links between trade and environment have not been neglected by the ASEAN

Table 6.1

Basic Indicators of ASEAN Compared with China and Japan

	Population	GNP per Capita	Exports	Imports	Total Trade
	(mid-1993, million)	(1993, US$)	(1994, US$million)	(1994, US$million)	(1994, US$million)
Brunei	0.3	n.a	2,162	3,142	5,304
Indonesia	187.2	740	37,958	30,589	68,547
Malaysia	19.0	3,140	58,748	59,555	118,303
Philippines	64.8	850	13,433	22,534	35,967
Singapore	2.8	19,850	96,419	102,210	198,629
Thailand	58.1	2,110	41,757	54,324	96,081
ASEAN6	332.2	1,334	250,477	272,354	522,831
Vietnam	71.3	170	4,706	8,607	13,313
ASEAN7	403.5	1,130	255,183	280,961	536,144
Cambodia	9.9	200	883	1,056	1,939
Laos	4.6	280	337	606	943
Myanmar	44.6	n.a	859	1,489	2,348
ASEAN10	462.6	n.a	257,262	284,112	541,374
China	1,178.4	490	120,822	115,629	236,451
Japan	124.5	31,490	395,201	274,123	669,324

Sources: World Bank, *World Development Report 1995;*

IMF, *Direction of Trade Statistics Yearbook 1995;*

Asian Development Bank, *Key Indicators of Developing Asia and Pacific Countries 1995;* Chia and Tan (1996), pp. 2–3.

governments which recognise that "... gains from trade liberalisation in certain sectors could be eroded if compliance with environmental requirements were to lead to cost increases or discrimination against their exports. Developing countries are in particular concerned that environmental requirements may be used for protectionist purposes (Vossenaar & Jha, 1996:55).

Clearly, exploitation of the rich natural resources of many ASEAN countries has contributed to the rapidly growing importance of trade. In Indonesia for example, over 40 percent of the gross domestic product and 50 percent of employment are derived from primary industries attributable to the downstream processing of natural resources or tourism and other closely related sectors (World Bank, 1990). Adjustment lending by the World Bank, with its increasing focus on environmental management in developing countries, is another source of concern for development planners in ASEAN (Seda, 1993). Adjustment lending aims to assist governments in working towards and achieving policy reform. Adjustment policies have had conceptually traceable impact on the environment. On the one hand, in reducing government intervention in marketing arrangements or revaluing the exchange rate, price reforms have encouraged the production of environmentally benign export crops in some countries (Wharford & Wheeler, 1993:23). In other countries, however, trade liberalisation leading to higher export prices have encouraged extension of the cultivated area thereby resulting in substantial damage to the natural vegetation cover.

An illustration of the impact on development in ASEAN member countries is the determination of the World Bank to emphasise environmental management as seen in the withdrawal of its support for a development project in Thailand. This project was seen to have a serious potential impact on one of Thailand's last remaining tropical forests and on six rare animal species (Seda, 1993:19). Similarly, large infrastructural development projects, such as hydro-electric power plants, usually require financing that has to be raised through loans. If financing by international aid agencies is involved, many of these projects would have to prove that they are environmentally sound.

Trade and Exploitation of Natural Resources

The impact of international trade on the natural environment of the ASEAN countries is best demonstrated in forest exploitation by timber and wood-related industries. The concern over the depletion of natural forests in the ASEAN region has been a consequence of rapid loss in recent years. Estimates are that annually, the Philippines loses 100,000 hectares compared to 23,000 hectares in Malaysia, 325,000 hectares in Thailand and 550,000 hectares in Indonesia (Ooi, 1987). This has meant the decline in Malaysia's forested area from three-quarters of the nation in 1958 to well under half in 1985; as well as the decline in Thailand's forested area from 53 percent of the nation in 1961 to 29 percent in 1985 (Hirsch, 1987).

In the ASEAN countries, the less developed Indochinese states and Myanmar, having introduced economic reforms, currently face difficult and complex resource use and environmental quality issues in the effort to attract foreign investment (Mya Than, 1991). There is concern that unsustainable resource exploitation practices are being transferred from other more developed ASEAN countries to the poorer countries. This, at least, appears to be the case with logging. After logging was banned in Thailand in 1989, Thai timber companies were being allowed to operate in Myanmar since it had no policy in place and its politicians were reportedly more concerned with ensuring an adequate supply of timber and keeping the prices down (Seda, 1993:4). Regional cooperation is necessary if such transfers are to be discouraged. There is ample evidence why such transfers should be actively discouraged in the region.

Impact of Deforestation

Since British colonial rule, Sabah's forestry has contributed significantly to export earnings and between 1980 and 1989, actually representing 40 percent of the state's gross domestic product (Mohamed & Ti, 1993). The sector has since been overtaken by the discovery of oil fields off the Sabah coast. Values of Malaysia's sawlog exports, however, remain high (see Table 6.2). These values indicate that logging is likely to prove attractive as a source of revenue for some time to come. Dwindling resources, as well as the periodic downturns in prices, are likely to prove deterrent. The indications are that so far both have not been effective in any major way as a deterrent to loggers.

Sabah and Sarawak of Malaysia have been leading exporters of tropical logs, with Japan as the main importer. It

Table 6.2

Malaysia's Production, Export and Price of Sawlogs, 1980–91

Year	Production ('000 cubic metres)	Export ('000 cubic metres)	RM*million	Unit value (RM/ cubic metre)
1980	27,916	15,152	2,621	173.0
1985	30,957	19,630	2,771	140.5
1986	29,869	19,055	2,876	150.9
1987	36,149	23,001	4,274	185.8
1988	37,727	20,552	4,010	195.0
1989	39,709	21,101	4,356	206.4
1990	40,000	21,000	4,200	200.0
1991	38,000	20,500	4,203	205.0

Source: Ministry of Finance, Malaysia, Economic Report 1990/91.
Mohamed and Ti, 1993: 116.

Note: * 1 $US = 3.8 Ringgit Malaysia (February 1998).

appears that logging activities are unlikely to respond to the pressure from environmental groups in Europe and the United States which have been trying to organise consumer boycotts on tropical timber and propose restrictions on tropical timber products (Seda, 1993).

Forest depletion in Sabah imply more than just the destruction of natural ecosystems. Reports on the impact in villages in Ulu Kinabatangan (Marsh & Gait, 1990) highlight the destruction of forests that provide for the livelihood of local communities involving shifting cultivation of hill paddy and vegetables and fruits together with hunting, fishing and gathering of forest produce such as rattan, honey, resins and bamboo. Furthermore, logging has ravaged land that falls under customary tenure and even damaged farmlands because the bulldozer operations of the loggers have compacted the soil leaving it largely uncultivable (Mohamed & Ti, 1993:128). At the same time, rivers upon which rural dwellers depend have been polluted.

In 1987, Malaysia arrested hundreds of members of the Penan indigenous tribe in Sarawak who were trying to stop logging activities (Seda, 1993). These arrests generated widespread publicity and a boost to the campaign in Europe and the United States to ban tropical timber imports. More specifically, the European Parliament called on its member states to ban the import of tropical timber from Sarawak although this was rejected because the ban would have hurt European timber importers equally. Two hundred city councils in Germany and almost half of the local governments in the Netherlands, however, stopped using tropical timber in 1989 (ibid.). A major implication of bans such as these is that exporting countries have to bear the costs although the benefits are for both the developed and developing worlds. ASEAN countries have rightly pointed out that a similar pressure does not exist for temperate forest products.

River pollution and other environmental problems resulting from logging activities are not confined to Sabah alone. Indonesia has one of the last remaining great stands of tropical forests, indeed, the largest in Asia. Such forests, like those in the Amazon, are important global assets as storehouses for "biological diversity". They are also important as "carbon sinks" in their contributions to controlling global warming. "Most of Sulawesi's best forests are already gone, and the provinces of Kalimantan are now realising that their timber-based economies are threatened by dwindling wood supplies. Unless returns are reasonably high, it is difficult to imagine how Indonesia will be able to rehabilitate the still growing area of degraded lands (McCauley & Lubis, 1993:40).

Logging constitutes just one of the many examples in which trade has had serious deleterious effects on the environment. Other areas include mining, coastal fishing zones with resources which can be affected by pollution and environmental degradation.

Industrialisation and the Environment

A newspaper report recently highlighted that toxic waste had killed more than 80,000 full-grown fish at a fish farm in Johor state of Malaysia (*The Straits Times*, 29 October 1997:33). The fish farmers blamed the contamination on nearby factories and workshops for the toxic effluents that had been washed into the farms after a shower of rain. Such an incident underscores the difficulty of managing the environmental impact of industrialisation in the ASEAN countries. Yet the failure to manage such impact has serious implications including the pollution of sources of drinking water.

Textile industry is a major import industry in both Indonesia and Thailand. Unfortunately, the total pollution load contributed by the industry to rivers is highly correlated with the robustness of the industry. In Indonesia, textile industry accounts for an estimated 70 percent of the total pollution load of the West Java rivers (Intal, 1996), although these rivers are included in the Indonesian government's Clean Rivers Programme. Similarly, the textile industry in Thailand accounts for 32 to 38 percent of pollution loading in the rivers running through where the industry is located.

Interestingly in ASEAN countries, such as Malaysia, the Philippines and Thailand, where semiconductor and the electronics industry comprise large shares of total exports, there are concerns about the treatment of the toxic substances. Phantumvanit 1994 observes that "[t]here are substantial health risks of improper utilisation and disposal of the toxic materials in electronics manufacturing. For example, lead levels in the blood and urine of electronics factory workers in Thailand in 1987 were very much higher than the levels in rural residents and Bangkok residents". The electronics industry is dominated by large multinationals and is very likely the most environmentally sensitive. Hence, the issue lies more with the provision of infrastructure for waste disposal in the countries in which the industry is located.

Environmental protection measures which are implicit in international standards, such as, ISO14000, may place the small and medium-sized enterprises especially in difficult positions, without access to facilities, technology and know-how, and capital to adapt to new environmental rules (Tay & Esty, 1996:5). Although the standards are voluntary and the ISO14000 process open to all countries, it has proven to be dominated by European and North American industry (Runnalls, 1996:173).

Small and medium-sized enterprises generally have difficulty in access to capital for environmental investments because of low or even negative returns. In addition, for some sectors such as timber and textile industries, which may not be competitive, internalising environmental costs is likely to drive many of the firms out of business. Hence, the role of the state and the market in providing for the infrastructure are crucial in environmental management. They play an important role in reducing the cost of compliance, particularly for small companies (Vossenar & Jha, 1996:62).

Furthermore, the growing number of eco-labelling schemes in developed countries represents an additional pressure on the local business sector to react to these schemes with resources in order to qualify for the labels. Failing to comply with these schemes will likely impair market access.

More than 30 countries now have some form of voluntary eco-labelling scheme, virtually all with different product requirements (Runnalls, 1996:173). Since each of the labels has very different requirements that are also based on a host of environmental, social and cultural conditions of the country implementing the label, it will be very difficult for products from developing countries to comply with the requirements. Many of the labels are implemented unilaterally by the countries in which the voluntary eco-labelling schemes have been introduced. Since these schemes are voluntary in nature, the onus of compliance is shifted to producers in developing countries including the member states of ASEAN.

Challenge for Regional Cooperation on the Environment

For many businesses which have had to internalise the costs of complying with environmental regulations, cooperation among the ASEAN member countries is anticipated to be translated into reducing price differentials which, on paper at least, would not disadvantage countries with higher costs because of compliance. There has also been a similar expectation regarding transboundary pollution. The haze, which is enveloping much of Malaysia and Singapore because of uncontrolled forest fires in Sumatra, Kalimantan and other parts of Indonesia, has again led to questioning the regional cooperation objectives that ASEAN should be working on.

There appears to be first, an urgent need for ASEAN member states to address the issues of Federal–State and Inter-Agency cooperation within each of their own countries. This is of particular importance in the areas of resource utilisation and regional planning and implementation. Once such coordination has been achieved within each member country, there can be more effort allocated to the implementation of policy guidelines arising from regional cooperation agreements.

The only certainty arising from the growing recognition of the link between trade and environment is that there will continue to be pressure on ASEAN member countries to incorporate environmental management into their development plans. Strong indications are that ASEAN will have no choice but to work on the process of emphasising environmental protection in line with its high economic growth objectives because there will be international as well as domestic pressures to do so.

REFERENCES

ASEAN Secretariat. (1994) *ASEAN Strategic Plan of Action on the Environment*. Jakarta: ASEAN Secretariat.

Chia, S.Y. & J.L.H. Tan. (1996) "An overview of ASEAN in the WTO: Challenges and responses". In S.Y. Chia & J.L.H. Tan (eds.), *ASEAN in the WTO: Challenges and Responses*. Singapore: Institute of Southeast Asian Studies. pp. 1–28.

Douglas, I. (1984) "Water and sediment issues in the Kuala Lumpur ecosystem". In Y.H. Yip & K.S. Low (eds.), *Urbanisation and Ecodevelopment with special reference to Kuala Lumpur*. Kuala Lumpur: Institute of Higher Studies, University of Malaya.

Goh, B.L. (1991) "Urban environmental management: A new challenge to local authorities in Malaysia". *Malaysian Journal of Tropical Geography*, 22(1):9–17.

Hirsch, P. (1987) "Deforestation and development in Thailand". *Singapore Journal of Tropical Geography*, 18(2):125–32.

Intal, P.S. (1996) "Perspectives from the Philippines and ASEAN". In S. Tay & D. Esty, *Asian Dragons and Green Trade*. Singapore: Times Academic Press. pp. 89–98.

Marsh, C. & B. Gait. (1990) "Effects of logging on rural communities in Ulu Kinabatangan". Abstracts of papers presented at the International Conference on Forest Biology and Conservation, Borneo, Kota Kinabalu, Sabah.

McCauley, D. & R. Lubis. (1993) "Economic development and environment in Indonesia". In P. Koomsup (ed.), *Economic Development and the Environment in ASEAN Countries*. Bangkok: The Economic Society of Thailand. pp. 39–64.

Mohamed, M. & T.C. Ti. (1993) "Managing ASEAN's forests — Deforestation in Sabah". In M Seda (ed.), *Environmental Management in ASEAN: Perspectives on Critical Regional Issues*. Singapore: Institute of Southeast Asian Studies. pp. 111–40.

Mya Than. (1991) "ASEAN, Indo-China and Myanmar: Towards Economic Cooperation?" *ASEAN Economic Bulletin*, 8(2):173–93.

Ooi, J.B. (1987) *Depletion of the Forest Reserves in the Philippines*. Singapore: Institute of Southeast Asian Studies.

Phantumvanit, D. & E. Olsen. (1994) "The relationship between business and environment". *TEI Quarterly Environment Journal*, 2(1):5–23.

Runnalls, D. (1996) "What the North must do". In S. Tay & D. Esty (eds.), *Asian Dragons and Green Trade*. Singapore: Times Academic Press. pp. 169–87.

Seda, M. (1993) "Global environmental concerns and priorities — Implications for ASEAN". In M. Seda (ed.), *Environmental Management in ASEAN: Perspectives on Critical Regional Issues*. Singapore: Institute of Southeast Asian Studies. pp. 1–54.

Spofford, W. (1995) "Resources for the future's China Program". *National Environment Enforcement Journal*, 10(2): 34–38.

Tay, S. & D. Esty. (1996) "Trade and environment: Context and controversy". In S. Tay & D. Esty (eds.), *Asian Dragons and Green Trade*. Singapore: Times Academic Press. pp. 21–32.

UNCTAD. (1991) "Environmental Trade". Report to Preparatory Committee of the United Nations Conference on Conference and Development, July 1991. Prepared by the United Nations Conference on Trade and Development.

Vossenaar, R. & V. Jha. (1996) "Competitiveness: An Asian Perspective". In S. Tay & D. Esty (eds.), *Asian Dragons and Green Trade*. Singapore: Times Academic Press. pp. 49–68.

Wharford, J. & D. Wheeler. (1993) "Environmental economics and development: A research agenda". In P. Koomsup (ed.), *Economic Development and the Environment in ASEAN Countries*. Bangkok: The Economic Society of Thailand. pp. 19–37.

World Bank. (1990) *Indonesia: Sustainable Development of Forests, Land and Water*. Washington, D.C.

Chapter 7

Urbanisation and Sustainability of Southeast Asian Cities

Wong Tai-Chee

Introduction

Urbanisation of Southeast Asia has been a well-researched area for more than three decades. From McGee's (1967) study of urban evolution and post-war urban patterns marked by pseudo-urbanisation, interest has shifted more recently to urbanisation trends, factors contributing to the formation of large megacities (see Jones, 1993; Pernia, 1992; Forbes, 1996; Dutt & Song, 1996), and urban management issues (Ruland, 1992). Indeed, from a relatively low urban base, Southeast Asian cities are growing rapidly both physically and in population size. Yet cities in Southeast Asia are largely responsible for environmental degradation given their high concentration of production and consumption (Haughton & Hunter, 1994:111), and the lagging behind in the provision of basic services to the urban poor. The high incidence of urban poor in the megacities of the developing countries has a direct relationship with urban environmental degradation (Mathur, 1994; Lee, 1994), though fundamentally through no fault of the poor themselves.

This chapter examines urbanisation in Southeast Asia in general and the sustainability issue in particular. Attention is centred on megacities in Southeast Asia in the light of their faster growth than lower ranking cities in the region, and the environmental problems they face in meeting rising demands from a burgeoning urban population. Furthermore, as ASEAN has expanded to include lower-income states, such as Vietnam, Laos, Myanmar and Cambodia, economic growth has inevitably appeared to be a priority aimed at strengthening the association's foothold as a grouping in the present increasingly competitive global economy. Will the economic pursuit and the strong demand for multinational capital contribute to additional adverse environmental effects? How then to balance economic growth with the need to sustain the environmental resource base in the region? The prospect of intergovernmental efforts in managing diverse environmental effects, largely of transboundary nature, is finally explored.

Urbanisation and Industrial Development in Southeast Asian Cities

Since the 1950s, industry has been looked upon by developing countries as a leading sector of productive economic development. Three basic factors have influenced policy-makers to think along this line. First, industry is seen as capable of producing multiplier effects with its forward and backward linkages that agriculture cannot provide. Second, growth potential is handicapped by the terms of trade for agriculture-based developing countries relying on the export of primary products. Third, industry can generate an increasing marginal return through economies of scale in the production process. Consequently, industrial workers are in a position to be more productive than farmers, in particular in developing countries dominated by subsistence farmers who are seen as "conservative" and reluctant to change.[1] High population growth coupled with massive unemployment in the 1950s and the 1960s further convinced the national élites, at the aftermath of decolonisation, of the need for industrialisation (see Knox & Agnew, 1989).

In Southeast Asia, modern industrial development, sharply contrasted with traditional cottage industry, is an imported production system after World War II. Largely because of the region's weak inherited industrial base, and because four states (Vietnam, Cambodia, Laos and Myanmar) have opted for an agriculture-based centrally planned socialist path, urbanisation rate in the region is relatively low. In 1990, Southeast Asia was 34.3 percent urban as against the world average of 45.2 percent (United Nations, 1993). Despite a low urbanisation rate, urban primacy is highly significant in the region. These primate cities (Jakarta, Manila, Rangoon (Yangon), Saigon (Ho Chi Minh City), Singapore[2]), developing from a colonial port base, are a product originating from a complex process of socio-political dominance at locations having the best attractions for central place activities, such as administration, import-export trade and manufacturing (Dutt & Song, 1996:107; World Resources Institute, 1996:10). These colonial ports saw their population size tripling in the 19th century and continuing to dominate in the 20th century (McGee, 1967:54). Though Thailand was exempted from direct colonial rule, it followed identical processes as other Southeast Asian port cities. Its capital city, Bangkok, endowed by a strategic location in the fertile Chao Phraya deltaic plain, is most pronounced of primacy development for making up more than half of the urban population in the country.

Persistence of Urban Primacy

The Southeast Asian capital cities, as centres of change, are often the first recipient of latest technology from more advanced states. They facilitate the diffusion of products, information and human resources between themselves and other subordinate settlements. As industry can be used as an instrument of political favouritism and patronage, national governments have strong biases in favour of capital cities in their decision-making process by making available resources and formulating policies to facilitate economic growth, reinforcing primacy as a result (see Pernia, 1992:235). Despite diseconomies caused by congestion and high land prices, the core urban region produces higher returns to investments than smaller cities, and will most likely remain so until "polarisation reversal" takes effect (see Jones, 1993:65–66). Foreign direct investments in Southeast Asia, particularly those from Japan, are highly concentrated in capital cities and their immediate surrounding areas, thus generating opportunities for business expansion and employment which, in turn, act as a "pole" in attracting further migrants, both skilled and unskilled. In Thailand in the mid-1980s, for example, more than 95 percent of the manufacturing firms and employment were found to be located in Bangkok and its suburbs (Knox & Agnew, 1989). The same holds true for Indonesia. In 1992, 17 percent of the nation's domestic industrial production, and 61 percent of its banking and financial services were located in Jakarta (World Resources Institute, 1996:6).

Whilst skilled labour fills up jobs mostly in the formal sector in the capital cities, the unskilled find it easier to settle down in the informal sector. Evidence has suggested that informal jobs are in one way or another integrated with the urban economy, though remuneration paid to workers in this sector are normally below those in the formal sector.

The dominance of primate cities in pro-capitalist Southeast Asia is persistent, and has been further consolidated following the formation of the monopolising political and business élite groups there who saw little interest in developing supporting yet balancing secondary cities in the post-independence era. The primate cities remain the main industrial capital absorber since import-substituting industrialisation began in the late 1950s, and export-led industrialisation emerged since the 1960s. They also benefit from high concentrations of financial, administrative facilities, and a higher-paying skilled workforce that supports a sizeable consumer market.

Table 7.1 shows the continued dominance of the capital cities as leading centres of Southeast Asian countries from 1960 to 1990 during which the urban population increased by 3.4 times. On average, the capital cities accommodated 30 percent of the region's urban population in 1960, 26 percent in 1990 and by the year 2000, are still expected to comprise a persistently high 24 percent. The proportion could have been even higher if the conurbations were included in the estimate.[3] In capital cities of pro-capitalist countries, urbanisation has been more rapid than that in centrally planned economies, and in-migration contributed to urban growth as much as natural increase. In Thailand, the Northeast, the poorest region of the nation, has been a major exporter of migrants to Bangkok and the more prosperous Central Region for over 20 years (United Nations, 1995a:184).

Urban growth has taken place more rapidly outside the city boundary. Indeed, suburbanisation is widespread in Kuala Lumpur, Bangkok and Manila, and reclassification of the city boundary has been frequent. In Jakarta, for example, annual growth within the city had slowed down from 3.9 percent during the period 1971–80 to 2.7 percent during 1980–90 (Forbes, 1996:40). There is, however, a marked difference in their residential form. With a stronger middle class in Kuala Lumpur, suburban houses in its suburbs are characterised by double-storey terrace houses or condominium blocks built by private developers. Where affordability is weaker and access to bank loans is less readily available in Jakarta, Bangkok and Manila, suburban housing is dominated by self-built houses with materials purchased at affordable prices.

Rates of urbanisation have been slower in the centrally planned socialist countries, where the state controls the bulk of economic activities and the extent of foreign trade. This is not only because of the residential control system used for regulating rural-urban flow, it is also due to lack of urban jobs in the informal sector which is again rigidly controlled by the authorities. In the mid-1970s, there was even a short stage of deurbanisation in South Vietnam and Cambodia, immediately following Vietnam's reunification and the installation of the Khmer Rouge respectively (Forbes, 1996). Both countries forcefully evacuated the cities flooded with refugees of mainly rural origins.

Table 7.1

Population Growth of Capital Cities, 1960–2000 (population in million)

Cities	1960		1970		1980		1990		2000	
Bangkok	2.151	(65.1*)	3.11	(65.5)	4.723	(59.3)	5.894	(61.3)	7.32	(54.0)
Jakarta	2.679	(19.1)	3.916	(19.1)	5.985	(17.9)	9.25	(16.5)	14.091	(16.4)
Ho Chi Minh City**	1.321	(25.9)	2.00	(25.6)	2.735	(26.5)	3.237	(24.4)	3.992	(21.7)
Kuala Lumpur	0.344	(15.9)	0.451	(12.4)	0.921	(15.9)	1.122	(12.6)	1.383	(10.8)
Metro Manila	2.274	(27.2)	3.535	(28.6)	5.955	(32.9)	7.968	(26.9)	10.801	(24.5)
Phnom Penh [a]	0.39	(69.6)	0.51	(63.0)	n.a.		0.97	(62.4)	n.a.	
Rangoon (Yangon)	0.944	(22.6)	1.419	(22.9)	2.215	(27.3)	3.302	(31.9)	4.506	(30.8)
Singapore	1.634	(100.0)	2.075	(100.0)	2.414	(100.0)	2.705	(100.0)	2.967	(100.0)
Vientiane [a]	0.13	(76.5)	0.16	(61.5)	0.24	(55.8)	0.40	(52.6)	0.67	(51.9)

Source: United Nations, 1995b. World Urbanization Prospects: The 1994 Revision. New York. pp. 88–89 & 136–37.
      [a] United Nations, 1989. Prospects of World Urbanization 1988. pp. 107 &144.

Note: * Percentage of urban population in brackets is computed.
      ** Hanoi, the capital city, was one-third of Ho Chi Minh City's population size in 1990.
      n.a. = reliable data not available.

Since the 1986 economic reform *doi moi*, a limited amount of non-organised spontaneous migration has been allowed in Vietnam. Attracted by higher-income jobs offered by emerging private businesses, spontaneous migrants often settle in poorly serviced city fringe areas, largely living in semi-permanent or temporary types of dwellings and using well water as the main source of drinking water (Doan & Trinh, 1996:14–15). Actual data in Cambodia is unknown. Understandably, the reportedly high unemployment rates and poverty in Phnom Penh are indications that the city's housing standards and basic services could not be better than in Ho Chi Minh City.

Industrial Growth and Environmental Sustainability

Intensification of industrial investments by multinational corporations in Southeast Asia occurred in the late 1960s, as a result of declining manufacturing profits in industrialised nations. Foreign direct investments (FDIs) from developed nations in the open economies in ASEAN were uneven, depending on the commitment, quality of local physical and financial infrastructure, tax concessions, government efficiency and other technical support services. Singapore has been highly successful in absorbing FDIs; it became fully integrated with world trade and experienced a heavy inflow of multinational investments and technology. High export-led growth of the city-state in the late 1960s encouraged Malaysia, Thailand, then Indonesia and the Philippines, to follow a similar strategy in the 1970s. By 1981–86, though small in population and physical size, Singapore received 50 percent of the total FDIs in ASEAN as against Malaysia (35.7 percent), Indonesia (11.6 percent), Thailand (8.9 percent) and the Philippines (2.7 percent) (Dixon, 1991). Between 1965 and 1988, achievement of industrial shares in the gross domestic product was significant, rising from 28 to 34 percent for the Philippines and for Indonesia, from 13 to 36 percent (Jones, 1993:49).

It is important, however, to note that environmental impact arising from industrial activities does not coincide with the extent of FDI in each individual country. This could be explained by two aspects in the industrialisation process. First, industrial investments in ASEAN are generally not the most polluting types, if compared to local small, sometimes informal sector industries, employing few measures to safeguard the environment. Second, environmental law enforcement that has become an official agenda of government departments since the 1970s, has helped to regulate and control industrial emission and discharges to the environment. The extent of environmental damage, therefore, is an outcome strongly associated with national governments' effectiveness in implementing policies and laws. In pro-capitalist Southeast Asian countries, with the exception of Singapore, expansion of the informal sector is closely associated with slums and squatter housing in the capital cities. Here, there is a serious lack of basic sanitary services, such as access to safe drinking water and decent waste disposal facilities. Squatter sites are largely located within city limits to facilitate travel to work, and the children to schools. Three brief cases of the primate cities Kuala Lumpur, Bangkok and Jakarta, will be examined here.

Environmental Issues in Kuala Lumpur

Industrial development and expanding export of primary products in the past two decades have bolstered growth in Malaysia. Growth of industries has contributed to a great accumulation of wastes of diverse types. Yet environmental health and industrial wastes have received low priority. Illegal dumping of wastes and incompatibility of land use are a common phenomenon. According to investigations by the Consumers' Association of Penang and *Sahabat Alam* Malaysia (1996:53), 57 percent of major rivers in Malaysia in 1994 were heavily polluted with suspended solids including mercury, lead, cadmium, zinc and copper. One of these rivers, Sungai Kelang, which flows through the capital Kuala Lumpur, is seriously contaminated. Other than solid, liquid and gaseous wastes, the study also found that Malaysian cities were disturbed by high levels of noise pollution of between 55 and 65 decibels. Coastal areas near major Malaysian cities were also widely polluted by oil and grease.

High economic growth has given rise to greater purchasing power and consumption, and thus larger volumes of solid waste. In 1989, an average Kuala Lumpur resident generated 1.29 tonnes of solid waste, almost 2 times as much as in Jakarta and 2.5 times as much as in Manila (Brandon & Ramankutty, 1993:51), the level was higher than an average Australian city. Greater affluence has also brought about heavy traffic congestion in Kuala Lumpur. Several factors have led to high car dependence, namely greater affordability due to rising affluence, inefficient public transport, dispersed suburban residential development, and inadequate road infrastructure.

Congestion and Pollution in Bangkok

Bangkok's serious traffic congestion is phenomenal, reflecting characteristically its negligence of the need to cope with the corresponding rise in traffic as a result of fast economic growth. Rapid growth in the last four decades had not been matched with proper physical planning of the city and implementation of plans. Much like Kuala Lumpur, public transport is hardly looked upon in Bangkok as an alternative to supplement private transport and to reduce its use in daily commuting trips. While the number of private vehicles tripled over the last 15 years, the city's road network has not been improved to support such traffic. Numerous fast expanding suburban housing estates still need to be properly linked to the city. As observed by Phiu-nual (1996:27–32) in a recent study, uncontrolled urban sprawl has left large tracts of undeveloped land between the city and the suburbs, which contribute further to extended commuting distance and higher travel expenses.

Bangkok's residents, especially those in the shanty towns, suffer from surface and ground water pollution, which result largely from untreated industrial waste and, through seepage of the Chao Phraya which receives large amounts of domestic waste discharge daily. To meet the increasing demand for water by the industry and residents, much water has been pumped out of the underground aquifers that the city is subsiding by

10 cm a year (Smith, 1994:294). Like Jakarta, Bangkok's water sources are being increasingly located further and further away from the city. The city is also treating water from polluted sources to meet its needs (Brandon & Ramankutty 1993:48–49). While water quality deteriorates, the city is also seriously affected by frequent floods, which is aggravated by deforestation in the north.

Jakarta's Pollution Hazards

Rise of pollution levels in Jakarta is comparable to Bangkok. For almost half of the year, levels of particulate matter in the city fall below health standards, with the source of pollution coming from vehicular emissions, burning of household solid wastes and industries. Consequently, fatal respiratory disease is high, representing some 13 percent of the city's mortality. Water quality for the city and for the 11.5 million inhabitants in its surrounding townships is generally poor. Domestic waste water contributes to 80 percent of surface water pollution, a factor strongly responsible for the city's 20 percent death rate for children below five years of age (World Resources Institute, 1996:6–7). Some progress has been made recently. Under the Kampung Improvement Programme, facilities such as standpipes, paved footpaths, sanitary services, garbage collection stations and public health centres have been established. An estimated 3.5 million of the city's population have benefited. However, greater efforts are still needed to reach a greater proportion of the population as well as to raise the reliability of the services and quality of their maintenance.

Jakarta's environmental degradation is at least partly attributable to a large influx of rural-urban migration in the last three decades. Control of in-migration implemented in Jakarta in the 1970s was ineffective despite rigorous measures being undertaken (Dutt & Song, 1996:109). As centres of high-pay jobs and other opportunities, Jakarta continues to grow primarily by migration comprising mainly younger and employment active groups.

Urban Environment in a Centrally Planned Economy: Vietnam

Vietnam is the largest economy of the Southeast Asian centrally planned economies comprising also Cambodia, Laos and Myanmar. Prior to Vietnam's reunification in 1975, the economy in both North and South Vietnam was predominantly agriculture-based. In the north, industry was resource-based, focused on infrastructure and mineral exploitation. It was, however, interrupted by the war in 1965 until 1975. In South Vietnam, light industries which had developed to some limited extent, were also disrupted by the war.

After 1975, industrialisation was on a self-reliant basis. Growth of the largest cities was controlled to prevent the widening of income gaps between urban and rural sectors. In the south, a rigid policy was introduced to restrict expansion of cities above 500,000. Income differential between urban and rural sectors was negligible (United Nations, 1993:120–22).

Economic Reforms and Industrialisation after 1980

Reforms since the early 1980s have stimulated industrial growth, though much emphasis was placed on an inefficient heavy industry. In 1988, the gross domestic product share of the secondary sector, which comprises manufacturing, construction, mineral exploitation, electricity and fuel, reached as high as 50 percent.

Largely for lack of incentives in its economic system, Vietnam introduced an "open-door" policy in December 1987 by enacting a new Foreign Investment Code (Jamison & Baark, 1995:276). This reform, apparently a duplicate of the Chinese reformist measures, saw the setting up of a number of joint-ventures between Vietnamese state firms and foreign companies. Industrialisation generates greater labour demand. Yet, in Vietnam, prior to the reform, stringent control of rural-urban migration had restricted growth of the four largest cities, Hanoi, Ho Chi Minh City, Danang and Hai Phong (Doan &

Trinh, 1996:3). They saw an annual growth of only 1.4 percent, between 1979 and 1989 for instance — much lower than the national average of 2.4 percent, thus contributing to a decline in the primacy index.

Like other primate cities in the pro-capitalist countries, Hanoi and Ho Chi Minh City, nevertheless, possess a high concentration of industrial activities. In 1989, they alone accounted for more than 40 percent of national industrial production (United Nations, 1993:128). This industrial bias inevitably acts as an incentive to induce rural migrants to flow into the metropolises, exerting pressure on the already overstressed infrastructure and social services. Consequently, levels of water and air pollution as well as congestion in Ho Chi Minh City and Hanoi are on the rise. There is a risk that the flood-gate might burst should the system of residential control become ineffective as a result of further liberalisation of its economy.

Environmental Concerns

As a late "door opener" and at a time of increased international concern about environmental degradation, Vietnam was well aware of the need to protect its environment as it started to welcome foreign investments in the mid-1980s. In 1986, the Vietnamese reformists drafted a National Conservation Strategy. Based on this, a new "Committee for Rational Utilization of Natural Resources and Environmental Protection" was created with the assistance of a Western organisation, the International Union of Conservation of Nature and Natural Resources (IUCN), and the World-wide Fund for Nature (Jamison & Baark, 1995:277). The Committee primarily promotes environmental awareness and acts as an educator for national to regional and local authorities in development projects. Interestingly, two processes are at work, one seeking growth through market reforms and the other being environmentalist in character, checking the operations of the other party motivated by profit-seeking entrepreneurs. Both, however, are supported by Western international institutions.

The results of environmental protection are yet to be investigated, given Vietnam's general lack of experience in safeguarding its environment.

Policy Measures for Urban Sustainability

Urbanisation Trend

As Southeast Asia is further integrated in the globalised economy, urbanisation will proceed in the new millennium. The pattern of urbanisation of the centrally planned economies is anticipated to converge with their pro-capitalist partners (Table 7.2). Primate cities are expected to expand further incorporating their conurbations in the process (see Jones, 1993). The opening up of the centrally planned nations in Vietnam, Cambodia, Laos and Myanmar to world trade will inevitably lead to further industrialisation in favour of leading cities which is likely to intensify the inequalities between leading cities and small cities within nations (Dutt & Song, 1996:110).

The general urban growth in Southeast Asia is expected to be moderate in the next three decades, falling below the world average. By the year 2025, more than 55 percent of the region's population will be living in the cities (Table 7.3). Compared to more developed regions, Southeast Asia would be much less urbanised by 2025, despite rapid growth of its megacities. By 2015, according to the United Nations projections, two of the region's cities are expected to be among the 15 most populous cities in the world: Jakarta is projected to rank fifth (21.2 million) and Metro Manila fifteenth (14.7 million). Megacities in developed nations would grow much slower (less than one percent) than those in less developed regions (over two percent of annual growth) (United Nations, 1995b:5). Southeast Asian metropolitan centres, particularly the megacities, will face rising environmental problems in the light of its management and technical capabilities that are yet to catch up with world standards. Whether this weakness in environmental management will lead to the future expansion of the informal sector in their key cities is too early to say. As

Table 7.2

Projected Urban Growth of Southeast Asia, 1994–2025 (Population in million)

Country	1994			2025			Projected Average Annual Growth Rate (1994–2025)*
	Total Pop.	Urban Pop.	% Urban	Total Pop.	Urban Pop.	% Urban	
Brunei	0.28	0.16	57.7	0.41	0.29	72.5	1.9
Cambodia	9.97	2.00	20.1	19.69	8.57	43.5	4.8
Indonesia	194.61	67.02	34.4	275.60	167.39	60.7	3.0
Laos	4.74	1.00	21.1	9.69	4.32	44.6	4.8
Malaysia	19.70	10.42	52.9	31.58	22.94	72.6	2.6
Myanmar	45.55	11.77	25.8	75.56	35.76	47.3	3.7
Philippines	66.19	35.18	53.1	104.52	77.62	74.3	2.6
Singapore	2.82	2.82	100.0	3.36	3.36	100.0	0
Thailand	58.18	11.49	19.7	73.59	28.76	39.1	3.0
Vietnam	72.93	14.98	20.5	118.15	46.14	39.1	3.7

Source: United Nations, 1995b. World Urbanization Prospects: The 1994 Revision. New York. pp. 75, 80–81.
* Computed.

Table 7.3

**Urbanisation Trend in Southeast Asia
and Other Regions, 1950–2025**

Region	1950 (%)	1970 (%)	1990 (%)	2010 (%)	2025 (%)
Southeast Asia	14.8	20.4	30.2	44.8	55.4
Less Developed Regions*	17.3	25.1	34.7	47.2	57.0
More Developed Regions**	54.7	67.5	73.6	79.3	84.0
World Total	29.3	36.6	43.1	52.7	61.1

Source: United Nations, 1995b. World Urbanization Prospects: The 1994
Revision. New York. pp. 78–81.

Note: * Comprises all regions of Africa, Asia (except Japan), Latin America
and the Caribbean, and Melanesia, Micronesia and Polynesia.
** Comprises regions of Europe, North America, Australia, New Zealand
and Japan.

discussed earlier, the informal sector has contributed to
environmental problems in the primate cities, it is best that
expansion of this sector be more systematically controlled.

Urban Sustainability Principles

The concept of environmental sustainability, as Thayer
(1994:99) suggests, is "a limitation on the degree and rate of
human impact such that the natural carrying capacity of the
earth's ecosystems can be perpetually maintained". City
ecosystem refers to a situation where residents can enjoy a
decent lifestyle of modern living, and yet not be victimised by
pollutive adverse effects that render urban living unpleasant,
stressful and physically unhealthy. At this stage, the debate is
still on as to how to set the minimum standard for urban
carrying capacity beyond which sustainability is perceived as
threatened and impossible. There is no consensus as yet for a
comprehensive assessment to set the carrying capacity limit.

The "perceptual" concept, most frequently considered in urban planning practices in terms of quality of life, includes aesthetic values, greenery, conditions of overcrowding, air, water and traffic noise pollution (Barton, 1997).

Sustainability Indicators

In the pursuit of profit maximisation in business undertakings, sustainable development can be seen as a trade-off for long-term benefits for humanity. Therefore, it is not proper to use gross domestic product as a yardstick to measure net economic progress because the adverse effects, such as natural resource depletion and environmental degradation, need to be accounted for (Mikesell, 1992:67).

For many developed nations, economic growth and environmental protection are widely perceived as non-contradictory and mutually compatible (Blowers, 1994). But it is obviously premature to expect low-income Southeast Asian nations, in particular those practising a self-reliant economy, to follow high-standard regulations of environmental protection. It was only a decade ago, if not less, that Vietnam, Cambodia, Laos and Myanmar began to accept foreign direct investments, which are moreover of limited scale. Newly open to world trade, they still lack a scientific information-base on the environment, and an administration capable of monitoring and enforcing environmental laws and regulations. Blowers's (1994:173) observation that the Third World in general would have a problem implementing and monitoring environmental laws applies to Southeast Asia, with the exception of Singapore. Southeast Asian nations will have problems in implementing externally-induced environmental targets, unless they set their own.

Imposing high standards may also hinder poor countries from industrialising which, as Haughton and Hunter (1994) argue, touches on the issue of "social justice". Their argument is that since poverty is a major cause of environmental degradation, denying a country from industrialising can mean ignoring the basic needs and common aspirations of poor nations that have little control over the distribution of world resources. Except for Singapore perhaps, Southeast Asia is a developing region. As environmental protection is an expensive enterprise, Southeast Asia would be less motivated to implement international environmental policies that require them to use their limited capital to import capital equipment and expertise.

Sustainability indicators are, nonetheless, indispensable if policies are to be translated into action. Indicators provide guidelines of measurement for policy-makers to identify issues, implement policy measures and to monitor progress towards set targets, whether they are international or minimum standards. They also help to encourage local communities to assume responsibility and be involved in sustainable development (Pinfield, 1997). As discussed above, given the varied capabilities of individual countries, there should be different sets of sustainability indicators for large cities so as to facilitate them to follow one that suits their ability. For developing nations, the idea of sustainability indicators should be applied as a developmental and incremental process towards an improved environment. A minimum standard of sustainability indicators may be set as a starting point at which action is necessary, and this threshold level will need to be supported by scientific and technical analysis.

Environmental Agenda in Southeast Asia

The post-Cold War since 1990 has seen an increasingly globalised economy, accompanied by a fiercely competitive international market place, particularly for high value-added goods and services (Blowers, 1994:169; Daniels & Lever, 1996). Globalisation has resulted in environmental effects that are more transboundary in character than ever before. A new environmentalism, though loosely bound with political structure, is expected to replace once strong political ideologies, such as Marxism, to become a dominant paradigm of the 21st century (see Boulding, 1994:5). This trend makes it more likely that Southeast Asia's two political groupings, once deeply divided over ideological differences, are prepared to work more readily together towards a common goal for an improved living urban environment.

For Southeast Asia as a whole, pursuing economic growth will remain a strong goal underlying the basis of environmental protection, without which mobilisation of adequate resources towards this objective will face hindrance. Besides reinforcing efforts towards environmental awareness and using appropriate technology, sustainable urban development should aim at producing "user-friendly" cities which are energy efficient and provide pleasant living (Elkin, McLaren & Hillman, 1991:12). Such sustainable cities will have to consume more renewable resources and less non-renewable resources, and involve less environmentally damaging activities (Haughton & Hunter, 1994:123). To minimise adverse impacts on surrounding areas, it is essential to understand the relationship between one city's ecosystem with those of the surrounding ones, including those outside national boundaries. In the longer term, the dream of the 1992 Rio Earth Summit would be realised: that international sustainable city networks be set up.

But thinking "green" is not sufficient. To be workable, at least in the nearer future, there is a need to merge the neo-liberal, market-led thinking that promotes growth and the environment-oriented ideals which emphasise "local" action and technologies. Ironically enough, new technologies, including environment-related technologies from advanced countries, can help developing countries to improve productivity, health and the quality of life, while reducing environmental risks (Smith, 1994:292). ASEAN, as a regional grouping, needs indeed three levels of organisational control to help achieve sustainable development:

1. **Intergovernmental cooperation** on the basis of common interests in the region. The haze pollution today originating from Indonesia reminds us that a great deal still needs to be done to enhance intergovernmental cooperation and capability in tackling transboundary hazards.

2. **Multinational operations**. Though there is currently wide disparity between ASEAN member states, there is a generally strong desire to attract international capital. As such, there is a need to reach consensus on how to regulate multinational operations in the region effectively.[4]

    The current monetary crisis which broke out in July 1997, arising from internal financial weaknesses and international speculative attacks, will enable affected countries such as Thailand, Malaysia and Indonesia to readjust their financial policies and strengthen their operational banking systems. As a result of regional currency depreciation which facilitates export, the ASEAN member states present even better investment opportunities for multinational corporations which are expected to increase investments in the region. It is equally an opportunity to encourage or guide, where possible, multinational corporations to increasingly reorient their production process to be "environmentally friendly", including waste reduction and product recycling, use of new materials towards energy and resource efficiency (Smith, 1994).

3. **Non-governmental organisations (NGOs)**. Local NGOs can work with international NGOs to draw public attention to problems, mobilise opinion and lobby for specific policies (see Blowers, 1994:181–82).

ASEAN's Resolution on Environment and Development

With trade blocs playing an increasingly important role, ASEAN as a region has seen the advantages of closer ties. On 18 February 1992, the Ministers of the Environment from the ASEAN member states signed a resolution for a better living environment. The ministers agreed in principle to promote regional cooperation towards sustainable development, for a harmonisation of standards, with a strong emphasis placed on appropriate technology (NPAG Online Internet, 20 October

1997, see Appendix 1 for more details). Transboundary issues such as air and water pollution and disposal of toxic wastes were examined, though no concrete measures were recommended. Solutions such as environmental education to promote public consciousness for a clean environment was discussed. Environmental education is a crucial issue as environmental degradation in the squatter or slum areas is partly caused by ignorance of residents who are less informed. There is scope to enhance the living environment of disadvantaged residents when their living standards are improved with better job skills and greater awareness. The private sector should also be actively engaged to help in urban management, and through collaboration, to reduce red-tape in government departments (Dutt & Song 1996:112).

Compact or Decentralised Urban Development

The issue of the primate city in Southeast Asia will remain a thorny one. Decentralisation in the name of equity and "spatial justice" in the past three decades have not proven to be effective, at least if gauged as a goal of economic development. At this juncture of globalisation where the main objective is economic efficiency, it makes it even more difficult for Southeast Asia to continue such a policy to any significant scale especially when capital resources are scarce (United Nations, 1993:134). Decentralisation of primate cities may mean suburbanisation or the construction of new townships around the urban core. Evidence has shown that unless suburban centres are self-contained and feasible enough to provide sizeable employment to local residents, traffic congestion caused by heavy commuting is likely to result — a phenomenon which is socially inequitable as commuters are largely restricted to car users (McLaren, 1992). Massive commuting again contributes to high energy consumption and heavy pollution. Hayashi's (1996) study of heavily car-dependent Bangkok reveals that the city's carbon dioxide level is 15 times higher than Nagoya where public transport usage is high. Nonetheless, for city dwellers to switch to public transport, it would depend on its quality and availability

(Giuliano, 1994:267). Consequently, a vicious circle is set in motion as provision of quality public transport requires the city governments to draw on scarce resources, which may be most difficult to find.

Conclusion

Southeast Asia is a dynamic region experiencing rapid growth. Its urban population, now relatively low in proportion, is growing fast, especially the capital cities for which primacy has remained persistent. It is in these primate cities that environmental degradation is most severe, a consequence of a dualistic economy whereby the poor is largely deprived of basic services, and where there is a strong concentration of industrial activities and wealth. These economic activities lead to serious air, water and noise pollution. Unless drastic policy measures are used to counter such trends, the long-term sustainability of the cities is in question.

As ASEAN has now englobed all 10 nations in Southeast Asia, the region has found itself in an increasingly competitive world for markets which emphasise urban efficiency, a situation which makes decentralisation as a strategy to relieve primate city congestion less appealing. Thus, a solution has to be found *in situ*. First, economic growth is needed to generate revenues for social services for the poor, and an improved management for transport, housing and urban living. For the poor, public awareness of the environment to safeguard their neighbourhood needs to be enhanced. Second, sustained urban growth in an increasingly integrated region must be supported by mutual concern and care of environmental problems which transcend borders. With regard to this objective, ASEAN member states have moved ahead, and the prospect of an improved regional environmental cooperation in the next century appears promising. Many obstacles have yet to be overcome however.

APPENDIX 1

Resolution on Environment and Development signed by ASEAN Ministers responsible for the environment on 18 February 1992 in Singapore

1. ASEAN member countries shall intensify cooperation in environmental management and protection in their common pursuit of sustainable development. Member countries shall work collectively towards the improvement of environmental quality, harmonisation of standards, and jointly promote the application, transfer and development of appropriate environmental technologies.

2. ASEAN shall continue to participate actively in and support international efforts in promoting the principles of sustainable development.

3a) Enhancing regional cooperation

   To enhance regional cooperation towards sustainable development, the ASEAN member countries agree to adopt the policies:

   i. introduce measures and promote institutional development that will encourage the integration of environmental factors in all developmental processes;

   ii. work closely on the inter-related issues of environment and development;

   iii. cooperate in setting basic environmental quality standards in the region, and adopt long term quantitative goals relating to ambient air quality and river water quality;

   iv. harmonise policy directions and step up operational and technical cooperation on environmental matters such as transboundary movements and disposal of toxic chemicals and hazardous wastes, and undertake joint actions to address the anti-tropical timber campaign;

   b) Information exchange

   i. encourage greater information and data exchange, particularly in air and water quality as well as greenhouse gas monitoring.

c) Institutional development

 i. strengthen the institutional and technical capability of national agencies to enable them to effectively integrate environmental considerations into development plans;

 ii. cooperate in capacity building of national institutions responsible for the environment through regional training assistance programmes, regular exchange of information and management data and a greater exchange of visits among officials and experts;

 iii. work with and cooperate in providing adequate training at all levels in public and private sector organisations, including NGOs, with the aims of improving their environmental management expertise and skills;

d) Technology cooperation

 i. continue to enhance cooperation in the field of environmental technology through sharing of technical information, initiate joint training and research programmes, and exchange expertise in environmental management and technology;

 ii. promote the application of appropriate and environmentally sound technologies, as well as encourage support from the business sector and the public for clean production and industrial practices.

e) Public awareness

 i. continue to promote public awareness of environmental issues so as to bring about broader participation in environmental protection efforts, and to do so through greater exchange of information and experiences on approaches and strategies in environmental education.

f) Programmes

 i. undertake to develop and implement specific programmes relating to haze caused by forest fires, air and water quality management, natural resources and environmental accounting, environmental economics, trans-frontier parks and other protected areas, a regional network for biological diversity conservation and protection of the marine environment in ASEAN seas.

Source: NPAG Online Internet, 20 October 1997

NOTES

1. Indonesia is a typical example. In the early 1980s, the country's agricultural share of employment was 55 percent whereas its GDP was only 24 percent (Jones, 1993:51).

2. Singapore was a key component of the economic entity of Malaya prior to Singapore's attainment of self-government in 1959.

3. Petaling Jaya is a satellite town, with a population of over 300,000, which adjoins Kuala Lumpur. It is, however, statistically a separate entity.

4. In the short run, it is expected that the labour-intensive industries will be shifted to low-wage socialist countries whereas the pro-capitalist Southeast Asian nations will be focusing on increasingly information-related, higher value-added industries which are more knowledge-intensive and skill-based. Within ASEAN itself, geographical division of labour is likely to concur with the different levels of technological ladder achieved. Low-wage countries (Vietnam, Cambodia, Myanmar) are expected to receive industrial investments in, for instance, textiles and clothing and shoemaking, from other more developed members, with Singapore in the lead.

REFERENCES

Askew, M. & W.S. Logan (eds.) (1994) *Cultural Identity and Urban Change in Southeast Asia: Interpretative Essays*. Geelong (Australia): Deakin University Press.

Barton, H. (1997) "Environmental Capacity and Sustainable Urban Form". In S.M. Farthing (ed.), *Evaluating Local Environmental Policy*. Brookfield (USA): Aldershot. pp. 78–96.

Blowers, A. (1994) "Environmental Policy: The Quest for Sustainable Development". In R. Paddison, J. Money & B. Lever (eds.), *International Perspectives in Urban Studies 2*. London: Jessica Kingsley. pp. 168–92.

Boulding, K. (1994) "Economic Ethics and the Environmental Crisis". In J.E. Hickey & L.A. Longmire (eds.), *The Environment: Global Problems, Local Solutions*. Westport, Connecticut: Greenwood Press. pp. 3–11.

Brandon, C. & R. Ramankutty. (1993) *Toward an Environmental Strategy for Asia*. World Bank Discussion Papers. Washington DC.

Briffett, C. & Sim Loo Lee. (1993) *Environmental Issues in Development and Conservation*. School of Building and Estate Management, National University of Singapore. Singapore: SNP Publishers.

Brookfield, H. & Y. Byron (eds.). (1993) *Southeast Asia's Environmental Future: The Search for Sustainability*. Tokyo: United Nations University Press.

Chia, Lin Sien. (ed.). (1987) *Environmental Management in Southeast Asia*. Singapore: National University of Singapore.

Consumers' Association of Penang and Sahabat Alam Malaysia. (1996) *State of the Malaysian Environment*. Penang (Malaysia).

Daniels, P.W. & W.F. Lever (eds.). (1996) *The Global Economy in Transition*. Harlow (UK): Longman.

Dixon, C. (1991) *Southeast Asia in the World Economy: A Regional Geography*. Cambridge: Cambridge University Press.

Doan, Mau Diep & Khac Tham, Trinh. (1996) "Survey of Spontaneous Migration to a Rural and an Urban Area in Viet Nam". Asian Population Studies Series, No. 142. New York: United Nations.

Dutt, A.K. (ed.). (1996) *Southeast Asia: A Ten-Nation Region*. Dordrecht: Kluwer Academic Publishers.

Dutt, A.K. & N. Song. (1996) "Urbanization in Southeast Asia". In A.K. Dutt (ed.), *Southeast Asia: A Ten-Nation Region*. Dordrecht: Kluwer Academic Publishers. pp. 95–115.

Elkin, T., D. McLaren & M. Hillman. (1991) *Reviving the City: Towards Sustainable Urban Development*. London: Policy Studies Institute.

Forbes, D. (1996) *Asian Metropolis: Urbanisation and the Southeast Asian City*. Melbourne: Oxford University Press.

Giuliano, G. (1994) "Equity and Fairness Consideration of Congestion Pricing". In National Research Council, Special Report 242. *Curbing Gridlock — Peak Period Fees to Relieve Traffic Congestion*. Washington DC: National Academic Press. pp. 250–79.

Hashimoto, Michio. (1992) *Economic and the Environment: The Japanese Experience*. Japan: Ministry of Foreign Affairs.

Haughton, G. & C. Hunter. (1994) *Sustainable Cities*. London: Jessica Kingsley.

Hayashi, Y. (1996) "Economic Development and its Influence on the Environment: Urbanization, Infrastructure and Land Use

Planning Systems". In Hayashi, Yoshitsugu & J. Roy (eds.), *Transport, Land-Use and the Environment*. Dordrecht: Kluwer Academic Publishers. pp. 3–25.

Jamison, A. & E. Baark. (1995) "From Market Reform to Sustainable Development". In I. Norlund, C.L. Gates & Vu Cao Dam (eds.), *Vietnam in a Changing World*. Richmond (UK): Curzon Press. pp. 269–91.

Jones, G. (1993) "Industrialization and urbanization in South-East Asia". In H. Brookfield & Y. Byron, *Southeast Asia's Environmental Future: The Search for Sustainability*. Tokyo: United Nations University Press. pp. 47–71.

Knox, P. & J. Agnew. (1989) *The Geography of the World-Economy*. London: Edward Arnold.

Lee, Yok-shiu F. (1994) "Myths of Environmental Management and the Urban Poor". In R.J. Fuchs, E. Brennan, J. Chamie, F.-c. Lo & J.I. Uitto (eds.), *Mega-City Growth and the Future*. Tokyo: United Nations University Press. pp. 390–411.

Mathur, O.P. (1994) "The Dual Challenge of Poverty and Mega-cities: An Assessment of Issues and Strategies". In R.J. Fuchs, E. Brennan, J. Chamie, F.-c. Lo & J.I. Uitto (eds.), *Mega-City Growth and the Future*. Tokyo: United Nations University Press. pp. 349–89.

McAndrew, C. & Chia, Lin-Sien (eds.). (1979) *Developing Economies and the Environment: The Southeast Asian Experience*. Singapore: McGraw-Hill International Book.

McGee, T. (1967) *The Southeast Asian City*. London: Bell and Sons.

McLaren, D. (1992) "Compact or Dispersed? Dilution is No Solution". *Built Environment*, 18(4):268–84.

Mikesell, R.F. (1992) *Economic Development and the Environment: A Comparison of Sustainable Development with Conventional Development Economics*. London: Mansell.

Ministry of the Environment. (1993) *Environmental Protection in Singapore (A Handbook)*. Singapore.

NPAG Online Internet. (1997) "Resolution on Environment and Development, Singapore, 18 February 1992". 20 October.

Pernia, E.M. (1992) "Southeast Asia". In R. Stren, R. White & J. Whitney (eds.), Sustainable Cities: Urbanisation and the

Environment in International Perspective. Boulder, Colorado: Westview Press. pp. 233–57.

Phiu-nual, Kunchit. (1996) "Congestion and Pollution in a Rapidly Expanding City of Southeast Asia: The Case of Bangkok". In Hayashi, Yoshitsugu & J. Roy (eds.), *Transport, Land-Use and the Environment*. Dordrecht: Kluwer Academic Publishers. pp. 27–45.

Pinfield, G. (1997) "Sustainability Indicators: A New Tool for Evaluation". In S.M. Farthing (ed.), *Evaluating Local Environmental Policy*. Brookfield (USA): Aldershot. pp. 49–64.

Rüland, J. (1992) *Urban Development in Southeast Asia — Regional Cities and Local Government*. Boulder (Colorado): Westview Press.

Smith, P. (1994) "Industrial and Environment". In T. Hewitt, H. Johnson & D. Wield (eds.), *Industrialization and Development*. Milton Keynes (UK): Oxford University Press. pp. 277–302.

Stren, R., R. White & J. Whitney (eds.). (1992) *Sustainable Cities: Urbanisation and the Environment in International Perspective*. Boulder (Colorado): Westview Press.

Thayer, R.L. (1994) *Gray World, Green Heart: Technology, Nature, and the Sustainable Landscape*. New York: John Wiley.

United Nations. (1989) *Prospects of World Urbanization, 1988*. New York.

————— (1993) *Urbanization and Socio-Economic Development in Asia and the Pacific*. Asian Population Studies Series, No. 122. New York: Economic and Social Commission for Asia and the Pacific.

————— (1994) *Population, Environment and Development: Proceedings of the United Nations Expert Group Meeting on Population, Environment and Development*. New York: United Nations Headquarters, 20–24 January 1992.

————— (1995a) *Trends, Patterns and Implications of Rural-Urban Migration in India, Nepal and Thailand*. Asian Population Studies Series, No. 138. New York.

————— (1995b) *World Urbanization Prospects: The 1994 Revision*. New York.

Weaver, J.H., M.T. Rock & K. Kusterer (1997) *Achieving Broad-Based Sustainable Development*. West Hartford (Connecticut): Kumarian Press.

World Bank. (1996) *Sustainable Transport: Priorities for Policy Reform.* Washington D.C.

World Resources Institute. (1994) *World Resources, 1994–95.* New York: Oxford University Press.

———— (1996) *World Resources, 1996–97.* New York: Oxford University Press.

Chapter 8

Managing Mobilisation and Migration of Southeast Asia's Population

Graeme Hugo

Introduction

In the 30 years since the founding of ASEAN, the demography of Southeast Asia has changed profoundly in many ways. Fertility and mortality levels have fallen dramatically, urbanisation has continued at a rapid pace, ageing has become a significant issue and family structure and functioning have been transformed. Yet one of the most striking changes in the population has been the huge increase in personal mobility of Southeast Asians as both a cause and consequence of the economic, social, political and demographic changes which have swept across the region. This has profoundly influenced the lives of many residents. Within the countries of the region there have been increases not only in the extent to which permanent redistribution of population is occurring but also in the scale, complexity and significance of non-permanent migrations (e.g. see Hugo, 1997a). Large-scale rural to urban migration has contributed to the urban population of the region which more than trebled from 30 to 113.3 million over the period of ASEAN's existence while the rural population increased by only a third from 204.7 to 320.2 million (United Nations, 1997a). In the present chapter however, the focus of attention is upon population movement *out of* and *into* countries within the region which has increased in scale and significance at a rate even greater than that of mobility within the ASEAN countries over the last three decades.

No region in the world has been more profoundly influenced by the upsurge in international migration which has accompanied, and been part of, accelerating globalisation trends in the last two decades than Southeast Asia. For many Southeast Asians, the labour markets within which they routinely search for work, and the destinations they consider moving to, overlap national boundaries both within and beyond the region. Whereas three decades ago this only applied to a small, mostly male, well-educated elite in the region, international migration is now within the calculus of choice of millions of people in the region regardless of education, skill level, gender, nationality and ethnicity. The resultant complexity is well illustrated in Malaysia which has in excess of two million workers from overseas not only from its ASEAN neighbours of Indonesia, the Philippines, Thailand, Myanmar and Cambodia, but also from Bangladesh and from more developed countries (MDCs) like Australia. Yet Malaysia too is a significant supplier of labour to nearby Singapore and also Taiwan and Japan and a source of permanent settlers to Australia.

The extension of Southeast Asian labour markets beyond national boundaries is partly a function of growing economic and demographic disparities between the ASEAN nations and the shrinking friction of distance in the region facilitated by more affordable international travel and rapid dissemination of information between nations. However, increasingly this movement is being enhanced and facilitated by two elements which, while influenced by economic and political forces, largely operate outside of them. First, substantial communities of foreigners have grown in several labour-short countries of the region and these are providing the anchors of social networks in labour-surplus nations along which even larger numbers of new migrants are travelling secure in the knowledge that their already established relatives and friends at the destination will ease their entry into the destination labour market and society generally. Second, an international migration industry has mushroomed in the Southeast Asian region made up of a complex interrelated myriad of recruiters, agents, travel providers, lawyers, labour suppliers, employers and government labour and immigration bureaucracies. These groups operate both within and outside legal immigration, emigration and labour regulations to initiate, encourage and facilitate movement of people and especially labour between countries in the region. The proliferating social networks and immigration industry will ensure the continued expansion of international migration in the region regardless of economic and political change.

The exponential escalation of international movement of people within the region has elicited a substantial response from governments in both the countries receiving migrants from overseas and those sending them. Governments have sought increasingly to influence, control and regulate the scale and composition of the flow of migrants and migrant workers, the recruitment process, the training of migrant workers, the conditions under which the migrants work, the remittances they send back and their return and readjustment to life at the place of origin. Nevertheless a great deal, probably more than half, of international migration influencing the region occurs outside of the official regulations and structures either through the clandestine entry of migrant workers, people entering without work visas but subsequently obtaining a job or through overstaying visitors. Attempts by governments of the region to intervene to influence international labour migration are increasing, yet policies and programmes are being formulated largely in a vacuum of knowledge about what the impacts and implications of existing international labour migration actually are upon the origin and destination countries, the migrant workers and their families. The present chapter begins with a summary of recent trends in international migration in Southeast Asia before considering some of the major policy issues relating to international migration in the region. Finally, it addresses some possible future development in international migration in the region and their implications for ASEAN. At the outset, it must be pointed out that such an analysis is greatly hampered by the lack of basic data relating to international labour migration in Southeast Asia and the lack of high quality research on it.

Evolving Trends in International Migration in Southeast Asia

Just how mobile are Southeast Asians? What is their propensity to move between countries. A recent United Nations (1997b) analysis shows that overall, Southeast Asia had a net migration loss of 502,000 persons over the 1990–95 period: equivalent to 6.4 percent of overall population growth of the region over that period. This however, is merely the tip of the iceberg of a vast array of international movements in and out of the region which can be demonstrated by examining international movements to and from a country which has high quality international migration statistics. Hence Table 8.1 shows the movements from the 10 Southeast Asian nations to Australia in 1980 and 1995–96 as well as those taking place inversely. Permanent migration from Southeast Asian countries to MDCs like Australia accelerated in the 1970s with the removal of discriminatory immigration policies in Australia, Canada and the United States. A major element in this was the resettlement of refugees from Vietnam and, to a lesser extent, the other former Indo-Chinese countries beginning in the late 1970s.

Nevertheless, it is clear from Figure 8.1 that other Southeast Asian nations have also been significant suppliers of settlers to the traditional immigration nations like Australia. The Philippines, in particular, has become one of the world's major emigration countries in the last two decades, as is evident in Table 8.2, which shows the rapid growth of the Filipino community in the United States, Australia and Canada. Nevertheless, there have also been significant outflows from other ASEAN nations, such as Malaysia and Singapore, as is evident in Figure 8.1.

Table 8.1

Growth of Population Movement Into and Out of Australia from Southeast Asian Countries 1980–96

	1980	1995–96	Percent Growth 1980–96
Arrivals			
Permanent	5,563	12,492	+124.6
Long Term			
Residents	1,613	8,574	+431.6
Visitors	3,888	23,641	+508.1
Total	5,501	32,215	+485.6
Short Term			
Residents	192,325	596,078	+209.9
Visitors	54,833	614,300	+1020.3
Total	247,158	1,210,378	+389.7
Departures			
Permanent	198	913	+361.1
Long Term			
Residents	1,306	9,749	+646.5
Visitors	2,931	12,207	+316.5
Total	4,237	21,956	+418.2
Short Term			
Residents	195,162	609,900	+212.5
Visitors	52,970	602,155	+1036.8
Total	248,132	1,212,055	+388.5

Source: ABS, 1981; 1997

The upturn in permanent emigration from Southeast Asian countries to MDCs is not the only dimension of the strengthening international migration relationship of Southeast Asia with Australia, North America and Europe. As Table 8.1 shows there has been an increase in the settlement of Australians in Southeast Asia. This involves two components (Hugo, 1994).

Figure 8.1

Settler Arrivals by Southeast Asian Birthplace, 1975/76–96/97

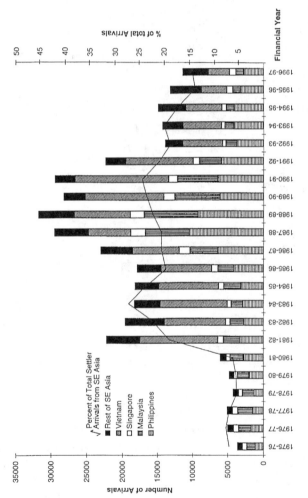

Notes: 1975/76–1980/81: "Rest of Southeast Asia" includes Burma (Myanmar), Thailand and Indonesia. Data not available for Vietnam.

1981/82–1996/97: "Rest of Southeast Asia" includes Myanmar, Laos, Cambodia, Thailand and Indonesia.

Sources: Australian Immigration, *Consolidated Statistics* (various issues).

Table 8.2

Growth of Largest Southeast Asian Communities in the United States, Canada and Australia

	USA			Canada			Australia		
	1980	1990	Percentage Change	1981	1996	Percentage Change	1981	1996	Percentage Change
Vietnam	231,000	740,000*	+220.3	50,640	113,595	+124.3	41,097	151,053	+267.6
Philippines	501,000	1,164,000*	+132.3	66,345	123,300	+85.8	15,431	92,949	+502.4
Malaysia	11,000	32,931	+199.4	7,740	16,105	+108.1	31,598	76,255	+141.3
Singapore	6,240	14,505	+132.5	3,015	6,285	+108.4	11,990	29,490	+146.0
Indonesia	30,820	49,786	+61.5	6,085	7,610	+25.1	12,463	44,175	+254.4
Laos	51,960	178,382	+243.3	8,850	14,440	+63.2	5,352	9,883	+84.7
Cambodia	18,620	120,985	+549.8	5,595	17,960	+221.0	3,589	21,549	+500.4
Thailand	62,620	120,206	+92.0	n.a.	n.a.	n.a.	3,346	18,936	+465.9
Brunei	820	524	-36.1	n.a.	n.a.	n.a.	n.a.	1,829	n.a.
Myanmar	12,200	20,408	+67.3	n.a.	n.a.	n.a.	7,294	10,139	+39.0

Sources: ABS, 1981 and 1996 Censuses; 1981 and 1991 Censuses of Canada;
1980 and 1990 US Bureau of Census and Current Population Survey
* 1996 Current Population Survey Data

- Return migration of former Southeast immigrants and their children.

- Migration of Australians to take up skilled jobs in Southeast Asian countries short of professional or highly skilled people.

It is especially evident in Table 8.1, however, that there has been a huge increase in non-permanent migrations between Southeast Asia and Australia. Long-term movement has increased fourfold over the last 15 years and includes particularly students and people on long-term transfer with companies. There also has been a huge increase in the short-term visiting by tourists and business people between Southeast Asia and Australia. Similar increases as these in short-term movement have occurred between the ASEAN countries but we do not have the data available to demonstrate it.

There is considerable variety in the international migration experience of the nations in the Southeast Asian region. For example, in the United Nations (1997b) lists of countries with the highest levels of immigration over the 1990–95 period only one, Cambodia, is from Southeast Asia although arguably, countries like Malaysia, Singapore and Thailand may have been included if data were available (Hugo, 1997a). With respect to the major emigration countries, the Philippines, Indonesia and Vietnam were among the world's leading countries in the United Nations (1997b:29) assessment. While, of course, all of the countries in the region are experiencing both immigration and emigration to some extent in the contemporary situation, it is possible to classify the nations of the Southeast Asian region according to whether they have significant gains or losses of migrant workers. This classification is presented in Table 8.3 and shows the larger nations of Southeast Asia in which the transition to low fertility did not commence until the 1970s or later hence remain labour-surplus areas. On the other hand, in Singapore, fertility decline was much earlier and economic growth has been more rapid and has sustained over a longer period. Despite strict immigration regulations the shortage of labour in these countries has led to major inflows of workers,

Table 8.3

Classification of Southeast Asian Nations on the basis of their International Migration Situation in the Late 1990s

Nation	Main Destination / Origin of Migrant Workers	
Mainly Emigration Nations		
Philippines	Middle East, Japan, Taiwan, Hong Kong, Singapore, Europe, US, Canada, Australia	
Indonesia	Middle East, Malaysia, Singapore, Hong Kong	
Myanmar	Thailand	
Vietnam	Europe, Russia, US, Canada, Australia	
Mainly Immigration Nations		
Singapore	Malaysia, Indonesia, Hong Kong, Europe, Philippines, Australia	
Brunei	Malaysia, Indonesia, Philippines	
Emigration and Immigration Nations		
Thailand	Emigrants	Middle East, Malaysia, Singapore, Taiwan
	Immigrants	Burma, Cambodia, Bangladesh, China
Malaysia	Emigrants	Singapore, Taiwan, Japan, Australia
	Immigrants	Indonesia, Bangladesh

both documented and undocumented. Singapore has experienced a rapid transition from being a primarily emigrant nation to being a major focus of labour immigration. This transition has been much more rapid than the similar transition in Europe and is a distinctive feature of the Asian international migration situation (Martin, 1993; 1994; Fields, 1994; Skeldon, 1994; Vasuprasat, 1994). Malaysia and Thailand are two countries in the region currently which are midway through this transition. They are both recording substantial emigration over a long period and also significant immigration of workers from nearby labour-surplus nations (Indonesia, Bangladesh and Myanmar especially).

Although migrations to MDCs, refugee flows and student migration have all been significant in Southeast Asia, there can be no doubt that the movement which has increased most in scale and significance in the region has been international labour migration. This type of movement has its roots in the international contract coolie movements in the region during the colonial period (Hugo, 1980) as well as in migrations associated with contractors, in the late 1960s and early 1970s, in the former South Vietnam undertaking large infrastructure projects as part of the strategy of "winning over" the local population importing labour, especially from South Korea, the Philippines and Thailand. However, the major impetus to international labour migration came in 1973 with the increase in oil prices providing the Gulf Cooperative Council (GCC) nations with the means to undertake large infrastructure projects. These projects often involved the same international contractors who had worked in pre-reunification Vietnam and their experience with Asian contract labour and recruiters facilitated the increased participation of Asian labour in the massive influx to GCC nations. While South Asian migrant workers had a long history of involvement in the Gulf area, after 1973 the numbers expanded rapidly and began to involve large numbers of East and Southeast Asians. In 1975, India and Pakistan contributed 97 percent of Asian workers to West Asia but this is now less than a third with the Southeast Asian share growing from 2 percent to more than half. This migration has continued through to the present with migrants originating from a greater number of these countries. Whereas workers in the early years were mainly involved in infrastructure development, those in more recent times have moved mainly into service occupations. Over time, women have become more significant in the migration flows with many moving into domestic service. During the last decade, the destinations of Asian migrant workers have become more diverse with Asian countries now accounting for more migrants than are directed to the Middle East. Much of the intra-Asia movement is undocumented and is not included in the available official statistics. Much of the movement is of unskilled and semi-skilled workers and again women are heavily involved.

The upswing in Southeast Asian migration to the Middle East is evident in Table 8.4 showing labour outflows from the major Southeast Asian origin countries. However, it will also be noted that whereas in the 1970s and the 1980s the Middle East was overwhelmingly dominant in the deployment of workers, in the 1990s other Asian destinations have increased in significance. While Japan, South Korea, Taiwan and Hong Kong have all become important destinations of workers from several Southeast Asian nations, from the perspective of ASEAN one of the most striking trends of recent years has been the increase in intra-ASEAN international movement. This is evident, for example, when we consider population movements to and from Indonesia depicted in Figure 8.2 and Appendix A. Indonesia is unquestionably a labour-surplus economy with more than 30 percent of its workforce underemployed and 7.2 percent unemployed in 1995 (Biro Pusat Statistik, 1996). Hence it is not surprising that there is substantial out-movement of workers. Figure 8.2 shows that among documented labour migrants more than half a million moved to Saudi Arabia between 1991 and 1996 and a similar number to Malaysia. There were also substantial flows to the other ASEAN nations of Singapore (103,209) and Brunei (11,179) as well as other Asian labour-short economies like Japan (18,558), South Korea (21,652), Taiwan (24,204) and Hong Kong (11,023). A distinctive and somewhat controversial feature of much of this movement, especially that directed towards Saudi Arabia and the United Arab Emirates and, to a lesser extent, Singapore and Hong Kong, is the predominance of women who work mainly as domestic maids. The official documented out-movement, however, is only the tip of the iceberg of the total emigration of labour migrants. Undocumented migration, especially to nearby

Table 8.4

Average Annual Number of Migrant Workers Originating in the Major Labour-Exporting Countries of Asia and Distribution by Region of Destination (1975–94)

	(Percentage)			
Sending country/ receiving region	1975–79	1980–84	1985–89	1990–94
Indonesia				
Western Asia	73.7	64.9	78.0	40.6
Other Asia	8.5	20.5	13.1	55.5
Outside Asia	17.8	14.6	8.9	3.9
Number of clearances	10,400	24,400	63,500	118,000
Myanmar				
Number of clearances	–	8,100	8,700	9,100
Philippines				
Western Asia	67.4	84.8	71.8	61.0
Other Asia	17.7	11.2	22.5	30.7
Outside Asia	14.9	4.0	5.7	8.3
Number of clearances (land based)	42,400	274,000	353,900	498,000
Thailand				
Western Asia	75.7	81.7	72.4	24.4
Other Asia	7.7	5.3	14.6	71.9
Outside Asia	16.9	13.1	13.0	3.7
Number of clearances	6,300	60,100	89,600	86,800

Source: United Nations, 1997b:80–81

Malaysia is cheaper and easier than legal migration and this significantly outnumbers it. Hence in the 1996 Indonesian elections, some 1.4 million Indonesians residing in Malaysia registered at the Indonesian Embassy to vote (Azizah, 1997). A recent crackdown on undocumented migrants in Saudi

Figure 8.2

Labour Migration From and To Indonesia 1991–96

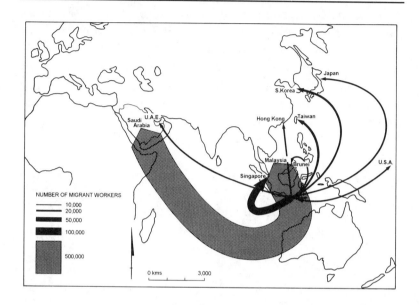

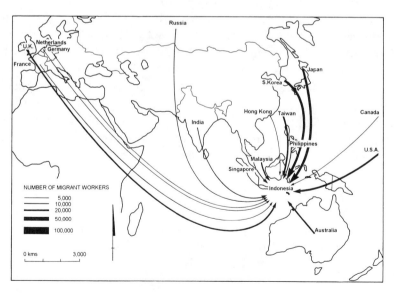

Source: Indonesian Ministry of Manpower, 1997

Arabia saw 25,000 illegal migrants detected and repatriated to Indonesia and it was believed that 150,000 illegals remained in Saudi Arabia (*Jakarta Post*, 10 November 1997:1). The Minister of Labour said that there were 1.95 million Indonesians working overseas in 1997 (*Migrant News*, 1997, 4(11):23). However, it would seem that a minimum of 2.5 million Indonesians are currently working overseas.

Perhaps, most surprising in Figure 8.2, is the significant amount of labour migration into Indonesia. This is quite different to the outflow of workers not only in its scale and the countries involved but also by virtue of the fact that:

- While the outflow is predominantly of unskilled workers, that of incoming workers is overwhelmingly of highly skilled, professional and technical workers.
- The "official" outflow is dominated by women whereas that moving into the country is male dominated.

In 1995, the number of registered newly incoming workers to Indonesia was 57,159, almost trebling since 1990 when 20,761 new workers were registered (Indonesian Ministry of Manpower, 1997). Moreover, as is the case with outgoing movements, there are many foreigners who have come to Indonesia and stayed for a long period so the stock is substantially greater than the annual flow of migrants. Also, there are foreigners who enter Indonesia as a tourist or visitor but subsequently work there. The burgeoning influx of workers seems paradoxical in the face of high underemployment and unemployment but is a function of two factors:

- The massive growth of investment by multinational operations in the region which has seen multinational corporations (MNCs) transfer large numbers of MDC origin staff into Asia. Hence, in 1994, there were 689,895 Japanese citizens officially regarded as living overseas (Okunishi, 1995:141) and between 3.3 and 6 million citizens of the United States (*Migrant News*, 1997, 4(11):27).

- The mismatches between the education and training systems and labour market skill needs in rapidly growing economies like Indonesia whereby, notwithstanding high levels of underemployment and educated unemployment, substantial numbers of specialists and professionals such as expatriate engineers, technicians, accountants, finance and management experts, have had to be imported (Hugo, 1996a).

The result has been an influx of highly trained people from the MDCs into the rapidly growing economies of the Asian region. Figure 8.2 and Appendix A show that the major origins of officially documented expatriate workers in Indonesia have been the nations from which MNCs have most heavily invested in Indonesia, such as Japan (33,798 workers moving in between 1991 and 1996), South Korea (31,170), the United States (25,657), Taiwan (8,474) and the United Kingdom (14,992). However, it will be noted that there were also quite significant influxes from Asian nations with well-developed educational systems which are producing professional and skilled workers in excess of local requirements, namely the Philippines (11,602) and India (9,580). Moreover, it is interesting to note that neighbouring Australia, where the economy in the 1990s has been quite flat, has supplied 16,904 workers to Indonesia. Malaysia (12,204) and Singapore (9,449) have also been significant suppliers of skilled and professional workers to Indonesia.

It is apparent from the Indonesian example that Southeast Asian countries are linked not only to many countries outside the region by migration flows but that international migration linkages between the members of ASEAN are not only strong but growing rapidly in scale and significance. These are overwhelmingly labour migration flows although in the 20-year period from 1975, there were substantial flows of boat and land people refugees from Vietnam, Cambodia and Laos to other Southeast Asian nations, especially Thailand. This involved more than 2 million people leaving the Indochinese nation and although other ASEAN nations were the country of first refuge, most were resettled in Western nations, especially the United States, Australia and Canada while some were repatriated. Although there have been some recent flows of Myanmar refugees across the border into Thailand the bulk of contemporary intra-ASEAN international migration involves labour migrants and the main flows are depicted in Figure 8.3. Table 8.5 shows that the pre-eminent emigration nation in Southeast Asia is the Philippines and although the bulk of out-movement is directed out of the ASEAN region, there are still significant flows to Singapore, Malaysia and, to a lesser extent, Indonesia.

The Philippines is one of the world's most significant contemporary sources of migrants with an estimated 5 million workers overseas in 1997 (Brillantes, 1998). They outnumber

Figure 8.3

Major Intra-ASEAN International Population Flows in the mid-1990s

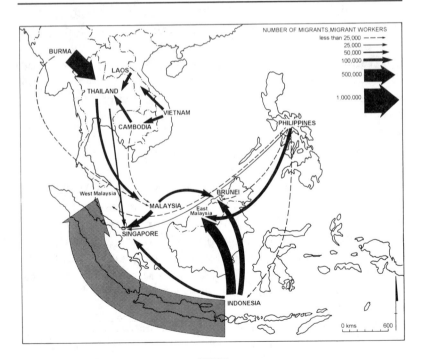

Table 8.5

Estimated Stocks of Migrant Workers in Southeast Asia the mid-1990s

Origin/Destination	Year	Stock ('000)	Source
Migrant Workers Absent			
Philippines	1997	6,100	Saywell, 1997:80
Indonesia	1997	2,404	Indonesian Ministry of Manpower
Thailand	1995	445	Stahl & PECC–HRD, 1996
Malaysia	1995	200	Azizah, 1997
Myanmar	1995	415	Stahl & PECC–HRD, 1996
Vietnam	1990	300	*Straits Times*, 10 May 1990
Cambodia	1996	30	ILO, 1997
Laos	1996	11	ILO, 1997
Migrant Workers Present			
Singapore	1997	450	*Migrant News*, 4(11):20
Malaysia	1996	2,300	Azizah, 1997
Thailand	1996	1,000	Stern, 1996
Brunei	1994	62	Stahl & PECC–HRD, 1996
Laos	1996	12	ILO, 1997

the migrant workers from all the other ASEAN countries currently deployed overseas. In addition, there are large communities of permanent Filipino settlers in the United States (1.16 million), Canada (123,300), Australia (92,949) and elsewhere (Table 8.2). The extent of the Filipino diaspora is evident in Figure 8.4 which depicts the main countries of origin from which remittances were made to the Philippines.

Figure 8.4

Origin of Remittances to the Philippines, 1994

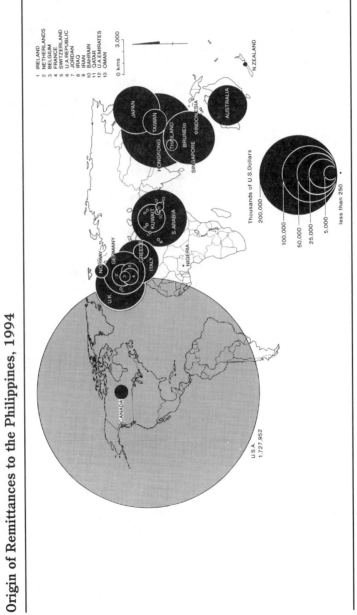

Source: Hugo, 1996b

These remittances have risen dramatically in recent years. While official remittances do not detect the full flow of hard currency associated with migration, Figure 8.5 shows that these figures increased from US$810.8 million in the mid-1980s to US$7 billion a decade later. This was equivalent to more than a third of total exports. Export of people has thus become a crucial element in the Filipino economy (Tiglao, 1997).

Vietnam is another major source of migrants in the ASEAN region. At present the bulk of the out-movement has been of permanent settlers who left Vietnam as refugees and were resettled in North America, Australasia or Europe after spending a period in refugee camps in other Southeast Asian countries. In early 1996, the Vietnamese government announced that there were 2.6 million ethnic Vietnamese living outside of the country and that this would exceed 3 million by the year 2000. They were spread over 80 countries with around 1 million in the United States, 400,000 in France, 300,000 in China, 160,000 in Australia, 150,000 in Canada, 120,000 in Thailand and 100,000 in Germany, Cambodia and Russia (*Japan Economic Newswire,* 29 March 1996). In addition, these communities have served as the nucleus for further Vietnamese migration under the family reunion components of the immigration policies and programmes of nations like Canada, the United States and Australia where, as shown in Table 8.2, there are now very large communities of Vietnamese-born people. The so-called Viet Kieu (overseas Vietnamese) are an important source of capital and growth to their relatives back in Vietnam and are being increasingly wooed by the Vietnamese government to invest in their homeland (Zielenziger & Rees, 1995). Return migration of some of the Viet Kieu has occurred but is on a very limited scale (Hugo, 1994). At present, there are only small numbers of Vietnamese migrant workers deployed overseas officially with 12,673 leaving Vietnam in 1996 and 36,000 over the 1990–96 period. However, some 220,000 were deployed overseas in the 1980s mainly to Eastern bloc nations. When the political changes of the late 1980s occurred, these jobs disappeared but many of the Vietnamese workers made their way westward into Europe (Geiger, 1995). There are apparently around 150,000

Figure 8.5

Overseas Contract Workers' Foreign Exchange Remittances in the Philippines, 1982–96 (in US$million)

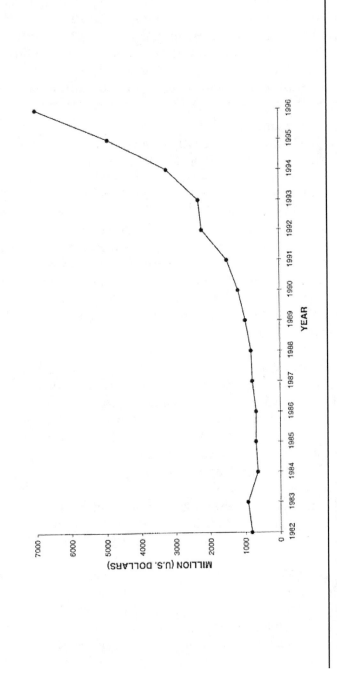

Source: Central Bank of the Philippines

Vietnamese undocumented workers overseas (ILO, 1997) and historical patterns of migration into Cambodia and Laos may have recommenced. It is likely that Vietnam will attempt to send more contract workers abroad in the near future with the increased pressure exerted by its rapidly growing workforce on limited job opportunities available locally.

Thailand has a long history of labour emigration (Sussangkarn, 1995). It was one of the earliest Southeast Asian nations to supply labour to the GCC nations following the 1973 oil boom but in recent years, it is apparent from Table 8.4 that other Asian destinations (particularly Taiwan and Japan but also fellow ASEAN countries like Brunei, Singapore and Malaysia) and Israel have become more important. While all ASEAN countries, even the non-labour exporters, have a significant inflow of skilled workers for the reasons outlined earlier, Thailand has experienced an influx of unskilled as well as skilled workers, especially from neighbouring Myanmar, and to a lesser extent, Cambodia and Laos. It is estimated that these were around 1 million foreign workers in Thailand in 1996, 75 percent of them from Myanmar (*Migrant News,* 1997, 4(11):21). An amnesty in 1996 resulted in the registration of 323,123 foreign workers and the issuing of 293,652 work permits. Although there is substantial cross-border labour migration from Myanmar into Thailand, the official outflow of official migrant workers from the former is minuscule (ILO, 1997:26).

Malaysia too is both an exporter and importer of labour. Table 8.2 shows that there has been significant settlement of Malaysians overseas, especially in Australia, although the tempo of that migration has slowed down in recent years. With respect to migrant labour, Malaysia is one of the most significant destinations of such movements in the world but it also exports workers (Table 8.5). Azizah (1997:13–15) estimates that there are around 100,000 Malaysians who work in Singapore; there are also significant flows to Brunei, Japan, Hong Kong and Taiwan. Pillai (1995) estimates the total number of Malaysians working overseas to be 225,000.

As is the case with emigration, estimating immigration to the countries of ASEAN is rendered difficult by the lack of completeness of the data and the large volume of clandestine movement. Malaysia is pre-eminent among the destination countries. The foremost scholar of Malaysian international migration, Azizah (1997:13) puts the number of immigrants and immigrant workers at around 2.3 million or around 11 percent of the total national population and over a fifth of the workforce. In particular, the flow from Indonesia into Malaysia, much of it clandestine, is among the largest international migration flows in the contemporary world. At the May 1997 Indonesian general election, around 1.4 million Indonesians in Malaysia registered to vote (*The Star,* 29 May 1997). Thailand too has become a significant magnet for migrant workers as has been explained above. The number of foreigners in Singapore are not released by the government but estimates range from 300,000 (Stahl & PECC–HRD, 1996) to 560,000 (*Straits Times,* 16 August 1997) out of a population of only 3.6 million in 1996, making Singapore proportionately one of the world's most significant immigration nations. In Brunei, too, migrant workers play a pivotal role making up more than a third of the workforce (Mani, 1995).

This chapter will briefly enumerate some of these evolving trends in international migration in Southeast Asia (for a more detailed analysis, see Hugo, 1997b), before considering some of the major emerging issues associated with this migration.

One distinctive feature of international labour migration in the region is the increasing involvement of women in that movement. Indeed, as Lim and Oishi (1996) point out, in several of the major emigration countries (e.g. Philippines and Indonesia), women outnumber men among legal overseas contract workers (OCWs). This trend has become more pronounced over time and is the subject of increasing controversy since many of the women move into jobs where they are particularly vulnerable to exploitation and abuse (e.g. domestic maids and entertainers).

- Undocumented migration is increasing exponentially. This includes both groups entering nations in a clandestine way as well as overstayers on visitor's visas. Illegal migration is sustained by the increasing involvement of criminal syndicates in international labour migration and trafficking of women and children. It is also facilitated by the development of social networks and the attempts of governments to intervene heavily to stop migration flows.

- Another feature is the increasing involvement of governments in the region, both at origin and destination, to regulate flows and, in some cases, attempt to encourage or prevent or restructure particular flows.

- The development of the "immigration industry" referred to earlier is expanding apace and is a major element sustaining a significant scale of movement.

The movement is becoming more broad-based in the range of skills of migrants. While the profile of the general flux of migrant workers is towards low-wage and low-skill 3D (dirty, dangerous and difficult) jobs, there are also flows of more skilled people.

Major Issues in ASEAN International Migration

International migration has only emerged as an issue of major significance in the ASEAN region relatively recently, yet it does have some important economic, social, demographic and political implications for the region and for the institution of ASEAN itself. Myers (1997:6) has highlighted the issue of international migration, especially of labour, as a critical ASEAN issue for a number of reasons:

- It is large, growing and will grow further.

- It is increasingly perceived as important by most, if not all, the ASEAN countries.

- It inevitably requires international cooperation in analysis and policy development.

- It is a very sensitive issue since it touches upon such things as national sovereignty and security, treatment of nationals by another country and trafficking in women and children.

- It is a "hard" issue because policies which have a favourable outcome for the destination end of the process may not do so for the origin and vice versa.

A few dimensions of the international migration issue in ASEAN are touched on here (see Hugo, 1998, for additional comments).

International Migration and AFTA

One of the paradoxical developments in the era of globalisation has been the emergence of regional blocs of nations (Lim, 1993). These include not only the well-documented European Community and the North American Free Trade Area (NAFTA) initiatives which have aimed to remove almost totally national barriers to the free flow of capital and goods in Western Europe and North America but also similar attempts in the southern cone of Latin America (MERCOSUR–Patarra, 1997), West Africa (ECOWAS–United Nations, 1992:185) and the Mahgreb in North Africa (AMU–United Nations, 1992:185). The member states of ASEAN have committed themselves to the ASEAN Free Trade Agreement (AFTA) which involves a reduction in tariffs at varying paces between 1995 and 2003 to encourage trade between the economies of the member states. Although there continues to be considerable debate within the region about the lowering of tariffs, it would seem that these moves will work towards encouraging greater flows of people between the nations of ASEAN.

The *raison d'être* of AFTA is that it will build upon the comparative advantages and complementarities of the ASEAN states by creating an integrated market of 500 million people. However, part of the complementarities and differences between the ASEAN economies are large and widening disparities between countries in, as Myers (1997:6) points out, "labour supply, demand and wages, workers' education and skills, population densities and natural resource endowments. These differences create strong incentives on both the demand and supply side for migration."

If we focus upon differences in the supply and demand for labour, Figure 8.6 shows that the age structures of the main labour importing nations of the region (especially Singapore and Thailand) are steep-sided in the younger ages so that the numbers entering the workforce ages are not expanding. In the labour-surplus nations on the other hand (e.g. Indonesia, Philippines), the age pyramids widens towards the bottom, indicating that the workforce is still growing quite rapidly: each year more young people enter the school-leaving age groups than the year before. Hence Table 8.6 shows that there is a considerable range in the annual rate of growth of the population aged 15–59 over the next 5 years, between countries of the region ranging from 0.8 percent per annum in Singapore and 1.31 percent in Thailand to 3.1 percent in Cambodia and 2.9 percent in Laos. These differences are maintained over the 2000–10 period.

Moreover, it will be noted that in the labour-surplus nations, the workforce will grow at a faster rate than the total population over the next 15 years. Hence there appears to be a divergence in the demographic situation of labour-surplus and labour-shortage countries with respect to growth of their labour force age groups over the next decade or so. This will obviously expand the potential for labour migration between countries in the ASEAN region.

Moreover, these demographic differences in the supply of labour are matched by equally substantial differences in the demand for labour. Table 8.7 shows that although economic growth rates are generally high across the region, there are variations and it is likely that Singapore, Brunei and Malaysia and perhaps, Thailand, will continue to experience shortages of workers with the rapid expansion of their economies.

The crucial question with respect to AFTA is to what extent the reduction of barriers between the Asian nations, in relation to the trading of goods and services, will place additional pressure on the barriers to movement of people between the countries. Unlike the EC, there are no elements in AFTA which relate to freeing up the movement of labour between member

Figure 8.6

Age-Sex Structure in Southeast Asia, 1995

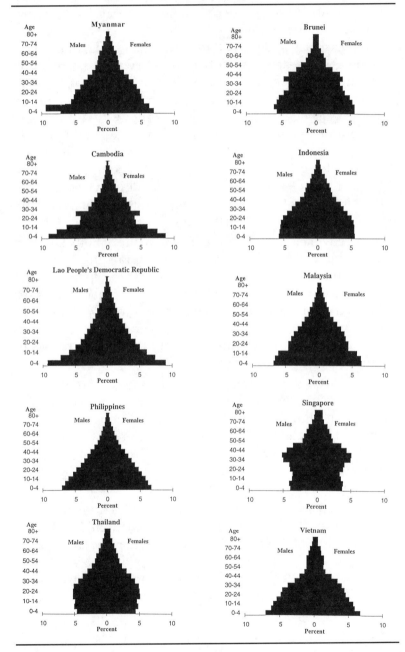

Source: United Nations, 1994

Table 8.6

Projected Growth of Labour Force Age Groups in Southeast Asia, 1995–2010

	('000)				% p.a. growth		Total Population % p.a. growth	
	1995	2000	2005	2010	1995–2000	1995–2010	1995–2000	1995–2010
			15 – 59 years					
Brunei	173	1,96	217	2,35	2.53	2.06	1.83	1.55
Cambodia	5,212	6,075	7,179	8,238	3.11	3.10	2.57	2.39
Indonesia	119,086	131,368	143,325	154,805	1.98	1.76	1.49	1.29
Lao People's Dem. Rep.	2,460	2,836	3,312	3,905	2.89	3.13	2.79	2.61
Malaysia	11,303	12,979	14,819	16,533	2.80	2.57	2.06	1.78
Myanmar	26,059	29,097	32,868	37,033	2.23	2.37	2.07	1.89
Philippines	38,085	43,196	48,501	53,852	2.55	2.34	1.99	1.79
Singapore	1,915	1,993	2,080	2,093	0.80	0.59	0.82	0.66
Thailand	37,702	40,235	42,541	43,887	1.31	1.02	1.04	0.89
Vietnam	41,143	47,267	53,763	60,788	2.81	2.64	2.09	1.87
Total	283,138	315,242	348,605	381,369	2.17	2.01	1.71	1.52

Source: United Nations, 1994

Table 8.7

Economic Indicators in the ASEAN Countries, around 1995

| | GNP per capita US$(1995) | % Growth GNP (1985–95) | % of GDP in Agricult. (1995) | % of GDP in Manufact. (1995) | % of Age Group Enrolled in Education (1993) | | |
| | | | | | Secondary Education | | Tertiary Education |
					M	F	
Philippines	1,050	1.5	22	23	71	75	26
Malaysia	3,890	5.7	13	33	56	61	7
Singapore	26,730	6.2	0	27	69	71	n.a.
Myanmar	n.a.	n.a.	59*	7*	23	23	n.a.
Thailand	2,740	8.4	11	29	38	37	19
Indonesia	980	6.0	17	24	48	39	10
Laos	350	2.7	52	14	19	31	2
Brunei	n.a.	n.a.	n.a.	n.a.	67	74	n.a.
Cambodia	270	n.a.	51	6	n.a.	n.a.	n.a.
Vietnam	240	n.a.	28	22	n.a.	n.a.	2

Source: World Bank, 1997; Population Reference Bureau, 1997;
UNESCAP, 1997

* 1992 Data

states. A number of scenarios would appear possible including the following:

- To the extent that AFTA results in greater specialisation of national economies in line with comparative advantage, labour-intensive activity may concentrate more in labour-surplus areas where wages are low while capital-intensive activity may concentrate more where skilled labour is available. This would result in a reduction of movement between nations.

- To the extent that AFTA produces greater linkages between private and public-sector employers in the member states, movement between nations will increase along these linkages.

Hence the effects of AFTA on international movement within ASEAN are unclear. Theory would suggest that in the short term, movement would increase but in the longer term, economic development in the poorer countries may lead to a reduction in the outflow (Martin, 1993).

International Migration and Economic Development

It is obvious that labour migration between ASEAN countries has the potential to assist the economic growth in origin and destination areas through a number of mechanisms:

- overcoming labour shortages in particular sectors;
- overcoming skill shortages in particular sectors;
- relieving local labour-surplus situations; and
- local creation of jobs through the influx of remittances (Taylor et al., 1996).

On the other hand, it could equally be suggested that there could be negative impacts on social and economic development as a result of migration:

- the loss of the most skilled and entrepreneurially oriented groups in the origin area depresses development prospects there;
- depressing of wages in destination areas;
- displacement of native workers at destination areas;
- increased income inequality in origin areas;
- excessive dependency on outside sources of income in origin areas; and
- social costs of separation of migrants from their families.

There is a general assumption in much of the policy development in the ASEAN region, especially in the labour-surplus countries, that the economic benefits of increased migration outweigh the costs. However, there is a dearth of empirical research to either confirm or contradict this assumption. Such research is needed if the undoubted potential economic benefits are to be maximised and the costs minimised. In these analyses, there is a need to take not only a national perspective but to also consider the impact of international migration upon regional development. In most origin countries, immigrants tend to be drawn from particular regions so that the impact of the migration is quite spatially concentrated. Often these areas are among the poorest and least developed in the country so that international migration can be an instrument of regional as well as national development strategy. For example, it is clear in Indonesia that some of the poorest areas in the nation (e.g. East and West Nusa Tenggara) are the major areas of origin of international labour migrants. Hence while remittances may make up only 2 or 3 percent of Indonesian national exports, they can be the largest incoming element in the regional balance of payments (Hugo, 1995a).

How Temporary is Labour Migration in ASEAN?

A crucial question relating to the burgeoning international labour migration impinging upon Southeast Asia is the extent to which the migration will remain temporary. At present, the bulk of workers return to their homeland upon completion of their contract and the countries of destination are very strict in enforcing this. Indeed, migrant workers in several countries are subject to restrictions which prevent them developing strong links to the destination. One example is immigrant workers are banned from marrying locals in several countries (Lim & Oishi, 1996). However, the policy-makers in destination nations are conscious of the experience with guestworkers in Europe in the 1950s and 1960s whereby temporary labour migration became transformed into permanent settlement (Castles, Booth & Wallace, 1984). These concerns emanate from a number of sources. In some nations, there is anxiety that a significant influx of permanently settling foreigners will disturb social cohesion or the "ethnic balance". In others the concern is with becoming overly reliant upon outside labour or having to support the foreign workers in the event of an economic downturn. Indeed, the Southeast Asian currency crisis of 1997 has resulted in the displacement of foreign workers. For example, in Thailand, it was announced that "At least 17,000 foreign workers, mostly in construction, lost their jobs in August 1997" due to the reduction in economic activity as a result of the financial crisis (*Migrant News*, 1997, 4(11):21). Similarly, the economic downturn in the late 1980s in Singapore saw the repatriation of a large number of foreign workers to Malaysia but these workers did not want the 3D jobs being filled by Indonesian workers despite the fact that the returning workers were unemployed (Hugo, 1993).

While there is little research into the settlement intentions of migrant workers, it is clear that in some cases permanent settlement has occurred. Many Indonesians and Filipinos in Sabah in East Malaysia, for example, have been there for extended periods and begun families (Hugo, 1996c). However, it is not clear how widespread this pattern is and it will remain a central concern of destination countries.

Bilateral Relations

It is apparent to any observer of the ASEAN scene in the last decade that international migration both influences, and is influenced by, bilateral political relationships between the ASEAN member states. Clearly the type and context of the movement are important in this as are the numbers of migrants involved and their characteristics, and whether or not there are reciprocal flows. International migration can be the basis for building up a wider set of mutually beneficial flows between nations. However, they can also be the basis for souring relations between countries where countries accept emigres fleeing from a neighbouring nation and where those emigrants continue to actively oppose the regime in their home nation, as is the case with some Burmese in Thailand for example. Similarly, the case of a female Filipino domestic worker in Singapore who was executed for the alleged murder of a fellow Filipino maid and her ward led to a significant cooling of relations between the two ASEAN partners (Arcellana, 1995). It would certainly seem that migration is going to figure more prominently in bilateral and multilateral relationships involving ASEAN countries.

In the Philippines, it has been argued (Brillantes, 1998) that the protection and the welfare of Filipinos overseas is now a major underpinning of the nation's Department of Foreign Affairs. Much of the day-to-day activity of that department is concerned with overseas workers. Indeed, a specific Act (Migrant Workers and Overseas Filipinos Act of 1995) charges Filipino missions abroad with protecting migrant workers' welfare.

Rights of Migrants

One very important issue which has not been given enough prominence in the region relates to the rights of migrants, especially migrant workers. The issue is made all the more difficult in Southeast Asia by the high level of illegal migration. Clearly, migrants in a foreign country where they do not have the rights of citizens of that country are vulnerable to the risk of exploitation, discrimination and abuse. This vulnerability is increased if they are undocumented migrants. While there are well-established regimes for dealing with some types of international migrants, such as refugees, they are not widely accepted and established regimes for dealing with other types of international migrants. This applies especially to international labour migration. Although there is a UN international charter of Migrant Worker Rights which could serve as a blueprint for such a regime, it has not been ratified by most nations in the region (only the Philippines in Southeast Asia). The difficult issue of protecting the rights of nationals in a foreign land is exacerbated when they work in contexts which are not even under the jurisdiction of local labour authorities, such as is the case with domestic workers or many workers in the so–called "entertainment" industry. The priority given to the protection of the rights of migrant workers is clearly low in most countries in the region, and this especially applies to women (Goldberg, 1996). There may be greater scope for involvement of non-governmental organisations (NGOs) in these activities.

The fact that many Asian women move to other nations for marriage, to work as domestics or in the entertainment and sex industries, means that they are often vulnerable to abuse and exploitation. The sex trade has also become a significant element in female international migration in Asia. Women are recruited to work as entertainers or prostitutes in other Asian countries or in MDCs, such as Japan and Australia. Thailand and the Philippines are important source countries of this movement. Brockett (1996) has shown that for Thai women, there is a circuit of movement involving Japan, Taiwan and Australia and social networks link the sex industry across several nations. One insidious element in this is the increased scale of trafficking of women. This trade is largely in the hands of organised crime, some of it involving diversification from the drug trade. There are an estimated 150,000 foreign sex workers in Japan alone, most of them Thais and Filipinas (Sherry, Lee & Vatikiotis, 1995:24).

Undocumented Migration

It is apparent that the role of undocumented migration has increased greatly in the Southeast Asian region. This is reflected in the fact that over the last year, Thailand and Malaysia have granted amnesties in an attempt to regularise the migration situation. It is apparent that organised crime has become increasingly involved in undocumented migration globally and certainly within Southeast Asia (Beare, 1997). Some spontaneous border crossing does occur but much of the undocumented movement is highly organised and presents a particular challenge to countries of origin and destination. In origin countries, it is clear that legal migration procedures are sometimes overly bureaucratic, time-consuming and expensive so that an illegal agent or recruiter may, in fact, be offering a cheaper and more convenient service. In other contexts, destination-end migration controls may be so strict that the only avenue open for migration to some aspirants is the illegal route. Large-scale policing and extensive crackdowns on illegal migrants can be expensive as Azizah (1997) has demonstrated in the Malaysian case. Very often too, such strategies end up penalising the victim (the migrant) and not the criminal (the recruiters or agents involved). Moreover, the literature would suggest that often such crackdowns are not very effective in controlling that movement. Certainly the control of illegal and criminal recruiting rings which exploit migrant workers is a significant global and regional challenge.

Social Implications

Much of the literature concerned with international migration in ASEAN focuses upon its economic and development consequences and neglects its significant social impacts. It is apparent, for example, that international labour migration can have detrimental effects on marriage and the family due to the long periods of separation involved. In Eastern Indonesia, the incidence of divorce among such families is high and some men maintain a wife at both origin and destination. Control over children can be difficult when one or both parents are away working overseas (Hugo, 1995b; 1996c). It is clear that the interrelationships between international migrations and changes in family structure and functioning are complex and little understood (Hugo, 1997b) but they need to be investigated in much greater detail than has hitherto been the case and taken into consideration in policy-making.

Data Issues

It has been pointed out earlier that one of the major constraints in developing appropriate policies and programmes in international migration in the ASEAN region is the lack of comprehensive and accurate data in virtually all of the member states. Accordingly, there is a pressing need for data collection processing to be developed in the international migration area. These data collection initiatives necessarily involve both origin and destination so there is a need for the initiative to be a regional rather than a nation by nation one (Bilsborrow et al., 1997). These data collection initiatives should consider:

- improvement of collection, storage and analysis of border control statistics;
- consideration of inclusion of international migration operations in national census;
- harmonisation of labour permit statistics across the ASEAN nations; and
- consideration of special data collection initiatives relating to undocumented migration as have been attempted in Mexico, for example (Bustamante, 1997).

A regional initiative for all of ASEAN incorporating each of these elements would provide a sounder basis for the development of national and regional policies in this area.

Existing research on international migration in the ASEAN region remains limited partly due to the poor quality of the data sources available. However, Myers (1997:6) has argued persuasively that research in ASEAN international labour migration would be greatly enhanced by a coordinated and collaborative approach among the states of the region and should address the following:

- flows, sources, numbers, gender and employment sector at departure and destination;
- employer behaviour, recruitment, wages, benefits, working conditions, job duration and security;
- migrant characteristics and behaviour, education attainment, job skills, wages, remittances, repatriation;
- impact on the sending country, reduction in surplus, labour, brain drain, remittances and investment and other behaviour of returnees, growth and poverty consequences; and
- impact on the receiving countries' growth, income distribution and poverty consequences, persistence of sunset export industries.

Many of these issues are equally significant for other types of international migration as well.

Conclusion

The regional currency crisis of the second half of 1997 will have some influence in dampening the economic growth rates and the rate of creation of job opportunities in several of the ASEAN countries. However, it is unlikely to stem the flow of international migrants in the region. This is partly due to the continuation of the wide economic and demographic differences and complementarities outlined earlier in this chapter. However, the continuation of flows will also occur because of a strengthening of some structural features of the existing regional migration system which will ensure that migration is likely to continue regardless of what economic conditions prevail or what government policies and programmes are initiated. These structural features include:

- The segmentation of labour markets in destination countries which have resulted in the concentration of many migrant workers in the low-wage 3D (dirty, dangerous, difficult) jobs which are eschewed by native workers. Past experience in the region (for example, in Malaysia in 1987 (Hugo, Lim & Narayan, 1989)) is that even in times of economic downturn, local workers are unwilling to enter low-wage low-status occupations (e.g. in the agriculture, construction, domestic service and plantation sectors) and prefer to remain unemployed and hold out to get a job in an air-conditioned factory or office.

- Migrant networks have developed and strengthened over the last decade or so. These linkages between origin and destination communities give a momentum to migration which allows it to operate regardless of the economic conditions. The connections at the destination allow the new immigrant to adjust in a familiar and supportive atmosphere and ease entry into the labour market even in difficult situations

- The immigration industry of recruiters, travel agents and so forth will continue to be highly active in encouraging and facilitating international migration.

Accordingly, we can expect international migration to remain of considerable significance in the region regardless of what the fallout from the currency crisis is and what interventions are made by countries of destination and origin.

It is apparent that one of the major constraints on expanding development in ASEAN relates to human resources. This not only relates to situations of national or regional labour surplus or labour shortage, but also to significant specific skill shortages which are creating bottlenecks in the development of particular sectors of the economy which are rapidly expanding. In some cases (e.g. Singapore), there is a shortage of workers which is especially pronounced in particular sectors identified by the government to be crucial areas of future expansion — e.g. information technology. In other cases (e.g. Indonesia), there is a mismatch in the skills needed in the contemporary labour market and those being produced by vocational training institutions and universities. There is clearly the potential for overcoming at least some of these human resource problems in the short term through international migration within ASEAN and with other parts of the world. There have been some suggestions that human resource development strategies in the ASEAN countries could benefit from integration and collaboration. This would involve not only having regional strategies for training in particular skills but also cooperation between countries in the deployment of the available skilled workers within the ASEAN region. While such discussions are only in the earliest of stages in ASEAN, it is likely that they will be given more prominence especially if AFTA is successful in breaking down barriers to flows of goods and capital between ASEAN countries.

ASEAN has had many achievements in the 30 years of its existence. The future challenges which it faces are manifold and among these, human resource issues will loom large. It is apparent that international migration, especially of workers, will be very important. Indeed, one commentator (Myers, 1997:6) has designated the international labour migration issue as a "test issue for ASEAN and AFTA. It will not go away." Clearly, international migration will present a significant challenge to ASEAN's researchers and policy-makers over the next decade.

Labour Migration To and From Indonesia 1991–96

Origin/Destination	In	Out
Malaysia	12,264	505,886
Singapore	9,449	103,209
Thailand	3,978	80 *
Philippines	11,602	12 *
US	25,657	17,385
Australia	16,904	818
Japan	33,798	18,558
South Korea	31,170	21,652
Taiwan	18,474	24,204
Hong Kong	5,231	11,023
India	9,480	14 *
Saudi Arabia	–	536,679
Brunei	–	11,174
Netherlands	5,688	4,919
UK	14,992	211
Germany	5,738	521
France	6,351	768
Canada	5,804	156 *
New Zealand	1,994	95 *
United Arab Emirates	–	15,872
Italy	–	302
Kuwait	–	3,103
Egypt	–	306
Monaco	–	1,253
Norway	–	221
Russia	6,967	160

Notes: * 1994–96

Source: Indonesian Ministry of Manpower, 1997

Notes

1. Defined as temporary visa-holders arriving and residents departing temporarily with the intention to stay in Australia or abroad for 12 months or more, and the departure of temporary visa-holders and the return of residents who had stayed in Australia or abroad for 12 months or more.

2. Filipino workers are deployed in more than 110 countries (Brillantes, 1998).

References

Arcellana, E.Y. (1995) "The Maga-Contemplacian case: Beyond forgetting". *The Manila Chronicle*, 4 June.

Australian Bureau of Statistics (ABS). (1981) *Overseas Arrivals and Departures*. Catalogue No. 3402.0. Canberra: ABS.

————. (1997) *Migration Australia 1995–96*. Catalogue No. 3412.0. Canberra: ABS.

Azizah, K. (1997) "International migration and its impact on Malaysia". Paper presented at the 11th Asia–Pacific Roundtable, Labour Migration in Southeast Asia: The Impact (Political, Economic, Social, Security)". Kuala Lumpur. 5–8 June.

Beare, M.E. (1997) "Framework paper: Illegal migration". Paper prepared for the CSCAP Study Group on Transnational Crime. Bangkok, Thailand.

Bilsborrow, R., G.H. Hugo, A.S. Oberai & H. Zlotnik. (1997) *International migration statistics: Guidelines for improving data collection systems*. Geneva: International Labour Office.

Biro Pusat Statistik. (1996) *Laporan Eksekutif Nasional Survei Penduduk Antar Sensus 1995*. Jakarta: Biro Pusat Statistik.

Brillantes, J. (1998) "The Philippine overseas program and its effects on immigration to Canada". In E.R. Laquian, A.A. Laquian & T.G. McGee (eds.), *The Silent Debate: Asian Immigration and Racism in Canada*. Vancouver: Institute of Asian Research, University of British Colombia.

Brockett, L. (1996) "Thai sex workers in Sydney". Unpublished MA thesis. Department of Geography, University of Sydney.

Bustamante, J.A. (1997) Mexico–United States labour migration: Some theoretical and methodological innovations and research findings. In *International Population Conference Beijing 1997*. Liege: IUSSP vol. 1:45–91.

Castles, S., H. Booth & P. Wallace. (1984) *Here for Good: West Europe's Ethnic Minorities*. London: Pluto Press.

Economic and Social Commission for Asia and the Pacific (ESCAP). (1997) *1997 ESCAP Population Data Sheet*. Bangkok: ESCAP.

Fields, G.S. (1994) "The migration transition in Asia". *Asian and Pacific Migration Journal*, 3(1):7-30.

Geiger, E. (1995) "Vietnamese in Germany wait to be sent home". *San Francisco Chronicle*, 22 June.

Goldberg, P. (1996) "International projections for migrant women as a human rights issue". In G. Battistella & A. Paganoni (eds.), *Asian Women in Migration*. Quezon City: Scalabrini Migration Center. pp. 165–82.

Hugo, G.J. (1980) "Population movements in Indonesia during the colonial period". In J.J. Fox, R.G. Garnaut, T. McCawley & J.A.C. Mackie (eds.), *Indonesia: Australian Perspectives*. Canberra: Australian National University, Research School of Pacific Studies. pp. 95–135.

———. (1993) "Indonesian labour migration to Malaysia: Trends and policy implications".*Southeast Asian Journal of Social Science*, 21(1):36–70.

———. (1994) *The Economic Implications of Emigration from Australia*. Canberra: AGPS.

———. (1995a) "Labour export from Indonesia: An overview". *ASEAN Economic Bulletin*, 12(2):275–98.

———. (1995b) "International labor migration and the family: some observations from Indonesia".*Asian and Pacific Migration Journal* 4, 2–3:273–301.

———. (1996a) "Brain drain and student movements". In P.J. Lloyd & L.S. Williams (eds.), *International Trade and Migration in the APEC Region*. Melbourne: Oxford University Press. pp. 210–28.

———. (1996b) "Remittances in Southeast Asia". Mimeo.

———. (1996c) "Economic impacts of international labour emigration on regional and local development: Some evidence from Indonesia". Paper presented at the Annual Meeting of the PAA New Orleans. May.

————. (1997a) "Changing patterns and processes of population mobility". In G.W. Jones & T.H. Hull (eds.), *Indonesia Assessment: Population and Human Resources*. Canberra: Australian National University and Singapore: Institute of Southeast Asian Studies. pp. 68–100.

————. (1997b) "International migration in the Asia-Pacific region: Emerging trends and issues". Paper prepared for the Conference on International Migration at "Century's End: Trends and Issues". Organised by the International Union for the Scientific Study of Population, Barcelona, Spain. 7–10 May.

————. (1998) "Migration and mobilisation in Asia: An overview". In E.R. Laquian, A.A. Laquian & T. McGee, *The Silent Debate: Asian Immigration and Racism in Canada*. Vancouver: Institute of Asian Research, University of British Columbia.

Hugo, G.J., L.L. Lim & S. Narayan. (1989) "Malaysian human resources development planning project module 11: Labour supply and processes". Study No. 4: Labour Mobility. First draft of Final Report. January.

Indonesian Ministry of Manpower. (1997) *Profil Sumber Daya Manusia Indonesia (The Human Resources Profile in Indonesia)*. Jakarta: Departemen Tenaga Kerja, Badan Perencanaan dan Pengembangan Tenaga Kerja.

International Labour Office (ILO). (1997) *Cooperation in Employment Promotion and Training in the Greater Mekong Subregion*. Bangkok: ILO.

Lim, Lin Lean. (1993) "Growing economic interdependence and its implications for international migration". Paper presented at Expert Group Meeting on Population Distribution and Migration. Organised by the Population Division of the Department of Economic and Social Development, United Nations. In collaboration with UNFPA, Santa Cruz, Bolivia. 18–22 January.

Lim, L.L. & N. Oishi. (1996) "International migration of Asian women: Distinctive characteristics and policy concerns". In G. Battistella & A. Paganoni (eds.), *Asian Women in Migration*. Quezon City: Scalabrini Migration Centre. pp. 23–54.

Mani, A. (1995) "Migration in Brunei Darussalam". In O. Jin Jui, C. Kwok Bun and C. Soon Beng (eds.), *Crossing Borders — Transmigration in Asia Pacific*. Singapore: Prentice Hall. Chapter 25.

Martin, P.L. (1993) *Trade and Migration: NAFTA and Agriculture.* Washington DC: Institute for International Economics.

————. (1994) "Migration and trade: Challenges for the 1990s". *Work and Family Life of International Migrant Workers,* 4(3):1-21.

Myers, C.N. (1997) "Labor migration in Southeast Asia". *Jakarta Post.* 19 October:6.

Okunishi, Y. (1995). "Japan". *ASEAN Economic Bulletin,* 12(2):139–62.

Patarra, N. (1997) "Economic integration, labour market and international migration: The MERCUSOR Case". Paper presented at the 23rd General Population Conference, China, Beijing. 11–17 October.

Pillai, P. (1995) "Malaysia". *ASEAN Economic Bulletin,* 12(2):221–36.

Population Reference Bureau. (1997) *1997 World Population Data Sheet.* Washington: Population Reference Bureau.

Saywell, T. (1997) "Workers' offensive". *Far Eastern Economic Review,* 29 May:50–52.

Sherry, A., M. Lee & M. Vatikiotis. (1995) "For lust or money". *Far Eastern Economic Review,* 14 December:22-23.

Skeldon, R. (1994) "Turning points in labor migration: The case of Hong Kong". *Asian and Pacific Migration Journal,* 3(1):93-118.

Stahl, C.W. & PECC–HRD Task Force. (1996) "International labour migration and the East Asian APEC/PECC economies: Trends, issues and policies". Paper presented at PECC Human Resource Development Task Force Meeting, Brunei. 7-8 June.

Stern, A. (1996) "Thailand's illegal labor migrants". *Asian Migrant,* 9(4):100–3.

Sussangkarn, C. (1995) "Labour market adjustments and migration in Thailand". *ASEAN Economic Bulletin,* 12(2):237–56.

Taylor, J.E., J. Arango, A. Kovaouci, D.S. Massey & A. Pellegrino. (1996) "International migration and community development". *Population Index,* 62(3):397–418.

Tiglao, R. (1997) "What Tiger?" *Far Eastern Review,* 23 October.

United Nations 1992. "International migration trends and policies". In *World Population Monitoring 1991.* New York: United Nations. pp. 170–212.

————. (1994) *The Sex and Age Distribution of the World Populations.* New York: United Nations.

————. (1997a) *World Urbanization Prospects: The 1996 Revision Annex Tables.* New York: United Nations Secretariat, Population Division.

————. (1997b) "Draft World Population Monitoring, 1997". Preliminary version prepared by the Population Division of the Department for Economic and Social Information and Policy Analysis of the United Nations Secretariat. New York: United Nations.

Vasuprasat, P. (1994) "Turning points in international labour migration: A case study of Thailand". *Asian and Pacific Migration Journal,* 3(1):93-118.

World Bank. (1997) *World Development Report 1997.* New York: Oxford University Press.

Zeilenziger, M. & J. Rees. (1995) "Back from the diaspora". *Far Eastern Economic Review,* 18 May:38–39.

Chapter 9

THE ROLE OF EDUCATION IN ASEAN ECONOMIC GROWTH: PAST AND FUTURE

GAVIN JONES

Introduction

The "second wave" of Asian tiger economies has heavily featured members of ASEAN. Singapore, of course, was one of the original "tigers", along with the Republic of Korea, Taiwan and Hong Kong. The second wave has featured Thailand, Malaysia and Indonesia. Throughout this period of intense growth, though its economy has been strengthening over the 1990s, the Philippines has remained out of the high-growth economies (Bautista & Lamberte, 1996). Vietnam and Laos also remain in the unspectacular growth league, while Myanmar (and Cambodia, which recently joined ASEAN) remain in the economic doldrums. It is worth stressing that, of the original ASEAN five, four countries experienced spectacular economic growth over the past three decades.

The serious financial and economic crisis that has gripped Southeast Asia since mid-1997 seems likely to seriously set back economic growth in ASEAN countries for at least two years and possibly much longer, and calls into question many basic aspects of their systems of governance and their economic development strategies. The crisis is likely to be most prolonged in Indonesia. Nevertheless, despite the severity of the current crisis, it should not be forgotten that Thailand, Malaysia, Singapore and Indonesia completed the three decades with a massively modernised infrastructure, profound changes in the structure of their economies and much higher levels of individual and family welfare than they started them. What were the reasons for this sustained growth?

The Role of Human Resource Development in the ASEAN Tigers

Growth theorists, economic historians and development economists have yet to agree on the answers to this question, but all seem to agree that the answers are embedded somewhere in the following list of factors: (i) substantial investment in infrastructure; (ii) an efficient absorption of advanced technology; (iii) a stable political environment; (iv) an impressive commitment to human capital formation (Ogawa et al., 1993:2). This chapter will stress the last of these, although the four factors are obviously closely interrelated.

The Southeast Asian tigers have benefited from their demographic dynamics (in particular, their declining dependency ratios as declining fertility halted the growth in numbers of children), and their long-term commitment to building human capital. Human resource development helps account for their rapid adaptation of imported technologies and thus rapid advance in productivity. Factors such as these have helped motivate a resurgent interest in formal theories of growth (Romer, 1986; Lucas, 1988; Barro, 1991). The new economic growth theories endogenize the rate of technological advance and population growth. They make the rate of physical capital accumulation (closely linked to the rate of technological advance) an increasing function of the level of human capital, in some cases making the *rate* of human capital accumulation also an increasing function of the *level* of human capital. These models' endogenization of the rate of technological advance through human capital accumulation, notably through formal schooling and informal skill development on the job, provide important implications for public education policy in ASEAN countries.

There is little doubt that broad-based human resource development has played a major role in the economic success of Asian economies such as the Republic of Korea, Taiwan and Thailand. The case for this conclusion was argued in detail in Ogawa et al. (1993), which noted that countries such as Japan, Korea and Thailand have profited from the early building of a literacy base, and declines in dependency rates induced mainly by reduced fertility have facilitated both rapid growth in physical capital per worker and human capital deepening. Many East and Southeast Asian countries have shown a strong commitment to schooling, investing a larger share of public resources in education than all the Western industrialised nations in the 19th century and almost all of the contemporary developing countries in Latin America and Africa.

It could be, though, that we give too much emphasis to the schooling aspect of human resource development. The Philippines provides a troublesome case for any theory prioritising human capital as an engine of economic growth. It had as good an educational endowment as South Korea in 1960 and a better one than Thailand. Yet its economic performance over the subsequent three decades fell way behind those two countries. This can be explained partly by unwise choice of macroeconomic policies, corruption and mismanagement, but a more interesting explanation has to do with the Philippines' failure to benefit much from on-the-job training because of its emphasis on import replacement strategies. The 1995 Nobel Laureate Robert Lucas, while agreeing that "the main engine of growth is the accumulation of human capital — of knowledge — and the main source of differences in living standards among nations is differences in human capital", then notes that "human capital accumulation takes place in schools, in research organisations, and in the course of producing goods and engaging in trade ... For understanding periods of very rapid growth in a single economy, learning on the job seems to be by far the most central" (Lucas, 1993:270). According to this argument, it is not so much the trends in schooling that explain the East Asian growth miracle, but rather their open, export-oriented economies that have required workers and managers to take on new tasks and move up the "quality ladder".

Recent Trends in ASEAN education

Now that Vietnam, Laos, Myanmar and Cambodia have been accepted as members of ASEAN, generalisations about ASEAN are much more difficult to make, and this is no less true of education than of economic growth or political matters. The original ASEAN five countries and Brunei have all achieved something approaching universal primary education,[1] and in this, they have been greatly assisted by sharp declines in fertility rates, which have led to actual declines in numbers in primary school ages in Singapore since the late 1960s, in Thailand since the early 1980s and recently, to a levelling off of such numbers in Indonesia. In Vietnam, the literacy level was raised by massive literacy campaigns in the late 1940s and 1950s, but universal primary school enrolment is still not attained: only 85 percent of primary school-aged children could be accommodated in schools, and fewer than 50 percent of pupils entering primary school completed it (Kinh, 1991). Although something approaching universal primary education is aimed for by the year 2000, this will be seriously hampered by qualitative deficiencies throughout the system: outmoded textbooks; poorly trained and poorly paid teachers, most of whom have to "moonlight" to make ends meet; physical facilities and teaching aids which, according to one observer, are "miserably poor" (Hac, 1991:37). Laos lags seriously in primary education. The net enrolment rate at the primary school ages of 6–10 was officially estimated to be 73 percent, up from 63 percent five years earlier.[2] The target is to reach 80 percent in the year 2000. But the net enrolment rate does not tell the whole story. A recent study showed that 46 percent of primary school students are overaged (World Bank, 1995);

repetition rates are estimated at 30 percent; and probably only 30 percent of children complete primary school.

Despite these continuing severe shortcomings in primary education in some countries, in general, the emphasis in the ASEAN region has shifted to secondary and higher education. Great progress has also been made at these levels (see Table 9.1). In 1970, Thailand and Indonesia lagged noticeably behind other Southeast Asian countries in secondary education, but they have made considerable progress since then, albeit following quite different trajectories of expansion. In Indonesia, progress over the 1970s and early 1980s was steady, but it slowed during the 1980s, culminating in an actual decline in secondary school enrolments in the late 1980s (Oey-Gardiner, 1997), a decline which flew in the face of official government policy. Far higher costs of education at the secondary than at the primary level meant that poverty was probably the main factor. Secondary enrolments began to pick up again in the last few years, before the economic crisis broke out in 1997, with the introduction of (theoretically) compulsory secondary schooling and intensified efforts to increase transition rates from primary to secondary school. Thailand's gross secondary enrolment ratio of about 29 percent was the lowest among the ASEAN5 in 1990, but educational authorities made great efforts to increase the transition rate from primary to secondary education, with remarkable success, raising this rate from about 50 percent in 1990 to 85 percent in 1995 (Sussangkarn, 1995:244). Opening lower secondary school classes in primary schools helped, as did parents' growing realisation that secondary education is essential for obtaining good jobs in the modern sector.

In both Indonesia and Thailand, the growth of the secondary educated population is proving to be one of the major trends of the 1990s. According to long-term planning projections in Indonesia, over the 20-year period between 1990–2010, the number of working-age population with completed lower secondary education will increase fourfold from 29 million to 120 million, and those with upper secondary education will increase fivefold from 15 million to 71 million (Oey-Gardiner & Gardiner, 1997). In countries such as the

Table 9.1

Enrolment in Secondary and Higher Education as Percentage of Age Group in Southeast and East Asia

	Secondary		Higher	
	1970	1992	1980	1992
Southeast Asia				
Indonesia	16	38	4	10
Philippines	46	74	28	28
Thailand	17	33	13	19
Malaysia	34	58	4	7
Singapore	46	72	8	n.a.
Vietnam	n.a.	33	2	2
Myanmar	21	n.a.	5	n.a.
Lao PDR	3	22	1	1
East Asia and Australia				
China	24	51	1	2
Korea, Republic of	42	90	16	42
Australia	82	82	25	40

Note: Secondary school age range depends on national definitions. It is most commonly considered to be 12–17 years. The age range for higher education is taken to be 20–24.

Source: World Bank, World Development Report, 1995, Table 28.

Philippines and Malaysia, the rise will be less dramatic because enrolment ratios in secondary education are already quite high.

According to the figures in Table 9.1, Vietnam and Laos have made considerable progress in secondary education, although the figure reported for Lao PDR appears to be distinctly too high.[3] In Vietnam, the gross enrolment rate at lower secondary school appears to be about 47 percent and at upper secondary level 17 percent.[4] It is claimed (Hac, 1991:68) that the network of lower secondary schools has spread to include every village. While this may be an exaggeration, there were 1,880 such schools in 1989–90.

It would be unwise to conclude from the above discussion that all is well with education in the ASEAN tigers, or that educational developments in these countries over the past two decades have been well fitted to the needs of their growing economies. Thailand and Indonesia are cases in point. Sussangkarn had long been stressing the shortage of middle-level manpower in Thailand and the failure of the Thai education system to expand rapidly enough at the lower secondary level (Sussangkarn & Chalamwong, 1989). Khoman (1993) made the same point, as did Jones (1993) and Warr (1997:19). The rapid rise in transition rates from primary to secondary school during the 1990s has come too late to enable Thailand to enter the 21st century with enough middle-level manpower to meet the needs of a rapidly industrialising economy. Indeed, it is projected that as far ahead as 2010, 62 percent of the labour force will still have only primary school education.

In Indonesia, despite the much-vaunted attainment of universal primary school education around 1990, to this day there remains a substantial drop-out rate and at least 10 percent of the children do not complete primary education, not to mention the very low quality of primary education offered in many schools (Jones et al., 1998). Therefore, in turning its attention to lower secondary education with the announcement of the policy of extending the period of compulsory education to nine years, the Indonesian government must continue to keep in mind that the primary education task is not yet completed; both completion of the level and quality of the education offered remain serious concerns (World Bank, 1997). At the secondary level, evidence of an actual decline in enrolment ratios at the lower secondary level in the late 1980s and early 1990s signals some problems for the policy of making education at this level compulsory. The available evidence, particularly in the poorest provinces, indicates that poverty is a major reason for the inability of children to continue at this level of schooling (Jones et al., 1998).

In terms of higher educational developments, Table 9.2 shows that tertiary enrolments in Southeast Asia have increased 13-fold since 1960, which somewhat surprisingly is only slightly faster than the increase in Australia (11-fold).

The growth multiple is biased in two partly offsetting ways. First, the Southeast Asian figure would be higher if students from the region doing their tertiary studies overseas were included; overseas study is a particularly important component of the tertiary education structure in Singapore and Malaysia. Second, the figures for Thailand and Indonesia are, in a sense,

Table 9.2

Students Currently Enrolled in Tertiary Institutions in Southeast Asia: 1960, 1981 and 1991

	1960	1981	1991
Indonesia	44,802	565,501	1,885,038
Malaysia	2,698	67,368	133,479
Philippines	271,791	1,335,889	1,656,815
Singapore	8,171	24,393	60,373
Thailand	45,548	911,166[1]	1,088,120[1]
Total ASEAN5	**373,010**	**2,904,317**	**4,823,825**
Brunei	n.a.	n.a.	1,299
Laos[2]	n.a.	n.a.	4,921
Myanmar[2]	13,600	165,000	195,333
Vietnam[2]	16,051	114,701	205,652
Total ASEAN	**402,661**	**3,184,018**	**5,231,030**
Cambodia	n.a.	0	7,839

Sources: *Statistical Yearbooks*, UNESCO, Paris, various years.

Yearbook of Statistics, Department of Statistics, Singapore, various years.

Notes: Notes in this table refer to students enrolled in all institutions, both public and private, at the third level of education; universities and equivalent degree granting institutions, teacher-training colleges, technical colleges, etc. As far as possible both full-time and part-time students are included.

1 Includes open admissions to Ramkamhaeng University and Sukhothaithammathirat (Open University).

2 Vietnam, Laos and Myanmar have become member states of ASEAN since 1991.

exaggerated by the inclusion of very large enrolments in o, universities, where the annual graduation rate is extremely lc

The quality of tertiary institutions in Singapore is probabl the highest in the region; in Malaysia and Thailand, it is reasonably good and improving; and in the Philippines, it is highly variable. Indonesia, Vietnam and Myanmar are on a lower plane, and university education in Cambodia and Laos is still embryonic.

A little more attention to Indonesia, as a middle range country of Southeast Asia in terms of the quality of its higher education, may be in order. While there has undoubtedly been improvement in the quality of various aspects of Indonesian higher education, serious deficiencies remain. There seems to be widespread recognition from those closely involved with Indonesian higher education that the rapid expansion of secondary and tertiary places has made quality improvement very difficult to achieve.[5] The level of training of staff in institutions of higher education, the budgets devoted to paying them and supporting them, the reward structures in place, which give little recognition to high quality research, and the limitations on freedom of expression combine to inhibit the improvement in the quality of higher education (Hill, 1991; Hull, 1994). The conclusion seems inescapable that, although graduate education has been expanding in Indonesia, in most cases, Indonesian students remain disadvantaged in terms of what tertiary education should offer if they pursue Masters and doctorate degrees domestically rather than travelling overseas to do so.

The Philippines faces a somewhat different set of problems, although the problems of low salaries and budgets and poor reward structures mirror those in Indonesia. Philippine tertiary educational establishments include some of the best in ASEAN as well as some very low quality institutions. The Philippines' very high enrolment rate in tertiary institutions is achieved largely through a system of private institutions, which account for 83 percent of tertiary-level enrolments, far higher than in other Southeast Asian countries (Pernia, 1991:141–43).

As noted earlier, it is difficult to generalise about education in a region as large and diverse as ASEAN, where there is an

nd quality. The Asian countries whose
.s are nowadays usually discussed with
are Japan, Korea, Taiwan and Singapore.
͵apore is in ASEAN. These countries share a
͵dition and all but Singapore have had a long
͵panese educational influence. As the East Asian
, including Singapore, have moved into the higher-
͵ogy end of manufacturing and into a more service-
͵ated economy, the content, style and quality of tertiary
͵ducation have become increasingly important. "The strength
of their educational system, with its emphasis on discipline,
facts and learning by rote, may also be its weakness" (*Economist*,
21 September 1996), by stifling creativity and inventiveness.
"Manufacturing, with its emphasis on systems and teamwork,
rewards the kind of disciplines and fact-filled students (they
produce). But what about the more creative service industries
in which Asian countries currently lag behind America — like
software design or entertainment?" (ibid.).

Nevertheless, the fact remains that children in such
countries perform better than Western children as measured by
test scores. (A recent international study of student ability in
mathematics and science rated Singapore, Korea, Japan and
Hong Kong above Australia, even though Australia ranked
among the top of the Western nations (Lokan et al.,
1996:Chapter 2)). Ethnic Chinese and other East Asians also
appear to outperform the general population in countries where
they have settled. In the United States, "the success of Asian-
Americans in gaining admission to the elite universities like
Harvard and the University of California has been so marked
that it has provoked rows about discrimination against Asians,
as the universities attempt to maintain an ethnic balance among
their students" (*Economist*, 21 September 1996:29). Over the
past five years, about 40 percent of the top 100 places in the
New South Wales Higher School Certificate examination have
gone to students with an Asian ethnicity, mainly ethnic Chinese
but also Vietnamese, Indians and others. This is far higher than
their proportion in the final year high school population.

Debate rages about the superior performance of East
Asians, both in their homelands and in countries such as the

United States and Australia (see, for example, Stevenson & Stigler, 1992). The explanation appears to be partly cultural, having to do with the seriousness with which the educational task is approached in Chinese, Vietnamese and other East Asian traditions, and partly structural. Children in East Asian countries have to work harder, with more days in the school year and more hours in the school day. Educational objectives are kept to a minimum. Teachers enjoy considerable respect and prestige, far more than in Australia. Examinations dominate the lives of the young, and if they fall behind, they are sent to cramming schools or given private tuition. All this may not be much fun for the children, but it achieves results.

But to what extent are these "East Asian" educational traits also characteristic of Southeast Asian countries? The East Asian traits are quintessentially those of Japan, Korea and Taiwan. Singapore is arguably very similar, and in the cities of Malaysia and Thailand, the pressure on students to perform is also very strong. But in Indonesia and the Philippines, the East Asian intensity of educational effort is hardly in evidence, except among the sub-group attending the top private schools.

Content of Higher Education

In Indonesia and Thailand, there has been a tendency to expand university education via open universities with unrestricted access. This needs reassessment, not only on grounds of the enormous "backing up" of students within the open university system (the ratio of students graduating in any year to total students enrolled is very low) but also on grounds of a possible distortion in fields of training and accumulation of the wrong kinds of human capital. Commenting on the situation in Thailand, a study by the Thailand Development Research Institute commented that graduates of open universities "are mainly arts, law and non-technical degree-holders. The employability of such graduates is uncertain at best, particularly if quality declines as quantity increases" (TDRI/Thammasat University, 1987:108).

Setting aside the particular problems of open universities, another problem is the slow adaptation of university course structures to changing labour market needs. Table 9.3 shows the mix of tertiary students by field of study in selected ASEAN countries and Australia. Although there will always be arguments about the mix of tertiary studies that is appropriate to the labour market and, more broadly, to the national development needs of different countries, the apparent anomalies detectable in the mix for some countries seem less striking than they did about a decade earlier (compare Table 3 with Table 5 of Jones, 1989). For example, in Thailand, total enrolment for engineering has risen and that for law has fallen, as befits its increasing level of industrialisation.

But anomalies certainly remain. In Indonesia and Thailand, law accounts for what appears to be an excessive share of total enrolment; in Thailand, "fine and applied arts" has a far higher share than in the other countries, and commerce and business administration account for twice as large a share of tertiary enrolments in the Philippines, Thailand and Malaysia as they do in Australia. Natural science and mathematics attract few students in Indonesia and apparently also in the Philippines. The Philippines has a particularly high proportion of enrolment in "medical and health-related sciences". Overall, in all the ASEAN countries except Singapore, science-based fields of study account for considerably less than one-third of all tertiary students and graduates. This compares with proportions of almost 40 percent in Italy and the United Kingdom, close to one-half in Germany and more than one-third in Australia but apparently less than one-third in the United States. Insofar as all ASEAN governments aim to build a strong, industrialised and internationally competitive economy, technical fields of study appear to require more emphasis in their tertiary education systems.

Education and the Labour Market

The rising educational levels of the workforce provide the opportunity for rapid increases in productivity induced by the

Table 9.3

Third Level Students by Fields of Study, around 1990 (% Distribution)

	Indonesia (1992)	Malaysia (1990)	Philippines (1993)	Thailand (1992)	Australia (1993)
Education	17.9 (26.8)	24.7	13.2	12.3	9.0
Humanities & Religion	3.0	8.4	11.9	3.6	7.9
Fine & Applied Arts	0.4	1.0	–	10.0	1.7
Law	8.2 (12.1)	1.9	0.9	9.3 (21.2)	2.0
Social & Behavioural Science	17.9 (9.7)	5.3	– (15.4)	9.0 (18.6)	2.7
Commercial & Business Adm.	27.0 (20.1)	20.4	26.3 (44.2)	28.7 (19.0)	14.3
Mass Communications & Doc.	0.8	1.5	8.6	2.0	15.8
Natural Science	1.2	7.2	–	6.7	8.2
Mathematics & Computer Science	0.7	3.8	–	0.1	2.6

continued next page

Table 9.3 continued

	Indonesia (1992)	Malaysia (1990)	Phillipines (1993)	Thailand (1992)	Auatralia (1993)
Medical & Health-Related Science	2.1	2.6	16.1	5.0	9.4
Engineering	11.4 (11.2)	10.5 (13.1)	13.4 (16.4)	9.1 (4.7)	12. 9 (7.0)
Architecture & Town Planning	1.6	2.0	–	0.2	4.1
Transport & Communications	0.4	–	–	0.0	3.5
Agriculture	6.3	3.5	3.5	2.4	3.4
Other & Not Specified	1.1	7.2	5.8	1.0	2.4
Total	100	100	100	100	100
Number	1,795,453	121,412	1,583,820	1,156,174	969,372

Notes: Category not used.

Figures in brackets refer to earlier years: for Indonesia and Malaysia, 1982; for Philippines, 1976; for Singapore, 1983; for Thailand, 1977. See Jones, 1989, Table 5.

Source: *UNESCO Statistical Yearbook 1995*, Table 3.11.

upgrading of human capital stock. Similarly, the rising share of workers in the total population provides the opportunity for such increases to be translated into even more rapid increases in real income per head. Both of these desirable outcomes are contingent on suitable work being available for the rapidly growing workforce. In recent years, the pace of economic growth and structural change has been sufficient in many parts of the region to turn attention from earlier concerns over job opportunities for the growing stream of better educated to worries about labour shortages, particularly at the unskilled end of the labour market. Indeed, in Malaysia, conditions have provided the incentive for a substantial inflow of foreign labour, numbering over one million workers in 1993, or about 16 percent of the economically active population (Abella, 1995). The number was estimated to have increased to 2.3 million in 1996 (Hugo, 1998:Table 6). Use of foreign labour is also increasing in Taiwan, Japan, Singapore and Thailand.

The dynamics of labour market changes in a number of major countries in the region (e.g. Thailand, Singapore, Indonesia, and to a lesser extent, Malaysia) are quite dramatic, and they have an important demographic element. Firstly, the volume of young workers entering the labour force is either about to level off, has already levelled off or in some cases (e.g. Singapore, Thailand) has even started to decline as a result of declining fertility rates in earlier years. However, the volume of *better-educated* younger entrants is increasing sharply as a result of educational advances. Despite the earlier concern about mismatch between educated labour market entrants and suitable jobs for them (Keyfitz, 1989; Jones, 1993), the rapid pace of economic growth and structural change has, on the whole, enabled these young workers to be absorbed and to contribute to rising productivity, although in Indonesia unemployment rates for the educated are increasing (Manning & Junankar, 1998). It should be stressed that in the absence of rapid economic growth, the combination of rapid growth of the youth cohort and rapid expansion of secondary education would have led to serious problems of youth unemployment.

Equity of Access

It is popular these days in population policy circles to emphasise the disadvantaged position of girls in access to education and the major contribution to fertility decline that can be provided by improving this access. These points are well taken in relation to some parts of the world — notably South Asian countries. But in Southeast Asian countries, with the exception of Laos, Cambodia and to some extent Indonesia, the sex ratio of enrolments in primary and secondary school is quite even (Knodel & Jones, 1996). Indeed, in the Philippines, a higher proportion of girls than boys is in secondary school. A much more serious problem is the inequity of access to education according to socioeconomic background.

Throughout Southeast Asia, there are wide disparities in educational enrolment ratios according to parents' occupation and income. In Asia as a whole, children of white-collar workers are overrepresented in higher education enrolments by a factor of 13 compared with children of farmers (calculated from Gertler & Rahman, 1994:Table 4.13). In Indonesia, enrolment ratios increase with income in both urban and rural areas, the disparity growing as level of education increases. Thus by age group 16–18 (the upper secondary age group), school enrolment ratios rise from 36 percent in the two lower quintiles of households classified by household expenditure to 53 percent in the third and fourth quintiles and to 65 percent in the top quintile, and the relative differences are even sharper at ages 19–25 (Gertler & Rahman, 1994:Table 4.16).

The lower income groups are disadvantaged not only by their much more restricted access to secondary education but also by the much lower quality of the schools, both at primary and secondary level, that they are able to access. The low reputation of these schools and the poorer quality of the education that they receive in these schools put them at a disadvantage in the job market once they have left school.

The small group of students who reaches postsecondary education receives heavy public subsidisation. A high proportion of this group is from white-collar backgrounds, who have higher family income levels (Tan & Mingat, 1992:84; 99–

101). Put together, these two facts indicate a heavy usage of public funds to benefit those who are already advantaged by socioeconomic background. In other words, the educational system — and educational funding — is helping to reproduce and reinforce the already heavily entrenched class structure in countries such as Malaysia and China. In an earlier paper, I stressed the need to search for

> ... ways of enhancing the access of bright children from disadvantaged backgrounds to more advanced levels of education. The present situation, in which "survival" to upper secondary and university education has more to do with social class than with inherent ability, is not only unjust but also extremely wasteful from a human resource development point of view (Jones, 1989:61).

This remains the case today, and poses difficult policy dilemmas. In principle, "user pays" approaches together with heavy subsidisation of students from poor backgrounds at all levels of the education system would be the logical way to deal with the issue. But even where the will is there to diminish socioeconomic inequities, it is not easy to convince the public that this is the best approach.

As noted by Pernia (1991), unit operating costs of public higher education are a multiple of those of primary and secondary education. The differences appear to be most extreme in the case of Malaysia (Pernia, 1991:Table 10.2). Private tertiary institutions provide a much larger share of all higher education in the Philippines and Indonesia than they do elsewhere in ASEAN. Once this is taken into account, along with the extent of subsidisation of private tertiary education and the extent of cost recovery through fees and other sources in both private and public tertiary education, it is possible to determine that the overall extent of private financing in higher education (both public and private) varied enormously among ASEAN countries. Philippines is highest at 86 percent, followed distantly by Indonesia at close to 50 percent, then Thailand at 27 percent and Malaysia 15 percent. This figure would rise to 35 percent if overseas education is considered. Pernia concludes that there remains ample scope for increasing private participation in financing higher education. This would not only address the issues of excess demand for such education, but would also allow for a reallocation of public resources to lower levels of education in accordance with efficiency and equity criteria. Part of the additional funds so released could be used to subsidise (for example, through scholarships) very poor but qualified and promising students to pursue higher education (Pernia, 1991:144).

The "Mismatch" Problem and Economic Slowdown

As mentioned earlier, the "mismatch" between the rising numbers of the educated and the slower increase in job opportunities, arising from the very rapid expansion of secondary and higher education in the region, has been prevented from reaching crisis proportions by the extraordinarily rapid economic growth, as well as evidence of some flexibility on the part of young people when their employment expectations cannot be fulfilled. But the issue of "mismatch" is always lurking there as a threat. There is a kind of "ratchet effect" to widened educational opportunities: once educational enrolment rates rise, they are unlikely to fall again. Large numbers of educated youth will therefore be entering the labour market regardless of the level of demand for their services.

If rapid economic growth was all that was holding the "mismatch" problem in check, then the current economic crisis (dramatic in Indonesia, serious in Thailand and Malaysia) could cause major problems. In the absence of a sharp downward revision of expectations, rates of unemployment for the young, educated population could be expected to rise sharply. This is a serious issue for the young people involved and their families; it is also potentially a major factor upsetting political stability: the role of educated youth in anti-government demonstrations that brought down previous governments in Thailand and the Philippines is well known, as well as their role in demonstrations that almost brought down the former regime in Myanmar. More recently, student demonstrations were crucial in bringing down the Soeharto regime in Indonesia. Although the role of unemployment has not been conclusively demonstrated to be crucial in such events, it seems reasonable to assume that the heightened frustrations arising from high levels of youth unemployment could "raise the temperature" and increase the likelihood that such expressions of dissatisfaction would gain momentum.

Much has been made of the potential for political instability of large youth cohorts (Moller, 1968). Although the period of particularly large youth cohorts is passing in countries such as Thailand, Indonesia, Malaysia and China, consequent on earlier declines in birth rates, the cohort of *well educated* youth continues to increase sharply in size in these countries because of the educational advances already discussed. This is important because where youth has played a major role in political change in Asian countries, a common element appears to have been the role of students or the educated unemployed (for some examples, see Jones, 1989:69).

The "Mismatch" Problem and International Labour Migration

A possible "escape valve" for educated youth who are unable to find suitable work is international migration. This is really only a widening of the option of moving to another region within the same country, such as from the northeast to Bangkok, from eastern Indonesia to Java or from the Visayas to Manila. However, it does have wider ramifications than does internal migration, because it has the potential to complicate international relations in various ways. For example, the large inflow of illegal Filipinos and Indonesians to Sabah and of Indonesians and Bangladeshis to Peninsular Malaysia has caused some tension in relations between Malaysia, on the one hand, and the Philippines, Indonesia and Bangladesh, on the other.

There is a more positive aspect of the international flow of workers in the region. The rapid and sustained economic growth in countries such as Singapore, Thailand, Malaysia and Indonesia, in recent years, has made it impossible for their educational systems to produce on demand the high-level manpower needed to sustain rapidly emerging industries. While it is important for educational and manpower plans to be developed to produce the relevant high-level manpower, in the short to medium term, the spectacular rates of economic growth attained have opened up many opportunities for highly trained workers from overseas. Some of these needs have been met from Western countries such as the United Kingdom, Australia and the United States, and from other Asian countries such as India and Bangladesh; well-trained workers from other ASEAN countries (notably the Philippines) have also been able to find work among their ASEAN neighbours. Not only this, but the rapidly growing local employment opportunities for highly trained workers are in some cases attracting workers, who were earlier lost through emigration by countries such as Singapore, Malaysia and the Philippines, back to their countries of origin (Hugo, 1998).

Conclusion

The achievement of mass education transforms many aspects of life in any country where it takes place. It has taken place in most ASEAN countries, and has undoubtedly played a major role in their economic development. Mass education provides many opportunities to the children of the poor, who traditionally were on the margins of society. But the serious gulf in quality of education between rural and urban areas and, in urban areas, between schools catering to the poor and to the wealthy, means that attainment of mass education certainly does not imply an equalisation of opportunity.

In the ASEAN countries, education is taken very seriously both by governments and by individual children and their parents. Some of the results were hardly at the forefront of the planners' minds: the increasing restiveness and political awareness of students in the cities; problems of "mismatch" between aspirations of educated young people and the kinds of work available to them; in some cases, rising levels of youth unemployment; and in other cases, potential for increased international mobility as dissatisfied young people seek better opportunities. The current economic crisis affecting much of the region will exacerbate these problems. Whatever the outcome on the economic front, the presence of large numbers of young people with secondary and tertiary education is now a fact of life, and will provide major challenges on both the political and economic fronts.

NOTES

1. Official statistics, particularly when expressed in terms of gross enrolment ratios (i.e. primary school enrolments related to numbers in the notional age groups from which primary school children should be drawn) generally suggest complete enrolment. This is not always the case when net enrolment ratios are used, which allow for over-age enrolments. In any case, enrolment data are frequently suspect. Data on grade to grade progression within primary schools indicates that a substantial proportion of children do not complete primary school in a country such as Indonesia, particularly in more isolated rural areas. See Jones and Raharjo, 1995, Chapter 8.

2. These data were supplied to the author by the Vice-Minister for Education of Laos at a briefing in August 1996.

3. Briefings in Vientiane in August 1996 indicated that the net enrolment rate at the lower secondary level is 15 per cent and at upper secondary level only 2 per cent.

4. These calculations were based on dividing the enrolment numbers reported in Dinh (1991), Table 1, by the numbers at the relevant ages from the 1989 Population Census.

5. An Indonesian report in the mid-1980s stated that the quality of the typical upper secondary graduate continued to decline to a level that was probably equivalent to lower secondary education before the beginning of rapid expansion of secondary education (IEES, 1986:77).

REFERENCES

Abella, Manolo I. (1995) "Asian labour migration: Past, present and future". *ASEAN Economic Bulletin*, 12(2):125–35.

Azizah, Kassim. (1998) "Intra-regional migration in Southeast Asia: Migration patterns and major concerns in Malaysia". In Eleanor

Laquian, Aprodicio Laquian & Terry McGee (eds.), *The Silent Debate: Asian Immigration and Racism in Canada*. Vancouver: University of British Columbia.

Barro, R.J. (1991) "Economic growth in a cross-section of countries". NBER Working Paper No. 3120. Cambridge, Mass: National Bureau of Economic Research.

Bautista, Romeo M. & Mario M. Lamberte. (1996) "The Philippines: Economic developments and prospects". *Asian-Pacific Economic Literature*, 10(2):16–31.

Dinh, Gia Phong. (1991) "General education in Vietnam". In Pham Minh Hac (ed.), *Education in Vietnam*. Hanoi: Ministry of Education and Training.

Economist, The. (1996) "Those educated Asians". 21 September.

Gertler, Paul J. & Omar Rahman. (1994) "Social infrastructure and urban poverty". In Ernesto M. Pernia (ed.), *Urban Poverty in Asia: A Survey of Critical Issues*. Hong Kong: Oxford University Press.

Hac, Pham Minh. (1991) "Educational reforms". In Pham Minh Hac (ed.), *Education in Vietnam 1945–1991*. Ministry of Education and Training of the Socialist Republic of Vietnam.

Hill, Hal (ed.). (1991) *Indonesian Assessment 1991*. Political and Social Change Monograph No. 13, Dept. of Political and Social Change, Research School of Pacific and Asian Studies, Australian National University, Canberra.

Hugo, Graeme. (1998) "Migration and mobilisation in Asia: An overview". In Eleanor R. Laquian, Aprodicio A. Laquian & Terry G. McGee (eds.), *The Silent Debate: Asian Immigration and Racism in Canada*. Vancouver: Institute of Asian Research, University of British Columbia.

Hull, Terence H. (1994) "Institutional constraints to building social science capability in public health research: A case study from Indonesia". *Acta Tropica*, 57:211–27.

IEES (Improving the Efficiency of Educational Systems). (1986) *Indonesia: Education and Human Resources Sector Review*. Economic and Financial Analysis, Ministry of Education and Culture/USAID, Tallahassee. Chapter 2.

Jones, Gavin W. (1989) "Expansion of secondary and tertiary education in South East Asia: Some implications for Australia". *Journal of the Australian Population Association*, 6(1): 57–72.

————. (1993) "Dilemmas in expanding education for faster economic growth: Indonesia, Malaysia and Thailand". In Naohiro Ogawa, Gavin W. Jones & Jeffrey G. Williamson (eds.), *Human Resources in Development along the Asia-Pacific Rim*. Singapore: Oxford University Press.

Jones, Gavin W., Laila Nagib, Sumono & Tri Handayani. (1998) "Issues in the expansion of high school education in poor regions: The case of East Nusatenggara, Indonesia". *Bulletin of Indonesian Economic Studies*, 34(3):59–84.

Keyfitz, Nathan. (1989) "Putting trained labour power to work: The dilemma of education and employment". *Bulletin of Indonesian Economic Studies*, 25(3):35–55.

Kinh, Nguyen Quang. (1991) "The eradication of illiteracy (EOI) and universalization of primary education (UPE) in Vietnam". In Pham Minh Hac (ed.), *Education in Vietnam 1945–1991*. Ministry of Education and Training of the Socialist Republic of Vietnam.

Knodel, John & Gavin W. Jones. (1996) "Post-Cairo population policy: Does promoting girls' schooling miss the mark?" *Population and Development Review*, 22(4):683–702.

Khoman, Sirilaksana. (1993) "Education policy". In Peter G. Warr (ed.), *The Thai Economy in Transition*. Cambridge: Cambridge University Press.

Lokan, Jan, Phoebe Ford & Lisa Greenwood. (1996) *Maths and Science on the Line: Australian Junior Secondary Students' Performance in the Third International Mathematics and Science Study*. Melbourne: Australian Council for Educational Research

Lucas, R.E. (1988) "On the mechanics of economic development". *Journal of Monetary Economics*, 22:3–42.

Lucas, Robert E. Jr. (1993) "Making a miracle". *Econometrica*, 61(2):251–72.

Manning, Chris & P.N. Junankar. (1998) "Choosy youth or unwanted youth? A survey of unemployment". *Bulletin of Indonesian Economic Studies*, 34(1):55–93.

Moller, H. (1968) "Youth as a force in the modern world". *Comparative Studies in Society and History*, 10(3).

Oey-Gardiner, Mayling. (1997) "Education trends and prospects". In Gavin W. Jones & Terence H. Hull (eds.), *Indonesia Assessment: Population and Human Resources*. Singapore: Institute of Southeast Asian Studies.

Oey-Gardiner, Mayling & Peter Gardiner. (1997) "The education explosion". In Gavin W. Jones & Terence H. Hull (eds.), *Indonesia Assessment: Population and Human Resources*. Singapore: Institute of Southeast Asian Studies.

Ogawa, Naohiro, Gavin W. Jones & Jeffrey G. Williamson. (1993) "Introduction". In Naohiro Ogawa, Gavin W. Jones & Jeffrey G. Williamson (eds.), *Human Resources in Development along the Asia-Pacific Rim*. Singapore: Oxford University Press.

Pernia, Ernesto. (1991) "Higher education in Asia: Indonesia in comparative perspective". In H. Hill (ed.), *Political and Social Change*. Monograph No. 13, Dept. of Political and Social Change, Research School of Pacific and Asian Studies, Australian National University, Canberra.

Romer, P.M. (1986) "Increasing returns and long-run growth". *Journal of Political Economy*, 94(5):1002–37.

Stevenson, Harold W. & James W. Stigler. (1992) *The Learning Gap: Why our Schools are Failing and What we can Learn from Japanese and Chinese Education*. New York: Summit Books.

Sussangkarn, Chalongphob. (1995) "Labour market adjustments and migration in Thailand". *ASEAN Economic Bulletin*, 12(2):237–54.

Sussangkarn, Chalongphob & Yongyuth Chalamwong. (1989) "Thailand's economic dynamism: Human resource contributions and constraints". Paper presented at the international symposium on "Sources of Economic Dynamism in the Asia and Pacific Region: A Human Resource Approach". Nihon University, Tokyo, November.

Tan, Jee-Peng & Alan Mingat. (1992) *Education in Asia: A Comparative Study of Cost and Financing*. Washington DC: The World Bank.

TDRI/Thammasat University. (1987) "Population Policy". Background paper for the Sixth National Economic and Social Development Plan. Thailand Development Research Institute and Human Resources Institute, Thammasat University, Bangkok.

Warr, Peter. (1997) "The end of the Thai miracle?" Thailand Information Paper No. 5. National Thai Studies Centre, Australian National University, Canberra.

World Bank. (1995) "Lao PDR Social Development Assessment and Strategy". Washington: World Bank.

———. (1997) *Indonesia: Suggested Priorities for Education*. Report No. 16369–IND.

Chapter 10

Lifelong Learning in ASEAN: Singapore's In-Service Programmes in Geography

Kalyani Chatterjea & Yee Sze Onn

Introduction

Lifelong learning in this chapter is defined as a process that helps develop a person through continued efforts of renewal and redevelopment throughout his life span. Lifelong learning, therefore, is associated with facilitating "re-tooling or upgrading workforce skills and increasing participation rates in learning programmes" (Hatton, 1997:vi). In this respect, lifelong learning equips a nation, its workforce and society to compete successfully and contribute effectively and positively towards economic development.

Lifelong learning equally applies to in-service teacher training. In-service teacher training programmes in each discipline have their own requirements and dimensions. This chapter focuses on geography teacher education in Singapore where analysis will be done in terms of a) retraining programmes of geography teachers; and b) the usefulness of in-service programmes as a strategy to provide "just-in-time" training to teachers of geography. The chapter also reviews the existing system of teacher support, and suggests some ways to reinforce the existing system and promote lifelong learning among teachers in Singapore. Finally, by examining the requirements of retraining opportunities for geography teachers in Singapore, the possibility of opening wider avenues of in-service programmes and fostering a culture of lifelong learning is explored for both Singapore and other ASEAN member states. For lack of information, this study is restricted to a discussion of Singapore, Malaysia, Thailand and the Philippines.

Rising Demand for Lifelong Learning

Learning throughout the life span, as pointed out by Hatton (1997), is possible and available in many instances. The awareness of the needs and benefits of such programmes has recently heightened within the Association of Southeast Asian Nations (ASEAN). Educational development programmes have long been viewed as an index of national development in the ASEAN countries, such as Thailand, Indonesia, Malaysia, the Philippines and Singapore. Each development programme views staff development as an important component (Ibe, 1990), and as an incremental process that requires reinforcement through continual follow-up support programmes. There is a rising awareness of the requirement for continuity in staff retraining. The Malaysian government, for example, recognises that " ... in order to face the challenges of the twenty-first century, new skills and fresh knowledge must be learned and re-learned on an on-going basis throughout life. [Further] ... education is a critical component [which] will directly determine the degree to which Malaysia is successful with regard to achieving its economic development goals" (Yip, 1997:130). To remain competitive and relevant, it is necessary that the people are able to continue learning beyond the pre-service schooling years. Malaysia, Yip (1997) argues, subscribes to the "concept of education for life" and as stated in "Vision 2020", focuses on development and, more importantly, on redevelopment in education. Indeed, as Lee and Wong (1996) observe, part of this expansion of educational opportunities in Malaysia is done through Distance Education to provide a second chance for those keen to improve their academic qualifications for a career shift or advancement. This is a "retooling" process that helps people to keep up with the industry's changing needs.

In the Philippines, too, continuing education among professionals is encouraged and lifelong learning is seen as an important and necessary platform. Gonzales and Pijano (1997) point out that the increased interest and emphasis on skills upgrading and professional updating are supported by the top-down encouragement and provisions provided by the Philippine Professional Regulations Commission. This helps professionals to keep abreast of developments in the various fields, although, as yet, not all professions are included. Upgrading and retooling are gaining acceptance in the Philippines and they are carried out through the University of Philippines Open University (UPOU) whose service has been extended to the whole country.

Education is a major area of concern throughout ASEAN. Lee and Wong (1996) have found that in Thailand, social demands for education are extremely high and the idea of distance learning is widespread. Despite variations in the application and implementation of lifelong learning programmes in individual ASEAN countries, there is a strong recognition of the rapid change and the need to engage the workforce to undergo periodic retraining and redevelopment towards the creation of a learning society. However, the programmes need to be better organised to ensure the widest possible access to learning opportunities.

Yoshio's (1997) study shows that even though many East and Southeast Asian economies have made profound positive changes in the quality of life in the past several decades, educational infrastructure has changed only slightly and that retraining and upgrading programmes are still very fragmented. The concept of lifelong learning should be at the core of the educational system and it should continually respond to the personal and professional upgrading needs of the people.

Yoshio (1997:268) pinpoints that retraining, up-skilling and refresher training are often available, but on an *ad hoc* basis and there is hardly any systems-wide coordination. He further laments that "the notion of seamless education throughout the lifespan ... remains for most of the workforce in the region, unheard of". As to his suggestion for a regional and borderless education and training support system, it must be pointed out here that efforts on a local basis have already been underway for some time. It is perhaps more pertinent to examine how such a system can be fine-tuned in order to optimise the benefits beyond mere rhetoric. This requires some introspection and close-up reviews of specific situations, for which interest is focused on Singapore.

Lifelong Learning in Singapore

It is argued that teachers, being at the helm of training the young minds of a nation, should be one of the prime targets for such efforts of lifelong learning so that the first organised form of learning (in schools) is carried out in a dynamic environment. The teachers' performance in school depends, among other things, on their mastery of the subject they have to teach. A study by Ng (1990) shows that an "expert" teacher's performance depended heavily on his "sound understanding of the fundamentals of the discipline" which can be reinforced "through years of cumulative learning". Even the highest degree of pedagogic training can fail if the teacher feels inadequate in the subject area and this feeling of inadequacy and insecurity in the subject area can be very easily transmitted to the students who, in turn, may lose initiative and drive in the process of learning. For a nation where people constitute the most important resource, having a vibrant and ever-inquisitive student-mind is essential to sustain economic well-being. With easy access to lifelong learning opportunities, teachers can provide the necessary conditions to nurture the inquisitive minds of their pupils, rather than shy away from the ever-changing and dynamic content area for lack of retraining opportunities.

For various reasons, as discussed later, pre-service training may only partially equip a teacher to face the classroom teaching environment. Moreover, subsequent to pre-service training, during the course of regular teaching duties, teachers may lose contact with the developments in the discipline if regular reinforcements are not readily available. The role of in-service programmes as a strategy for providing "just-in-time" training to teachers can create an environment of lifelong learning and pave the way for the development of a learning society.

Geography Retraining Programmes: Training Demand in Singapore

Retraining programmes for maintaining a high standard of education and to perpetuate an environment of continual learning is not new in Singapore. The need to maintain the lead in the fast changing world in East Asia requires concerted efforts to promote lifelong learning since accelerated growth and continuous obsolescence of information require trained personnel to seek further retraining to keep up with the dynamics of change. University education cannot and should not be the terminal point of learning (Pan, 1997). Such need for revalidation and periodic updating has been emphasised, among others, by the Organisation for Economic Cooperation and Development (OECD, 1995).

Lifelong learning through "discontinuous, periodic participation in educational programmes" (Candy & Crebert, 1991:6) can be well executed for the teaching community through in-service teacher training programmes. Under these programmes, graduate teachers who have had some exposure in the required discipline can periodically plug into the necessary courses run by organisations, in this case the teacher training institutions, in order to update or reinforce their knowledge in the content area. For the purpose of this chapter, the training needs of teachers in geography are analysed. It is hoped that this will provide a forum for further research and improvement efforts.

However, an analysis of the specific situation is vital in order to translate intentions into effective systems. It may be pointed out that at this point the rationale behind having well-organised in-service training programmes is universal. Each discipline needs to analyse its own area of requirement in order to yield effective results. Courses and other programmes need to cater to the specific requirements of the recipients rather than present generalised and hence futile efforts.

Pre-Service Geography Teacher Training in Singapore

Currently, there are two streams of student training for geography teachers. The Post-Graduate Diploma of Education (PGDE) programme is a 10-month pedagogical programme offered by the National Institute of Education, Nanyang Technological University which recruits degree holders from the National University of Singapore (NUS) and overseas universities. The NUS graduate students include those on Public Service Commission's (PSC) Teaching Scholarships who would be teaching upon graduation, as well as others who opt for the teaching profession. The Bachelor of Arts with Diploma of Education is another programme offered by the National Institute of Education to A-level holders. This programme which extends over four years provides a smaller source of teachers.

The NUS Geography Department has no course pre-requisites and core modules, except for Year One. There are three main reasons for this. First, the Department faces stiff competition from other social science departments for students. Second, to some extent, there is a constraint of staff availability for certain modules due to staff mobility. Third, giving students flexibility in module selection is congruent with the University's goal in providing broad-based quality education catering to the needs of the entire economy. After Year One, students have the freedom to choose modules across both physical and human geography. This practice of free choice, sound as it is in principle, poses problems for effective teacher training, which is now discussed.

As the present situation stands, many students in the Faculty of Arts and Social Sciences, where geography belongs, feel uncomfortable with subjects in the hard sciences. A good number of students prefer to take courses that do not require outdoor activities, probably due to the local hot and humid climate. Preference is given to more humanities-oriented human geography. For graduates who opt for careers outside teaching, this is not seen as a problem. But, there are problems when teaching is the option.

In Singapore, the secondary school geography curriculum covers both physical and human aspects of geography. A free choice of modules does not produce well-rounded graduates who are able to handle any given teaching situation within geography. There is a small minority who chooses only "physical" modules offered over all the years, thus graduating with little exposure to the "human" segment of the discipline. Most students deliberately choose the "human" modules, avoiding the "physical" modules which are perceived as scientific and more demanding. Students often ask course coordinators if the module requires mathematics or any outdoor fieldwork which they tend to avoid.

It is only after graduation and joining the teaching service that they are faced with the uphill task of understanding the basic concepts of physical geography, which are key to the understanding of various geographical phenomena. An introductory course in physical geography in the first year is inadequate and long forgotten in the absence of any follow-up in the subsequent years. As a result a graduate teacher, theoretically trained in geography, in practice enters the classroom only partially prepared in the content area. New teachers have time and again expressed diffidence in teaching topics, such as sea-floor spreading, plate tectonics, rocks and minerals and the various geomorphic processes. As a result, such teachers feel a lack of confidence in handling these topics and get frustrated while trying to cope with the understanding and delivery of such topics.

The second scenario of teacher-training woes has evolved from Singapore's system of education which, as Pan (1997:37) aptly points out, "rewards success and allows little margin for failure ... discourages exploration and ... saps the vitality of the inquiring mind ... Little wonder that students soon learn to be more concerned with the grades than with learning ..." Emphasis on examinations and grades does not allow much time for in-depth thinking or involved analysis on individual topics and puts a rather high importance on covering more ground within a short stipulated time. The outcome is a typical Singaporean student who is reward-driven, very capable of finding the path of least resistance to steer through the course at the surface-level (Chang, 1994; Wee & Huan, 1991), and is selective about what is to be learnt, rather than enthusiastic about developing an understanding of the discipline. The result is a graduate who has good grades but not always the required knowledge in the subject area.

The problem is further aggravated by the rapid changes and developments in the discipline. Geography, as a whole, and physical geography, in particular, have undergone changes in its content and approach. It is necessary to keep up with the latest development in the university curriculum as well as the secondary school syllabi which are regularly revised. This usually creates a gap in the knowledge of the teachers who have graduated earlier. Consequently, teachers lag in content knowledge. Therefore, supporting teachers through in-service programmes becomes a necessary strategy to maintain a quality learning environment.

In-Service Programmes for Geography Teachers

In-service programmes satisfy teachers' demand for self-improvement which, in turn, help them assume personal responsibility for their own continuing development. The programmes motivate the teacher-learners to learn arising from their own need to improve. The teachers' role now changes from a "surfer of course materials" to a "searcher for better understanding", and from a "searcher of so-called easier (more comfortable) modules" to one looking for "field-oriented" geography experience. This transformation in attitude is attributable to a change in driving force, from the pursuit of a university degree to job satisfaction and professional development.

In-service training programmes can be seen as a "just-in-time" strategy to compensate for the deficiencies and weaknesses, as well as to provide updated information, in the subject area. They provide the required support to teachers and help create a satisfying teaching environment. It must be emphasised that in order to maintain the interests of the teachers, teaching must be made a satisfying experience, just as for students learning needs to be pleasurable, if the current high attrition rates are to be reduced.

Motivation behind In-Service Programmes

In-service education is seen universally as a tool to enhance teachers' knowledge to teach effectively. With these goals in mind, in-service programmes must be planned to satisfy the needs of the participants. As Palmer (1978) points out, the teaching performance is enhanced through both "extrinsic" and "intrinsic" motivation of the teacher. An "intrinsic" motivation is the ideal situation where the teacher feels the urge and finds a way to update himself even if no external avenues are provided. However, the "extrinsic" motivation which, according to Palmer (1978), drives not so well-equipped teachers to ask for in-service courses is an area that needs careful consideration. Even though such extrinsic motivations do come from teachers from time to time, without a well-coordinated long-term plan to provide the necessary support and enrichment in the content area, the full benefit of in-service training cannot be realised. In order to establish and maintain a well-balanced learning environment, especially in Singapore where human resources are of paramount importance, nurturing of this extrinsic motivation of teachers becomes essential.

In-service should be taken as a system that teachers can and should regularly fall back on so that motivation to learn and teach the subject is maintained and improved. However, it has been found that if programmes are mounted based solely on the teachers' so-called extrinsic motivation (bottom-up demand for a course), then commitment to teaching and to the system may become weaker. This may result in a high turnover rate when there are alternative offers of employment which do not demand a thorough content knowledge or where inquisitive young minds do not have to be negotiated everyday. However, few people are intrinsically motivated. For the general teaching population, some help must be available and available readily to nurture extrinsic motivation, so that teachers obtain/experience satisfaction from the profession as it should be.

The Existing Teacher Support System: The Response Mechanism

In-service training courses in various aspects of geography, especially physical geography, have been mounted from time to time by organisations like the National Institute of Education (NIE)/Nanyang Technological University (NTU) and the National University of Singapore (NUS). Such courses have, hitherto, been conducted in the form of workshops, field trips and seminars to update geography teachers. Yee (1988) recorded a number of such courses during the period 1983–87 offered in response to requests made by the heads of division of secondary schools. Generally these courses, programmes and workshops can be grouped under the following categories:

a) Part-time courses: run weekly for a total of 30 contact hours, usually covering a wide range of topics relevant to geography taught in secondary school; conducted by university lecturers.

b) Field trips on specific topics: run on demand; conducted by university lecturers.

c) Talks or workshops by guest speakers organised from time to time by the Singapore Geography Teachers' Association (GTA) or in collaboration with geography lecturers.

On the whole, in-service training programmes have been organised by the Ministry of Education (MOE), NIE/NTU and GTA to keep teachers up-to-date and to address their specific needs. So far, response from teachers has been good. However, such bottom-up response also has its shortcomings as discussed below.

Segmented Coverage

Courses mounted in response to teachers' requests often lead to fragmented aids, without addressing the broad-based problem. For example, a course on "geomorphic processes" can help secondary school teachers understand the various physical concepts in geography and also help them to analyse landforms and explain physical phenomena. This course will definitely be of great help for teachers who either had not studied physical geography or have since forgotten the intricacies of the major concepts that rule the physical world. Another demand from teachers is "map interpretation", or "field trip", which have been conducted by NIE/NTU, NUS and GTA. The map interpretation course often ends in some kind of frustration because teachers lack knowledge in geomorphology. It is futile to attempt to interpret landforms in terms of spatial relationships without understanding the geomorphic processes.

Overlap of Course Contents

Repetition of course contents results in waste of the available human resources involved in the training.

Uneven Training of In-service Teachers

Bottom-up reactive programmes also mean that only enthusiastic teachers, who have asked for retraining, engage in continuing professional development, while others, who do not have the intrinsic motivation will not benefit. This means an uneven training of teachers. It is usually the "not-so-motivated" teachers who need more immersion in an upgrading programme. A failure to provide this much needed help might reduce the effectiveness of the retraining programmes.

Ad-hoc *Nature of Courses*

In-service courses are conducted on an *ad-hoc* basis. Although several in-service courses have been mounted on various relevant areas of geography, they have largely been in response to sporadic, discrete needs voiced by the teachers, without any long-term planning. In the absence of any long-term, coordinated planning, there will be no comprehensive retraining of teachers and some areas will not be covered.

Towards a More Systematic Lifelong Learning

The sporadic and disconnected nature of in-service courses stems from the lack of an integrated approach towards providing a continuum of teacher development. The programmes mounted to satisfy bottom-up responses, in spite of their strength of being learner-oriented, cannot be controlled or steered towards a programmed direction. The long-term benefits for such courses are therefore not fully realised, especially since all teaching personnel cannot benefit equally from such an *ad-hoc* approach.

In-service programmes should be seen as a means to achieve an effective learning environment, benefiting learners as well as the society as a whole. Such programmes should be proactive through prior and effective planning to support teachers and striking a balance between bottom-up demands and top-down decisions. Course coordinators should also be included in the decision-making process so that such a balance can be rationally established.

Indeed, the effective planning of in-service programmes relies, to a large extent, on the right choice of materials (provided by the teachers through the bottom-up responses), and the curriculum design of the programme (drawn up by the policy-makers in conjunction with the service providers). Therefore, a strong commitment from all concerned is essential, both in planning and implementation of such programmes.

It is suggested that the present system of *ad-hoc* course offerings be replaced by a coordinated programme to facilitate the continual retraining of all teachers. However, in-service programmes are meant to re-tool and upgrade teaching staff and should be planned with the teachers' need in mind. They must not become an additional burden forced on the already overstretched teachers. From past experience, it is possible to identify several retraining areas, as follows:

a)   Geology
b)   Geomorphology
c)   Climatology
d)   Fieldwork Techniques
e)   Soil and Vegetation.

In line with such demands and to provide some guiding principles for geography teachers in secondary schools and junior colleges, the following broad-based courses are suggested.

a)   *Initial content modules*

- Geomorphology
- Selected aspects of Climatology
- Selected aspects of Soils
- Selected aspects of Vegetation

b)   *Applied modules: Techniques*

(Pre-requisite: adequate prior knowledge of the content modules)

- Fieldwork techniques and laboratory analysis
- Information technology in teaching
- Pedagogy of physical geography

- Each of these proposed modules is for a duration of 30 contact hours.

- In order not to increase the teachers' workload excessively, the course is offered to those who could be released from duties once a week to attend classes. Hence, further development of teachers can take place without much disruption to school teaching.

- In-service courses should be conducted regularly and on a long-term basis. Teachers can attend classes according to their professional needs.

- The whole course can be stretched over a period of two to three years.

- Although the teachers are expected to benefit from attending such a course, it is felt that a formal recognition for their efforts may provide an added impetus. Therefore, it is suggested that credits, which can contribute towards the award of a higher diploma, be awarded for the successful completion of each module. Teachers can plan their own pace towards the completion of the retraining programme. The study of Law and Low (1997) shows that adult learners are more likely to participate when learning can be done intermittently and is formally recognised. Such extrinsic reinforcement may go a long way in establishing a culture of lifelong learning among the teaching community.

Conclusion

Economic development in the last three decades has created a fast-changing environment, and a re-examination of the present educational policies and practices is necessary to sustain the pace of development and change. Much in line with the advocacy of the United Nations Educational, Scientific and Cultural Organisation (UNESCO), the creed of "lifelong learning" has, at least in principle, been accepted by the ASEAN countries. The concept of providing educational opportunities "from the cradle to the grave" has caught on, judging by the numerous conferences and debates on the topic over the last two decades. Faced with the prospect of keeping up with the changing world, ASEAN has responded in many ways to provide avenues for continual self-development of its people.

Several significant conclusions can be drawn regarding the responses of the various ASEAN countries to the concept of lifelong learning. Bigger countries within ASEAN, like Malaysia and the Philippines, have embarked on programmes of distance education. Even though this system primarily provides an educational option to those who are not able to participate in classroom learning, it may well be useful to extend the facilities for retooling and upgrading programmes. Similarly, the distance education "tool" in Thailand may well be the vehicle for inculcating the culture of lifelong learning.

Distance education is also used in Malaysia as a "retooling" process (Lee & Wong, 1996). But, more importantly, the awareness and the provisions of continuing education beyond the initial years create the culture of continual self-development, which is essential for lifelong learning. In this respect, all efforts in the ASEAN countries to provide an after-school learning environment carry a highly positive connotation. In Malaysia, as Taib and Khadijah (1994) assert, there is a shortage of trained teachers, in spite of the efforts and provisions of the teacher-training colleges. Added to this is the usual requirement of keeping up with the changes in the education scene that requires sustained efforts to retrain the existing human resource. Malaysia's "Vision 2020" makes special reference to the development of this human resource. Therefore, the urgent need for instilling the culture of lifelong learning is accepted. Retooling and upgrading of the existing human resource through education has taken the same platform as economic development in "Vision 2020". Being in the forefront of the education system, teachers are, therefore, the prime targets for any upgrading programme.

As has been pointed out in this chapter, teachers in Singapore have been frequent targets for retraining programmes. Obviously, the small size of Singapore and the proximity to learning centres have been an advantage in the planning of retraining programmes. Even though distance education is increasingly being offered as an avenue for further development in a number of fields, in-service programmes organised by various organisations have so far been the usual mode of staff development for the teachers in Singapore.

Despite the general awareness for lifelong learning and some significant positive steps taken in this area, there continues to be some lag between what has so far been achieved and what could be done. In some cases, shortage of funds has been pointed out as a stumbling block (Gonzales & Pijano, 1997; Lee & Wong, 1996). But from the planning and organisational points of view, one of the main problems appears to be the lack of proper coordination and systematic planning amongst the various bodies involved. Much effort is required to minimise overlap and maximise the use of resources. This lack of coordination has been identified by several researchers such as Gonzales and Pijano (1997) and Yoshio (1997). Analyses of the Singapore scene by the present authors reveal the same. Retraining and refresher training efforts, presently available on an *ad hoc* basis, have produced fragmented results due to a lack of system-wide coordination. Closer coordination and continuous communication among the relevant bodies are essential to achieve the goal of lifelong learning and retain the continuum of development.

In-service programmes should be adopted as a long-term strategy to achieve development in education in line with societal and national development. It must be realised that upgrading the quality of education to keep up with the times is only possible through continuous efforts from all the partners in education: the policy-makers, programme providers and the teacher learners. Retraining programmes need to be (1) specifically suited to the learner requirements; (2) well coordinated; (3) on-going to provide support to the entire teacher population; and in addition, be (4) dynamic and (5) relevant. It must be emphasised that an analysis of the retraining possibilities in physical geography is an example of how specific need analysis may be done to suit teacher requirements. To keep up with changing socioeconomic conditions, education systems of all countries need to be revamped from time to time. To keep pace with these changes, certain revisions in the school curriculum are inevitable. These will alter the requirement profiles of the learning situation. Teachers, who are the executors of this changing education system, will need regular retraining, whether through classroom-based in-service programmes, as done in Singapore, or through distance education, as the specific situations require. The coming years will see an increasing need for retraining programmes. Therefore, it is not just a stop-gap measure to sustain any particular content area, but the concept of lifelong learning through in-service education that needs to be adopted to foster a learning society. Without the sustained professional development of the teachers, the fruits of a good education system will not be realised.

REFERENCES

Candy, P.C. & R.G. Crebert. (1991) "Lifelong Learning: An Endearing Mandate for Higher Education", *Higher Education Research and Development*, 10(1):3–17.

Chang, A. (1994) "Rapport or Compliance". Paper presented at the seminar on Excellence in Science Teaching, National University of Singapore, Singapore. 21–22 October.

Gonzales, Ma. Celeste T. & Ma. Concepcion V. Pijano. (1997) "Non-formal Education in the Philippines: A Fundamental Step towards a System of Lifelong Learning". In M.J. Hatton (ed.), *Lifelong Learning: Policies, Practices and Programs*. APEC publication. School of Media Studies, Humber College, Toronto. pp. 230–40.

Hatton, Michael J. (1997) *Lifelong Learning: Policies, Practices and Programs*. APEC publication. School of Media Studies, Humber College, Toronto. pp. v–vi.

Ibe, M.D. (1990) "School-based Staff Development Programmes: Theoretical Bases and Realities". In Ho W.K. & R.Y.L. Wong (eds.), *Improving the Quality of the Teaching Profession: An International Perspective*. A selection of papers from the Thirty-sixth World Assembly of the International Council on Education for Teaching, Singapore. 27–31 July 1990. pp. 67–74.

Law, S.S. & S.H. Low. (1997) "An Empirical Framework for Implementing Lifelong Learning Systems". In Hatton M.J. (ed.), *Lifelong Learning: Policies, Practices and Programs*. APEC publication. School of Media Studies, Humber College, Toronto. pp. 112–27.

Lee, M.N.N. & S.Y. Wong. (1996) "Different Functions of Distance Education: A Comparative Study of Five Asian Countries". *Pendidikan Tinggi — Higher Education*, 3:43–49.

Ng, M. (1990) "A Profile of an Expert Economics Teacher". In Ho, W.K. & R.Y.L. Wong (eds.), *Improving the Quality of the Teaching*

Profession: An International Perspective. A selection of papers from the Thirty-sixth World Assembly of the International Council on Education for Teaching, Singapore. 27–31 July 1990. pp. 526–28.

OECD. (1995) *Learning beyond Schooling: New Forms of Supply and New Demands*. Paris: Centre for Educational Research and Innovation.

Palmer, T.M. (1978) "In-Service Education: Intrinsic versus Extrinsic Motivation". In Louis Rubin (ed.), *The In-Service Education of Teachers: Trends, Processes, and Prescriptions*. Boston: Allyn and Bacon, Inc. pp. 215–19.

Pan, Daphne Y. (1997) "Lifelong Learning: The Whole DAMN Cycle — A Singapore Perspective". In *Lifelong Learning: Policies, Practices and Programs*. APEC publication. School of Media Studies, Humber College, Toronto. pp. 34–53.

Taib, M.K. & Khadijah bte Zon. (1994) "Embracing UNESCO's 'Education for All' Ideal by Expanding Tertiary Education Opportunities in Malaysia through Distance Education". *Pendidikan Tinggi — Higher Education*, 1:37–46.

Wee, T.S. & C.H. Huan. (1991) "Physics Students' Perception of Teaching and Learning". Proceedings of the Seminar on Teaching Science at the Tertiary Level, National University of Singapore, Singapore. November.

Yee, S.O. (1988) "Continuing Education of Geography Teachers — The Singapore Experience". Paper presented at the Commission for Geographical Education Symposium on Skills in Geographical Education, Brisbane, Australia. August 1988. pp. 14–20.

Yip, K.L. (1997) "Lifelong Learning and Vision 2020 in Malaysia". In M.J. Hatton (ed.), *Lifelong Learning: Policies, Practices and Programs*. APEC publication. School of Media Studies, Humber College, Toronto. pp. 128–39.

Yoshio, Jiro. (1997) "Thoughts on a Regional Approach for Lifelong Learning". In M.J. Hatton (ed.), *Lifelong Learning: Policies, Practices and Programs*. APEC publication. School of Media Studies, Humber College, Toronto. pp. 266–79.

NOTES ON CONTRIBUTORS

Kalyani **CHATTERJEA** is Assistant Professor in the Division of Geography, National Institute of Education (NIE), Nanyang Technological University (NTU). She received her Bachelor and Master's degrees in Geography from University of Calcutta and her doctorate from the National University of Singapore. Before joining NIE/NTU in 1997, she taught geography at the National University of Singapore. She specialises and does research in geomorphology, especially soil erosion and slope stability. Another area of research is geography education and teacher development. Her research papers have appeared in the journals *Earth Surface Processes and Landforms, Land Degradation and Development,* and *Singapore Journal of Tropical Geography.* She has been involved in in-service training and has developed web-based in-service training packages for school teachers.

Dean **FORBES** is Professor of the School of Geography, Population and Environmental Management at Flinders University, Adelaide, Australia. He chairs the Flinders University International Board and is an elected member of the Academy of Social Sciences in Australia. He has published numerous books and research articles on geography, and his current research work is on economic restructuring and postcolonial representations of Pacific Asia. He is author of *Asian*

Metropolis (1996), co-editor of *Multiculturalism, Difference and Postmodernism* (1993), and *China's Spatial Economy* (1990).

GOH Chor Boon is Assistant Professor in the Division of History, National Institute of Education, Nanyang Technological University. He served for 10 years as an education officer in the Ministry of Education, Singapore, before joining the Institute in 1986 and subsequently, pursuing his PhD in Australia. His research interest is focused on history of science and technology. Among his recent publications are "Science and Technology in Singapore: The Mindset of the Engineering Undergraduate" (1998) and "Creating a Research and Development Culture in Southeast Asia: Lessons from Singapore's Experience" (1998).

Graeme HUGO is Professor in the Department of Geography, University of Adelaide, and Fellow of the Academy of Social Sciences in Australia. In 1995, he won the prestigious Stephen Cole the Elder Prize for outstanding scholarship, University of Adelaide. He is also a member of the International Scientific Study of Populations Committee on International Migration and the International Geographical Union's Famine and Food Crisis Committee. Besides teaching and academic research, he has worked with a number of international organisations (United Nations, World Bank, World Fertility Survey, International Labour Office) as well as many Australian government departments. He is the author of some 100 books, articles in scholarly journals and chapters in books. His recent books include *Immigrants and Public Housing* (with Hassell) (1996), and *Worlds in Motion: Understanding International Migration at Century's End* (with D.S. Massey) (forthcoming).

Gavin JONES is Professor and Head of the Division of Demography and Sociology in the Research School of Social Sciences at the Australian National University. He has worked extensively on Southeast Asia, and as a consultant to government agencies in Thailand, Malaysia and Indonesia. He has published widely, and has written many books and papers on aspects of population and development, urbanisation, human resource development, and demographic transition. Among his most recent books are *Marriage* *and Divorce in Islamic South-East Asia* (1994), *Urbanization in Large Developing Countries* (edited with P. Visaria) (1997), and *Indonesia Assessment: Population and Human Resources* (edited with T. Hull) (1997).

Linda LOW is Associate Professor in the Department of Business Policy, National University of Singapore. She has published widely and her research focuses on public sector economics, social security, privatisation, trade and regionalism in ASEAN and the Asia Pacific, telecommunications and information technology, education, manpower and labour policies, health economics and ageing and human resource development. Her most recent books are entitled respectively *Housing a Healthy, Educated and Wealthy Nation through the Central Provident Fund* (1997) and *The Political Economy of a City-State: Government-made Singapore* (1998).

Mya Than is Senior Fellow in the Institute of Southeast Asian Studies (ISEAS), Singapore. He is one of the editors of the Institute's journal, *ASEAN Economic Bulletin*, and coordinator of the ASEAN Transitional Economies Programme. He specialises in ASEAN economic affairs. Among his many publications, the most recent ones include *Lao's Dilemmas and Options; The Challenges of Economic Transition in the 1990s* (co-editor) (1996), *Myanmar's External Trade: An Overview in the Southeast Asian Context* (1992), and "Economic Transformation in Southeast Asia: The Case of Myanmar", in *Burma: Myanmar in the Twenty-First Century* (edited by J. Brandon) (1997).

OOI Giok Ling is Senior Research Fellow in the Institute of Policy Studies, Singapore. After obtaining her PhD from the Australian National University, she worked as a research officer in the Housing and Development Board, Singapore, before being posted to her current post. During 1995–97, she was seconded to the Ministry of Home Affairs, Singapore, as Director of its Research Division. She is currently also Adjunct Professor at the National University of Singapore. Her main research interests are on urban environmental management, public housing policy and ethnic relations. Her most recent work was *City and the State: Singapore's Built Environment Revisited* (edited with K. Kwok) (1997).

Mohan SINGH is currently Senior Lecturer in the Division of Geography, National Institute of Education, Nanyang Technological University. He won the Rockefeller Foundation Re-Entry Fellowship Award in Population Sciences. He undertook his doctoral research in the Australian National University, and was subsequently Research Fellow in the University of New South Wales. His recent publications include *Changes in Marriage Practices: A Micro-Demographic Assessment* (1996), *Divorce in a Rural North Indian Area: Evidence from Himachali Village* (1997), and *The Future of Ageing Populations: Health in Latter Life* (1997).

Tin Maung Maung Than is Fellow in the Institute of Southeast Asian Studies (ISEAS), Singapore. He obtained his PhD in politics at the University of London, and is a member of the International Institute for Strategic Studies, London. He was a civil servant and consultant in Myanmar before his relocation in Singapore. His latest publications include *Myanmar: Economic Growth in the Shadow of Political Constraints* (co-author) (1997), and "Economic Development and Democracy in the ASEAN Region" (1997).

WONG Tai Chee is Senior Lecturer in the Division of Geography, National Institute of Education, Nanyang Technological University. After completing his doctoral research in the Australian National University, he was Research Fellow in the Institute of Southeast Asian Studies, and subsequently executive Planner in the Urban Redevelopment Authority of Singapore. His research interests are on urbanisation, information technology developments and transport and land use planning. His most recent research publications are "Workforce Productivity Enhancement and Technological Upgrading in Singapore" (1997), and *Land Transport Policy and Land Use Planning in Singapore* (1998).

YEE Sze Onn is Associate Professor in the Division of Geography, National Institute of Education, Nanyang Technological University. He teaches courses in geography education, and has been actively involved with the in-service training of geography teachers in Singapore. His research also focuses on geography teaching methodology and issues related to education and student learning.

INDEX